Jochen

Jochen Gerz

Res Publica

The Public Works 1968–1999

HATJE CANTZ PUBLISHERS

Jochen Gerz – Res Publica
The Public Works 1968–1999

CATALOGUE
Edited by
Museion – Museum for Modern Art, Bozen/Bolzano
Concept
Andreas Hapkemeyer, Marion Hohlfeldt, Jochen Gerz
Editorial staff
Andreas Hapkemeyer, Marion Hohlfeldt,
Brigitte Unterhofer-Klammer
Descriptions of the works
Marion Hohlfeldt, with the use of the first volume
of the catalogue raisonné *Jochen Gerz*,
Verlag für moderne Kunst, Nürnberg 1997
Bio-bibliography
Marion Hohlfeldt, with the use of the
catalogue *Get Out of My Lies*,
Museum Wiesbaden, 1997
Translations
Henry Martin
Brigitte Dix-Kuessner
Rosanna Albertini
Graphic design and production
Gabriele Sabolewski
Production
Dr. Cantz'sche Druckerei, Ostfildern-Ruit

Published by
Hatje Cantz Verlag
Senefelderstraße 12
D-73760 Ostfildern
Tel. (+49-711) 4 40 50
Fax (+49-711) 4 40 52 20
Internet: www.hatjecantz.de

Distribution in the US
D.A.P., Distributed Art Publishers, Inc.
155 Avenue of the Americas, Second Floor
USA-New York, N.Y. 10013-1507
Tel. 0 01/2 12/6 27 19 99
Fax 0 01/2 12/6 27 94 84

ISBN 3-7757-0884-7 (English)
ISBN 3-7757-0883-9 (German)

EXHIBITION
Direction
Pier Luigi Siena, Hans-Werner Schmidt,
Ove Mogensen, Helga Pakasaar
Curators
Andreas Hapkemeyer
Marion Hohlfeldt
In collaboration with
Jochen Gerz
Organization
Brigitte Unterhofer-Klammer
Secretary
Katja Vigl-Fink

Cover reproduction
Attenzione l'arte corrompe, 1968, p. 41

Photo credit
Atelier Jochen Gerz
Fréderic Delpech, Bordeaux
Die Farm, Rainer Krause, Bremen
Joachim Fliegner, Bremen
Elisabeth Hackenberg
Markus Hofbauer, Sidney
André Lützen, Hamburg
Heinz Pelz, Karlsruhe
Photo Kleinefenn, Paris
Photo Lasvenes
Regionalgeschichtliches Museum (T. Rössler),
Saarbrücken
Bernhard Schmitt
Esther Shalev-Gerz

Lenders
Galerie Chantal Crousel, Paris
Land Berlin, Senatsverwaltung für
Wissenschaft, Forschung und Kultur

Die Deutsche Bibliothek – CIIP-Einheitsaufnahme

Jochen Gerz – Res publica : the public works
1968–1999 / Museion – Museum for Modern Art,
Bozen/Bolzano ... [Red.: Andreas Hapkemeyer –
Übers.: Henry Martin ...]. – Ostfildern-Ruit : Hatje Cantz,
1999
Dt. Ausg. u.d.T.: Jochen Gerz – Res publica
ISBN 3-7757-0884-7

Contents

Foreword

The collective efforts of four museums have made it possible to realize the project, which all of them have nourished for quite some time, of holding an exhibition of the work of Jochen Gerz. As well, we are particularly happy to have grasped the opportunity to prepare a comprehensive survey of the artist's works for public spaces. This theme, until now, has never been the subject of a one-man exhibition, even while perhaps representing the aspect of Gerz's work which at present receives the most attention.

Gerz's works for public spaces first began to appear at the end of the 1960s, next to photo/text works, installations, videos and performances, and in the course of the last twenty years they have made a decisive contribution to the shape of the whole of his *oeuvre*. Ever since the time, at the very latest, of his *Monument against Fascism* for the city of Harburg–a work designed to disappear as a result of the active participation of the city's inhabitants and visitors–Gerz has enjoyed an international reputation not only as an artist who breaks with former notions of monuments, memorials and public spaces, but also as one who conceives of such spaces as active entities which are called into existence by the human beings who live within and animate them.

The desire to organize this exhibition reflects the conviction that Gerz's strategies for dealing with public spaces radically question all previous public sculpture, and therefore need to be more attentively explored. He employs all available media from photography to video and the internet, to newspapers, radio, and television, and in doing so–just as with his photo/text works–he always reveals that a principle of his work is to be found in breaching the divisions that separate the media. The exhibition–of which the various sections primarily offer a documentation of the works of the 1980s and 1990s–makes use of on-site photographs to show the works in the places for which they were first conceived. In addition, since Gerz's monuments and memorials remain essentially invisible even at their original sites, their exhibition in museum spaces is more than simply a way of renewing awareness of the work; it also constitutes a new manifestation of the work itself, which finds its true site in our thoughts and reflections.

The fact that this exhibition is a collaborative effort on the part of four museums in four countries–Italy, Germany, Denmark and Canada–can itself be taken as proof of the international level of interest that Jochen Gerz's work arouses. The artist is here to be thanked for all of his generous collaboration. We likewise express our gratitude to the two curators, Andreas Hapkemeyer and Marion Hohlfeldt, as well as to Olivia Morel, who as Gerz's assistant has served as a link between the museums and the artist, and again to all the others who have made a contribution to the exhibition's realization.

Pier Luigi Siena
MUSEION–Museum for Modern Art, Bozen/Bolzano

Helga Pakasaar
Art Gallery of Windsor

Hans-Werner Schmidt
Kunsthalle Kiel

Ove Mogensen
Sønderjyllands Kunstmuseum, Tønder

Preface

Works in public spaces hold a central position among the activities of Jochen Gerz. But whereas other groups of works in his *oeuvre*—especially the photo/text works and the installations—have already been widely exhibited, there has been no previous presentation, for understandable reasons, of his works in public spaces. Most of these undertakings are site-specific interventions, and moreover of a largely ephemeral nature; so, a number of obstacles to their presentation in museum settings is inherent to the work. Works in public spaces are linked to the places that host them. Their tasks and meanings derive from a real and specific context which can't be reproduced in other, institutional spaces. But it is also true that many of these works remain (or have become) invisible even on their original sites, and that the question of their presentation must therefore be seen from numerous point of view. Both the catalogue and the exhibition have attempted to stress the processes which have brought the individual works into existence. The resultant overlappings of performance, video, photo/text work, installations, posters, newspaper announcements and the internet within the framework of the larger theme of works for public spaces not only make it clear that Jochen Gerz has constantly altered the borders that separate genres, but also that the reproposal of works, and their transfer into ulterior contexts, is finally an essential component of the whole of the artist's activity.

Even while surveying a variety of media in the attempt to grasp an "off-site" process, the exhibition also aspires to achieve an overview of these works as a whole. The catalogue is therefore careful to note the important role that earlier pieces have played in the development of works for public spaces, thus bringing into relief a relationship which the lively debates of the last few years on the artist's monuments and memorials have allowed to slip into the background. The premises for the use of the various means which Gerz has employed in his works for public spaces—inclusive, as well, of the recent works which exploit the possibilities of the internet—are already to be found in his earliest works: on the one hand, he has always been committed to an exploration of the inherent possibilities of the various media; and, on the other, he has always thought of public spaces as places of true and interactive communication between real human beings. Such spaces, as he sees them, are in no way static, and that attitude has been quite clear ever since the time, at least, of his *Monument against Fascism*; for the city of Harburg.

The series of works for public spaces remains on-going, and Jochen Gerz is currently at work on various projects that pursue and develop new perspectives. The use of the current media, from television to electronic billboards, to the internet, is all the proof one needs. Yet, the ways in which they are used also reveals the fundamental skepticism with which Jochen Gerz regards them. With an overview that covers a span of more than thirty years, the exhibition and the catalogue hope to contribute to a better understanding of this aspect of his work. For the documentation of the individual works, we are very grateful to have had the opportunity to refer to catalogue raisonné of the work of Jochen Gerz which Michaela Ebbinghaus, Renate Petzinger, and Volker Rattemeyer of Museum Wiesbaden are now in the course of preparing. We sincerely thank them for their generous support.

Andreas Hapkemeyer Marion Hohlfeldt

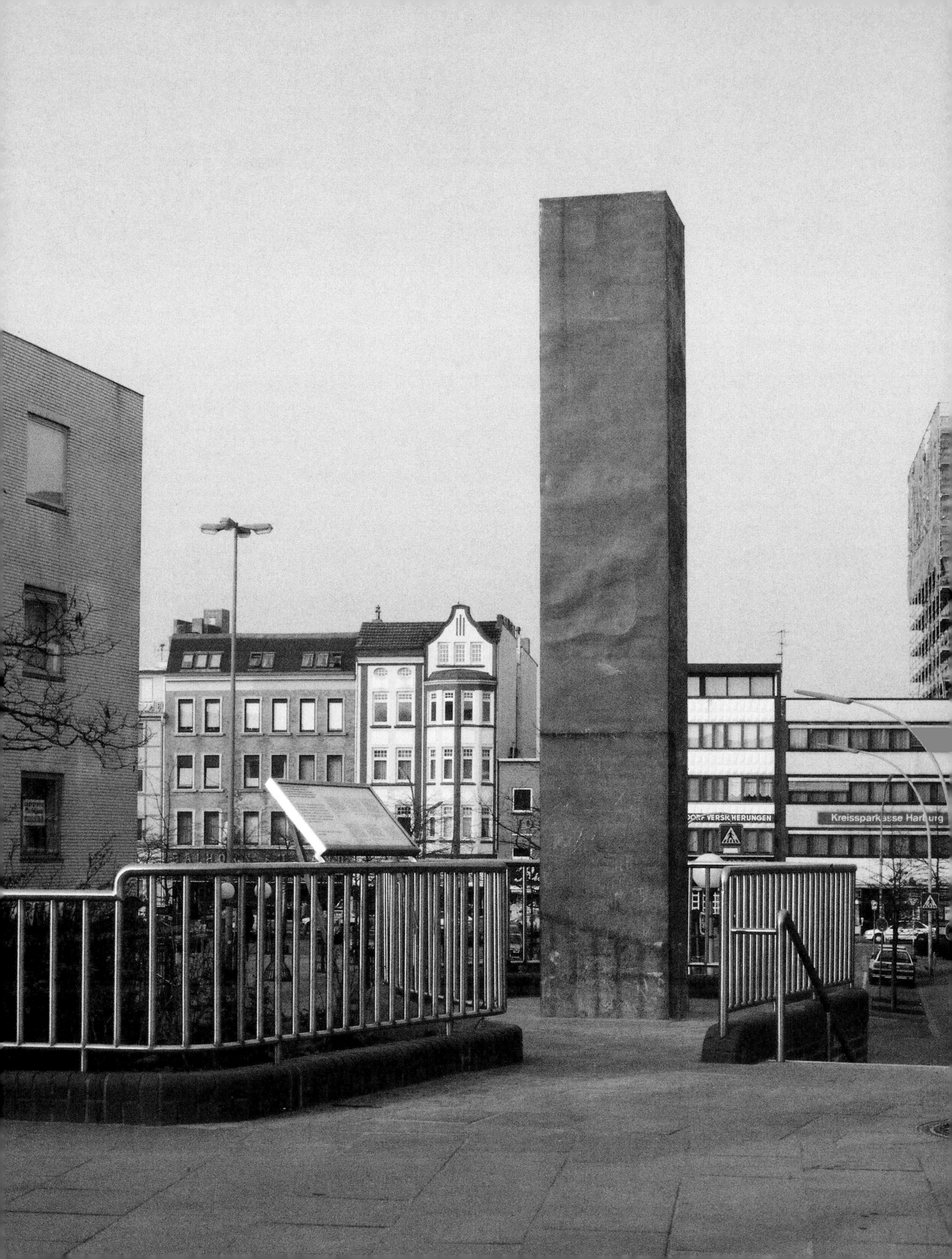
Kreissparkasse Harburg

Caution Art Corrupts:

Reflections on the Meaning of Public Spaces in the Work of Jochen Gerz

Marion Hohlfeldt

I'm a person who goes public. Jochen Gerz

If you want to be public, you have to be private. Vito Acconci

Jochen Gerz's first work for public spaces also remains his best known. It counts as the emblematic gesture, the symbolic act, that seems most tellingly to express the artist's attitudes in the years around 1968. It was in fact in 1968, the year of uprisings and new departures, that he pasted a small sticker with the words *Caution Art Corrupts* onto Michelangelo's *David* in Florence, and thereby laid the cornerstone for creative activities which consciously attempt to stand apart from categories, and which dare to formulate interventions that respect no strict separation of genres. *Caution Art Corrupts* is a work that addresses art while also extending beyond it: a single sentence, a single gesture, which makes it clear that the conditions for art in the era after 1968 can no longer be retrieved from art alone. "The difference between art and the world, between art and life," as Daniel Buren wrote in October 1968, "lies in the fact that the world and life are recognizably real. [...] The artist who wants to contribute to the creation of a different society should therefore begin by raising doubts about art, and fundamentally so, so as personally to experience the impact of its total collapse."[1] Raising doubts about art is also equivalent, at much the same time, to turning one's attention to what lies beyond it; and this, in turn, can be a question of beating back the language of art, with an eye to the creation of a state of "linguistic anarchy" (Germano Celant) that might lead to the development of a "non-authoritarian language" (Marie-Luise Syring).[2] Roland Barthes remarked that, "To speak–and, to an even greater degree, to engage in a discourse–doesn't result, as is all too often asserted, in communication, but, rather, in an act of submission."[3]

Language as an instrument of power and domination was already denounced and attacked by the Dadaists. The return to pre-verbal resources, such as we find it in the sound poetry of Hugo Ball or in Kurt Schwitters' *Ursonate*, can now be seen as well to link with internal needs of the work of Jochen Gerz. Gerz's reflections on pre-verbality and the birth of language are to be found in the manuscript *Die Schwierigkeit des Zentaurs beim vom Pferd steigen* (The Centaur's Difficult Task of Dismounting a Horse) of 1976. He writes, "One can imagine that consensus (or the suspicion of consensus) arose in the following way: two men, or two horses, were standing there and listening to themselves. Both of them were deeply engrossed in the task. There were no words, back then, and therefore, as well, no word for 'consensus.' Each of them was totally and always concerned with listening down into himself, and we have no way of knowing if they lived for a long enough time to be able to get to the end of it; they may have died earlier than that." Like Marcel Duchamp or the Fluxus artists, Jochen Gerz committed himself to a process that raises fundamental doubts about art through new uses of language which hinge on "semantic disjunctions" that derange all customary definitions of meaning.[4] The notion of the semantic disjunction, as formulated by Claude Levi-Strauss, refers to an alteration of meaning by way of a shift in context: words and objects in isolation are seen to be of little importance, or clearly in a secondary place, with respect to the relationships that hold between them on whatever the occasion on which they're used. Adorno reminds us that the (linguistic) structures which assert themselves in the social space of the page (of the book) are functions, in turn, of the principles that determine social order. "The liberation of form, which is the goal of all genuine new art, is first of all symbolic of the liberation of society, since form, or the aesthetic inter-relationship of all its individual elements, is the artwork's proxy for the body of social relationships; this is why newly liberated forms are in conflict with those that existed previously."[5] The use of linguistic signs, or the fusion of word and image which results in visual poetry, makes it possible to abandon the spaces defined by specific genres, and to shift the act of semantic disjunction from the precincts of the text, and out into the spaces of the real world. Vito Acconci, for example, describes a course of development which is similar to that of Jochen Gerz: "When I understood that I was interested in the page of the book only as a field of action, I concluded that I no longer needed it."[6] He speaks of a decision which led him from the page out into another dimension: "Breaking free of it was a question of abandoning the page in favor of concrete space, real space."[7]

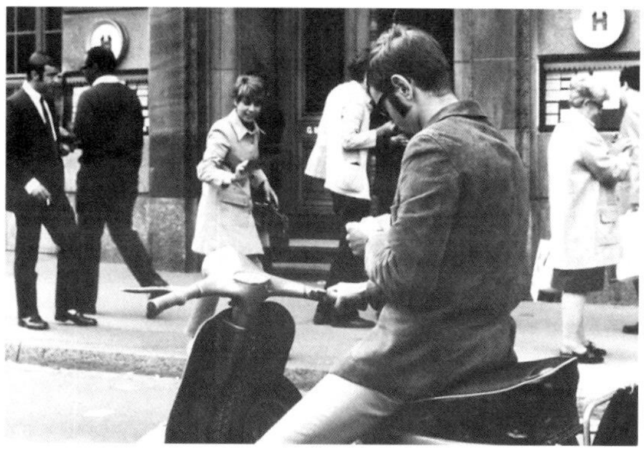

329 The Book of Gestures,
Basel, 1969

Jochen Gerz's work develops out of writing, and from this point of view his interventions in public spaces can be seen as extensions of the printed page. Like other artists of his generation, he regarded the page of the book as an already public space, and his goal was to alter its structure. But the notion of the page as a place of social interchange, and as such subservient to the same conventions that control the use of all such spaces, also implied the possibility of its use in those other spaces, without in any way ceasing to be subversive. *Caution Art Corrupts* is an example of the kind of textual (contextual) transgression that Jochen Gerz described in 1971: "Progression-texts are away-from-paper-texts, out-into-the-squares-streets-houses-and-toward-the-people-texts, and once-again-back-onto-paper texts. They nest in books like parasites. They don't come into existence on paper, and they take place everywhere, always, and publicly. They have countless, anonymous reader-authors. Their life span isn't of the length of turning pages or reading-to-the-end-of-it, and is circumscribed instead by the moment of their perception in daily life."[8] *Caution Art Corrupts* is no longer, in fact, to be seen as a text in any classical sense. Scattered throughout the environment of everyday life, and at the same time embedded in an art context, this sticker was concerned with art and as well with the notion of public space as a place of social intercourse. The artist's decision to place his sticker on Michelangelo's *David* was neither innocent nor accidental, since the role of this sculpture, from the moment of its very inception, has always been essentially political.[9] Wolf Vostell was able to assert, in 1958, that "Theater is in the streets."[10] Interventions in public spaces aimed to release passers-by from passivity and to empower them to play an active role in determining the nature of the environmental spaces in which they live. Majakowski had declared, "The streets are our brushes, our palettes are the squares,"[11] which is also to say that the artist's descent into real life must as well be understood as a rejection of the museum and as an act of allegiance to an expanded concept of art: a concept that attempts to eliminate, or at least to question, the traditional gap between work and viewer, art and life. Artists' interventions in the spaces of daily life were also intended to be irritating, for the purpose of suspending conventional modes of behavior. This also implies the artist's conscious appropriation of the ephemeral quality of reality, or of what Clément Rosset, for example, has described as "the insignificant and ephemeral character of all the things of the world [...] the nature of this reality as unique, and therefore as *irremediable* and *irrevocable*."[12] "Art as experience"[13] now becomes a part of the experience of all the other events of daily life. And as artistic activities move closer to reality, they also take on its typical quality of simultaneously presenting itself as both inconspicuous and extraordinary, as both a process and something transitory. Art makes itself more similar to the rest of the lives we lead.

Jochen Gerz's progression-texts and texts on cards also bring to mind the nomadic exhibition created in 1962 by Robert Filliou, with his *Galerie Légitime*: a hat which hosted little objects–on the order of some of the works of Ben Patterson, the American Fluxus artist–to be extracted and presented for perusal on demand. The *Galerie Légitime* makes one think of smuggled goods and clandestine sales on the black market in much the same way that plastering up small stickers in unauthorized places is reminiscent of the ubiquitous notice *Défense d'afficher*–Post No Bills–on the walls of the buildings in Paris. One likewise remembers Debord, who in as early as 1958 spoke of such things as *dérives*, or as "experimental forms of behavior that reflect the conditions of urban life."[14] The urban context, which remains untouched by the high-art traditions which until now have been received, becomes a space of experimentation. So these interventions in public spaces–in opposition to artworks in public spaces, such as monuments, equestrian statues, busts and fountains–take on the nature of ephemeral operations which stand outside of usual categories. The primary meaning of these public spaces can thus be derived from the artist's gesture, which attempts to fracture the boundaries[15] that separate the work of art from the fullness of life around it. *329 The Book of Gestures* is exemplary of such a use of public spaces. By scattering small cards with printed texts throughout the center of the city of Heidelberg, the artist diverted attention from art to life, and he did so *by way of art*. A similar relation to public space is also found, already at an earlier date, in the postal action *Is There Life on Earth?*, in which the artist made a random selection of names in the telephone book, and mailed each of them a small plastic bag, accompanied by a note that asked the recipient to send back a personal object. In all of these cases, the sphere of public space is coupled with the private space of the text, or with the individual's use of a potential space which the text makes publicly available. Michel de Certeau's impressive study of public space calls attention to the fact that all narrative structures make use of a syntax that depends on notions of space. In paraphrase, he tells us that a place (*lieu*) becomes a space (*espace*) by virtue of the occurrence of a transaction, a movement, an interactive process; a place is lifeless, whereas the distinguishing feature of a space is a "geography of transactions."[16] Just as words unfold on the page of a book, Jochen Gerz's texts on scattered cards unfold in public space, leaving behind traces and marking spaces where something has occurred or come to rest in the labyrinth of an otherwise primal and undifferentiated space. The artist's intervention leaves a mark on the "pages" of the city, and bears a message that departs from the context in which it was created and enters another by way of *metaphorai*, as the means of public transportation in the city of Athens are still called today.[17]

The reality of a transition from a (private) place of production to a (public) place of reception is in many ways precarious in the work Jochen Gerz. First of all, the production of the work, to an ever more thorough degree, is itself a question of actions performed by an inter-active public.[18] And, secondly, the reception of the work can be far from clear and obvious.[19] There are numerous works which exist as a process that only at a later date could be perceived as actions in a public space, thanks their having been documented by photographs or video tape. The photo/texts of the early 1970s–which here hold a somewhat special status–already made it clear that the perception of an action plays a highly important role for the way in which the work of Jochen Gerz attempts to abandon the space of art. As Acconci too remarks, photographs offer the possibility of "breaking out of the kind of isolation which is inherent in the space of the writer: the table and the sheet of paper. Of stepping outside the room and going out into the streets, into the world."[20] Like other artists of his generation, Gerz came to look upon the Jardin des Plantes in Paris as a special place for experimental "field research." As a space with a "half-public" quality, it was particularly suitable for almost intimate studies of the altered ways in which the private is perceived in public spaces.[21] One of his most essential concerns was for his work to able to integrate time. He writes, in an unpublished statement on art in public spaces, "This recuperation or reintroduction of time into art is the true precondition for works like these." Or again, "Multi-media art, works that make use of the media, works that deploy chronological information like texts, film, video or noises, don't find it easy to dwell on a positive, glorious, victorious past. Multi-media art much more readily thinks of itself as having a non-identity, rather than any new identity. It seems nearly to feel guilty for having relinquished the painting's pursuit of timelessness, even though having done so constitutes its base. It seems as though the discourse always has two sides. On the one hand, time is a theme that permits the criticism of human nature; on the other there's a feeling of guilt, concerning a loss of identity, or of the innocence of the timeless artwork."[22] The integration of the factor of time in works for public spaces in many ways expresses opposition to traditional public images, just as the adornment and elevation of public spaces were originally intended to function as a bulwark against forgetfulness and the transitory quality of life. Images in public spaces were intended to create visibility and enduring symbolic presence.

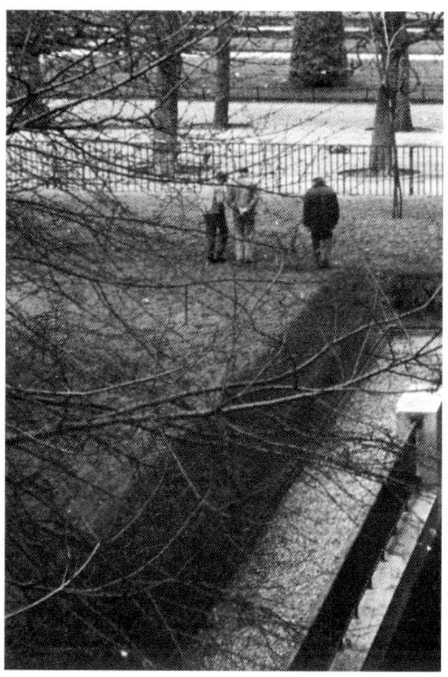

Piece for 1, 2, 3, 4,
Photo/text, Paris, 1971

Yet, careful accretions of apparently minor phenomena direct attention to the only thing that's of any meaning in art: life itself. So, one is therefore tempted to remark, in the company of Jean Atali, "If art allows the sharing of a public space, that space may nonetheless have no other choice than at first to develop from out of a private space. Nothing can ever be public from the very start."[23] From this point of view, the photo/texts of the early 1970s can be seen as public recordings of an intimate world which reveals itself only to the *flâneur*: to Benjamin's figure of the stroller who sharpens his eyes on ostensibly banal things. The works in the Jardin des Plantes are indicative of the transition from the private to the public insofar as they stem from the immediate environment of a private individual. *Piece for 1, 2, 3, 4* of 1971 was taken, for example, from one of the windows of Jochen Gerz's apartment, which at the time was in one of the buildings that flank the garden. But at the very same time, these works–referring again to *Piece for 1, 2, 3, 4* as well as to *Piece with a Blind Man*, of 1970, or to *Giving Water*, of 1971–consist of such minimal displacements as to allow them to escape from the realm of "creative alteration," and thus to shed a light that shows human gestures in all of their absurdity. While lending unexpected attention to inconspicuous events, this "strategy of the isolated gesture,"[24] as Roald Nasgaard has termed it, alters their dimension and allows the absurd to make its appearance as a part of human existence. But at the very same time, this world of apparently banal things becomes a place with which the artist regularly keeps appointments. The regularly repeated gesture becomes the fact that lends authority to the subjects photographed in *12 x La Santé* or *Defoliation*, both of 1971. Here too the important thing is the sense of time which finds expression in the repetition of (nearly) identical things. Whereas the classical artwork aspires to timelessness, Gerz deals in these works with that "zone of partial narrative" in which he was always interested as a writer. Repetition and the sense of time also find expression in the serial scansions of the recordings of his performances, and they likewise play an important role in the photo/text works.

The approach to public space by way of the spirit of writing makes the works nearly unconditional in their commitment to the sense of process. And in this regard, two features or conditions have always played an essential role in the structure and life of these works: invisibility and interactivity. The concept of public space is understood in the broadest possible terms; and the displacement of the page of the book into public space makes it clear that these terms are finally conceptual. Gerz warns that "Art in public spaces is not necessarily or automatically public simply by virtue of having been sited in public spaces." Nor indeed it is necessarily bound to any physical space. Gerz, indeed, makes use of all possible media, inclusive of the internet, in order to make it clear that there are various systems which define what's "public" in various different ways. Space is never seen as anything other than a potential space, or as a space where actions can occur, in the sense of possibly becoming a space in which people interact. Sculptures in public places, as Musil once remarked, can become entirely invisible: "...the most notable thing about monuments is that nobody notices them."[25] They only become visible through active participation, through the appeal of the work to its public, and through the way the public responds to it. Questionnaires, invitations, mailings, requests for an act of participation: what "viewers" see in these works amounts to no more than what they themselves put into them, take out of them, or contribute to them. This is especially true with the monuments and memorials which Jochen Gerz has been making since the beginning of the 1980s. As de Certeau has written, "The nature of a space depends upon its use. Thus, the streets laid out on the geometric plan of a city planner are transformed into a space by the passers-by. And much the same can be said of the space produced by the frequentation of a place created by a system of signs, which is to speak of a text."[26] Such a thought is essential for the works of Jochen Gerz, and especially for his monuments and memorials. A space has no existence until someone completes it, or as Jochen Gerz has put it: the visitor visits him/herself. Without active participation–without being completed and reflected upon–the work becomes a lifeless landmark: a simple signal that announces the name of a place, and which itself is consigned to non-visibility. The Harburg *Monument against Fascism*, which Esther and Jochen Gerz created in 1986–93, is an exemplary formulation of this perception. Without the actions (the interaction) of those who left their marks on it, the monument still today would continue to stand where it stood, but as a place which had gone unnoticed, and abandoned to the same condition in which the artists left it on the day of its inauguration. So, the decisive thing is that the work in fact disappeared. One can ask, in the phrase of Maurice Blanchot, "Where is literature headed?" But he also furnished the reply, "Literature is headed to itself, to its essence, which is disappearance."[27]

1 Daniel Buren, "Faut-il enseigner l'art?" in: *Galerie des Arts*, October 1968. **2** See: *um 1968. Konkrete Utopien in Kunst und Gesellschaft*, Städtische Kunsthalle Düsseldorf, Cologne 1990, especially pp. 62–99. **3** Roland Barthes, *Leçon/Lektion*, lecture on entering the Collège de France (1978), Frankfurt am Main 1980, p. 21. **4** Claude Lévi-Strauss in: Georges Charbonnier, *Entretiens avec Claude Lévi-Strauss*, Paris 1961, pp. 97–101. **5** Theodor W. Adorno, *Ästhetische Theorie*, edited by Gretel Adorno and Rolf Tiedemann, Frankfurt am Main, 1993, p. 379. **6** "Lorsque j'ai compris que la page ne m'intéressais que comme champ d'action, j'ai pensé que je n'avais plus besoin d'elle." François Pluchart, "Entretien avec Vito Acconci," in: *Artitudes*, No. 2, November 1971, p. 22. **7** "... en sortir signifiait quitter la page pour l'espace concret, l'espace réel." Hans-Ulrich Obrist, "Entretien avec Vito Acconci," in: *Hors limites, l'art et la vie*, Centre Georges Pompidou, Paris 1994, p. 303. **8** Jochen Gerz, *Annoncenteil. Arbeiten auf/mit Papier*, Neuwied/Berlin 1971, unnumbered page. **9** On the meaning of Michelangelo's *David*, see, for example: M. Weinberger, *Michelangelo the Sculptor*, vol. II, London 1967. **10** Wolf Vostell, *Das Theater ist auf der Straße*, Paris 1958, an intervention in a public space, see: Jürgen Schilling, *Aktionskunst. Identität von Kunst und Leben? Eine Dokumentation*, Lucerne and Frankfurt am Main 1978, p. 116. **11** Ibid., p. 119. **12** "... le caractère insignifiant et éphémère de toute chose du monde, [...] le caractère unique, et par conséquent *irrémédiable* et *sans appel*, de cette réalité [...]." Clémént Rosset, *Le principe de cruauté*, Paris 1988, p. 32. **13** John Dewey, *Art as Experience*, 1934 **14** "... mode de comportement expérimental lié aux conditions de la vie urbaine." Guy Debord, *Internationale Situationniste*, No. 1, June 1958. **15** On the notion of aesthetic boundaries, see: Ernst Michalski, *Die Bedeutung der ästhetischen Grenze für die Methode der Kunstgeschichte*, Kunstwissenschaftliche Studien, vol. XI, Berlin 1932; Gottfried Boehm, "Plastik und plastischer Raum," in: *Skulptur*, Westfälisches Landesmuseum für Kunst und Kulturgeschichte, Münster 1977, vol. 1, p. 23–47; Wolfgang Kemp, *Der Anteil des Betrachters. Rezeptionsästhetische Studien zur Malerei des 19. Jahrhunderts*, Mittenwald 1983. **16** Michel de Certeau, *L'invention du quotidien. I. Arts de faire*, revised edition, presented by Luce Giard, Paris 1990, p. 170–171. **17** Brief mention should here be made of the concept of "Vehicle Art" which was defined at the beginning of the 1960s by Joseph Beuys. He espouses the notion that the physical signal of an object, primarily with reference to multiplied objects, can transport or "vehicle" the ideas inherent within it, thus anchoring mental contents in something material, even if the object in itself is of no special worth. Beuys saw this as "a game [...] a kind of mnemonic device" (as quoted in Jörg Schellmann (ed.), *Joseph Beuys–Die Multiples: Werkverzeichnis der Auflagenobjekte und Druckgraphik 1965–1986*, Munich 1992, p. 9.) **18** The reference here is to an early work like *Is There Life on Earth?*, 1968–70, to the Harburg *Monument against Fascism*, 1986–93, or to the internet work *Berkeley Oracle. Questions Unanswered*, 1997–99. **19** The reference here is to works like *Exhibition of Jochen Gerz beside His Photographic Reproduction*, 1972, or *Hand-Writing*, 1972, or the work in Saarbrücken, *2146 Stones. Monument against Racism*, 1990–93. **20** "... de sortir de cette espèce d'enfermement qu'est l'espace de l'écrivain: la table et la feuille de papier. Sortir de sa chambre, aller dans la rue, dans le monde." Claude Gintz, "Vito Acconci: l'impossibilité de l'art public–interview," in: *Art Press*, No. 166, February 1992, p. 17. **21** One remembers, among other endeavors, the promenades of Boltanski, Le Gac and Gette. See, for example: Catherine Millet, *L'art contemporain en France*, Paris 1987, "Promenades et collections," p. 187–195. **22** Jochen Gerz, "Zeit als Zeit in der Kunst," in: Jochen Gerz, *Drinnen vor der Tür. Reden vor Studenten*, Hatje Cantz Publishers, Ostfildern, now being readied for publication. **23** "Si l'art fait partager un espace commun, il est possible qu'il ne puisse d'abord s'établir qu'à partir d'un monde privé. Ce qui est public n'existe jamais d'emblée." Jean Attali, "La commande d'œuvres d'art destinées à l'aménagement de lieux publics," in: *Programme Art et Architecture*, Caisse des dépôts et consignations, 1994, as quoted in: Noëlle Chabert, "Préface," in: *Monument et modernité. À Paris: art, espace public et enjeux de mémoire 1891–1996*, Fondation électricité de France and Espace Electra, Paris 1996, p. 19. **24** Roald Nasgaard, "The Book of Gestures," in: *Jochen*

Gerz–People Speak, Vancouver Art Gallery, Vancouver 1994, p. 35: "The theoretical background here for what we might call the strategy of the isolated gesture, is Hugh Kenner's analysis of the clownish gestures of the characters in Samuel Beckett's novels and plays–characters who have forsaken, we might say, modernist beliefs in progress and perfectibility." **25** Robert Musil, "Nachlaß zu Lebzeiten" (1936), in: *Gesammelte Werke*, vol. 7, Reinbek 1978, p. 506–509. See also: Jochen Gerz, "Kein Kommentar!," in: *Magazin KUNST. Das aktuelle Kunstmagazin*, year 13, No. 49, spring 1973, p. 12: "When I am out in the streets, I exercise no influence on the events I have set in motion. The people who are there at the same time, are simply there by chance, which isn't, however to say, that chance is charged with any special power. It's entirely possible that they don't perceive, or only partially perceive, what I am doing. And that's their perfect right. Sometimes someone asks me something. But this doesn't happen often, and I've made a habit of giving no answer. I simply continue, as undisturbed and with as little provocation as possible, to continue with what I've begun." **26** "l'espace est un lieu pratiqué. Ainsi la rue géométriquement définie par un urbanisme est transformée en espace par les marcheurs. De même, la lecture de l'espace produit par la pratique du lieu que constitue un système de signes–un écrit." Michel de Certeau, *L'invention du quotidien*, op.cit. (see note 16), p. 173. **27** Maurice Blanchot, *Le livre à venir*, Paris 1959, as quoted in: Jean-Pierre Salgas, "Die Kunst der Erinnerung fordert die ganze Erinnerung der Kunst," in: Esther und Jochen Gerz, *Das Harburger Mahnmal gegen Faschismus*, Ostfildern 1994, p. 62.

Jochen Gerz – Reminders and Posters

Hans-Werner Schmidt

Gerz was born in Berlin in 1940. In 1966 he moved to Paris, which has been the hub of his life ever since. Although he decided to study abroad twice–in London in 1959 and in Basel, Switzerland from 1961 to 1966–he belongs to a generation which experienced the Fifties in Germany as a continuum that didn't end with the decade itself but rather led up to a different social atmosphere at some time around 1968.

In his study of persons born between 1938 and 1948, Heinz Bude characterizes this generation as follows: "As long as no other history exists, the generation of children born during the war will have to bear their parent's history."[1] The activities of the critical-minded representatives of the generation are motivated by the desire not to identify themselves with their parents. "The children born during the war could not share the mentality of unconditional economic development because they witnessed the emotional costs of this 'maniac reversal of history,' as Alexander and Margarete Mitscherlich wrote in 1967."[2]

Gerz holds on to the war when reflecting on his childhood memories: "I don't come from the happy appearance of art, but from memory, disappointment, clarification."[3]

Around 1968 Gerz experienced the politicizing of the general public. Streets and squares turned into platforms for discourse that broke away from the course of ritualized dialogue. The city was the locale for a debate which was conducted by persons and groups who no longer represented classic interest groups. Looking back upon this time Gerz states in an interview: "1968 primarily meant relief for me, because I could be part of it... 1968 was a success."[4] At that time Gerz worked in the field of experimental literature. He founded Agentzia, a writers' publishing company and composed visual texts. But 1968 was also the year in which he started his projects in public spaces, which he called *pièces* (in the sense of "theater pieces") because passers-by could become actors in them. At that point in time Gerz could not yet look back upon an artistic *oeuvre,* as other artists did, which was put up for discussion and moreover was subject to self-questioning in view of graffiti found on walls proclaiming that "art is crap." Gerz didn't find himself at this turning point but visual poetry moved to the sidelines vis-à-vis the fantasy that was propagated by the rebels and that was accompanied by fantasies of power. "1968 sounded the death-knell for the small literary avant-gardes, be it visual poetry or concrete poetry, for everything that derived from situationism, lettrism or surrealism."[5]

In symbolic acts visions are radically transformed into reality–for a day, powerful and without any authorship. The barricades in Paris were set up during the night of May 10 to 11, 1968 without any plan or functional aim. They are historical citations of barricades. "They don't possess an instrumental but rather an expressive character."[6] Once Sorbonne University and subsequently the Ecole des Beaux Arts as well as the Odeon Theater had been occupied by protesters–artists creating happenings, such as Jean-Jacques Lebel and the founder of the Living Theater Julian Beck still played a decisive role in this context–the symbolic acts rapidly fizzled out into disorganized activism. Underestimating the symbolic momentum of such a seizure, the organized leftist movement summed up the events: "... Sorbonne University was occupied in order to test whether one was able to occupy Sorbonne University."[7] In 1968 Gerz also distrusted the symbolic power of art. When he posted reminders on cultural monuments stating "Caution Art Corrupts", this was not a critical voice that could only be attributed to the debate about the mechanisms determining the art market and the presentation of art in museums separated from its context within society. When he attached this statement to the portal of Florence Cathedral, the doors of the baptistery and the pedestal of the *David* by Michelangelo he was concerned about art, endlessly reproduced and thus visually vitiated, which overlaid the topical reality of Italy somewhat like a film. Here he also voiced doubts about the quality of art which transforms reality into a system of abstractions, which in turn don't have the power to leave an imprint on reality.[8] But Gerz didn't turn his back on the discussion about the significance of art, he didn't act in other social fields but went his own way in the field of art and its appreciation.

In 1974–six years after 1968–there was a show by Gerz at the Kiel Museum of Art. Looking back on the series of shows that Gerz held during the previous six years, one realizes that the Kiel show was his first exhibition in a museum. Karlheinz Nowald, the show's curator, wrote in the preface of the catalogue that Gerz raised the subject of what can be considered a book and ultimately literature or art: "His books and his works of art are different from other books and other works of art. They try to perforate the given medium, to subvert or to go beyond its scope."[9] A substantial number of catalogues and other publications on Gerz have accumulated since 1974–the authors invariably discuss the artist's verbal and figurative vocabulary, which is never quite compatible with the vocabulary of interpretive writing. Any attempt verbally to pinpoint Gerz's intentions and methods poses the threat of translating them into a poorer version of themselves.

Since his childhood Gerz has labored over forms of communication which don't permit easy understanding but require an ability to decode. The left-handed schoolboy submitted himself to the drill at school so as not to deviate from the manual "goosestep." Once released from this duty, he could concentrate on free exercises using his left hand and in doing so committed the flowing script as a mirror image to paper. Thus the scribe's tool challenges the reader's tool, namely the mirror. Nor is it easy to decode the photographs by Gerz, whose special merit consists in their quality as snapshots. At first glance the motifs appear familiar but by grouping the matter into similar pairs or duplicates, by avoiding studied artistic interventions Gerz achieves an effect as if drawing a transparent veil of unfamiliarity. If Gerz forms columns of lines to supplement illustrations, suggesting a correspondence between text and image, the reader very soon arrives in a no-man's-land in which he tries to locate the meaning of the two only seemingly related information systems. Following Mallarmé, who showed less interest in words than in the white spaces between them, Gerz said: "I'm interested in the non-visual intermediate zone developing from the operation, which is neither text nor image."[10]

Gerz demonstrates this absence of interlocking in communication by various activities–a conversation in two languages in which the partners do not understand each other's language, the exchange of objects which only find their place in a subjective spectrum of meaning so that the act of exchanging does not correspond to a simple communicative act. Here, understanding always requires the ability to empathize and an imaginative capability.

In contrast to politically involved artists of the 60's and 70's who considered art as a weapon to be wielded in the everyday debates in the arena of social policy, Gerz pursues a more radical approach by continually calling communications systems into question not as neutral instruments but as elements of an existing order. Texts and images are used to examine the function of texts and images. His photo/texts resemble a riddle more than having the quality of directing messages for purposes of communication. In trying to understand, possible questions and new answers join together. The riddle ultimately conveys more communication than bite-sized tidbits of information.

In 1970 Gerz created a stamp to disseminate the message "Turn your back on the media–live." "I've got something against the media, against all media and the work I do is leveled against the media. I don't believe in the media. I believe in a society in which people are the media. I only believe in a human being as the medium...."[11] With his interventions, Gerz, who doesn't consider himself an author or a visual artist but rather as someone who "goes public", moves against a veil obscuring reality, beginning with the arts and extending to the reproducing mass media. Peter Sloterdijk's characterization of the information society is very much to the point: "In modern information-bathed minds conditions have developed compared to which the former ignorance was crystal clear."[12]

In this media-oriented society Gerz sets out as someone who "perforates" information systems, turning to the public with posters. If a poster is supposed to work as a medium in public, then it must characteristically convey condensed information of visual and textual clarity via an unimpeded channel of understanding while the promotion of the offer must contain the promise of satisfying a need. This holds true for material goods as well as for mental supports. Gerz thus uses a medium which he himself counteracts constantly–not only in this context but at all times and everywhere.

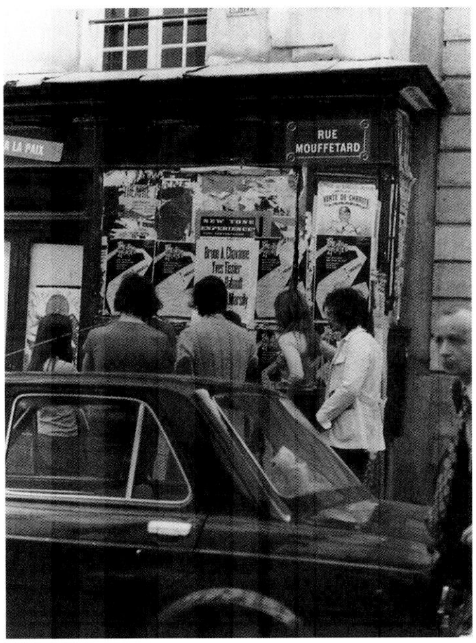

The Exhibition of 8 People Living in Rue Mouffetard, Paris, by Way of Their Names, on the Walls of Their Street, Paris, 1972

In 1972 Gerz posted two placards with the title "The exhibition of eight people living in rue Mouffetard, Paris, by way of their names on the walls of their street."[13] They are posters showing four names each, printed in brown type amidst authorized and unauthorized items of poster information. Gerz classified this poster project as belonging to the group of his "pieces," since the posters had an origin and an effect and therefore were only gradations on the scale of the artistic concept. It is said that: "This piece was realized in cooperation with students of the Ecole Nationale Supérieure des Arts Décoratifs of Paris. Eight names were copied randomly from mailboxes on Rue Mouffetard in Paris and printed on posters. The play began when the posters were put up in various places on Rue Mouffetard and ended when they were pasted over."[14]

The movement in May of '68 produced a flood of political posters, directly commenting on or forcing the pace of events. It is exactly in this realm of articulation that the imagination wanting to rise to power showed its traditionalism. Contemporary iconography of rule and rebellion became the focal point in order to rock the boat: de Gaulle is shown as a military "apparatchik" assisted by a police force that goes to fight in the streets adorned with the insignia of Hitler's SS troops and in contrast to that there are fists rising from smokestacks and throwing off all shackles.[15] Four years later Gerz reacted to this programmatic picture by publishing eight names which appear like abstract likenesses of individuals to the general public (of precisely those who live there). At the time this "piece" was a resolute step, a low but clear voice articulating itself in the political surroundings of the former 1968 protest movement that was becoming more dogmatic and formalized. Originally, the movement had expressed its criticism of society as cultural criticism. Spontaneous protest sustained by individual rebels attacked politicians who were unable to handle anything unexpected that went beyond the rituals of confrontation. The kind of reporting about the nights of protest and barricades was also new. Live coverage by RTL had the effect that every "individual was, in a way, objectively upgraded by the report about their actions and subjectively encouraged, reassured."[16] Four years later, Gerz's columns of names on Rue Mouffetard don't radiate any nervous reporting or broadcasting of individual voices at the center of events. The eight names do, however, seem to join the chorus of those who put forward the objective factor of subjectivity against the cadre formation of the former anti-authoritarian and anti-institutional movement. The historical subject "... no longer wants to be identified with historical large groups ... but demands self-constitution in the various spheres of everyday life."[17] Gerz's publication of individual persons in the immediate context of their lives, namely on their street, only calls a voice of opposition to the scene. A few years later, Gerz remarked about this: "... It was a provocation by silence, since it didn't fit into the context of a street, where there is a caption, a title, a certain explanation to everything ... The names of the people living in the street were as lovely as a poem. There is the relationship between an individual and the street where he lives, which is something like an extended kitchen for him, and in addition I intended to create an identifying relationship with the person's name.... some of them may have said: 'I am a star as well, so what?,' others felt persecuted and sued me like the editor of the *Nouvel Observateur* who walked downstairs and into the street at night to remove his name."[18]

...

A continuation of this article can be found at the following web sites
http://www.museion.it and http://www.uni-kiel.de/kunsthalle

It contains sections on *Exhibition of Jochen Gerz beside His Photographic Reproduction* (1972), *It's No Mystery* (1982), *Those Who Know Will Say Least* (1984), *The Golden Section* (1987), *The Annexation of Graz–Today is Yesterday* (1988), *Immobility* (1989), *The New Derision* (1989), *Pictures at an Exhibition* (1989), *Freedom for Stalin, Freedom for Coca Cola* (1990), *Comment vivre–How to Live?* (1992), *Free* (1992), *People Speak* (1993), and *The Witnesses* (1998).

...

The current poster project by Gerz is being undertaken in Weimar, only at the end of the year will it be possible to evaluate the project as an entity. Gerz deals with a rumor about a light. This rumor has it that a green light shines from Belvedere Palace to Buchenwald "on especially clear, moonlit nights," touching the city in doing so. "After all, Weimar is better known for Buchenwald in the twentieth century than for Goethe. Nowhere else does our culture meet its shadow so suddenly and immediately."[19] If one focuses on one historical chapter, the other becomes shady. Despite their different intentions, repression and ritualized commemoration will cause shadowing. Light, talking about the light prior to exposure invades the land of shadows. Personages from the political and cultural scene of Weimar comment on the light shed upon Weimar. These comments (seven posters all in all) subsumed under the title *Artist's Dream* will be shown at ten different locations in Weimar at intervals of five weeks until the end of the year. At the same time the newspaper *Thüringer Allgemeine* will publish the posters, while the *Thüringer Landeszeitung* will print additional comments, which corresponds to Gerz's distribution of the media with the aggregate state of his concepts changing simultaneously. In doing so, Gerz is not possessed by an educational desire to reach everyone. The presence of the messages isn't tantamount to a visual loudspeaker. "I imagine that passers-by, standing in front of the poster or walking past it, will become part of the poster for others without even looking at it or realizing it, they will move through the picture turning it into a *tableau vivant*."[20]

Besides mounting shows in museums and galleries, Gerz has also been working in public spaces since 1968–accompanying this with "publications" which range from the print media to the Internet and which he himself advocates by personally attending performances, discussions and lectures. Until today, the experiences pertaining to the context of 1968 continue to serve as motivation and reference point for reflection but without transporting stereotypes or routine actions over the years.[21] The fundamental attitude of questioning communications systems, which perceives the form of communication in its content dimension, again and again lets him arrive at results that seem like tilted everyday reception behavior. This is not the right place to analyze Gerz's socialization during early childhood so as to reveal some roots of his literary and pictorial works of art. One fact should be mentioned here, namely that Gerz was unable to speak for more than one year after having experienced a bombing in 1943. Gerz withdrew and lingered at the beginning stages of life before language acquisition. Gerz remained in the state of reality acquisition in which an immediate contact to material things wasn't screened by words, which in turn would make them rigid because of the linguistic concepts. The semblance of clear words threatens to obscure reality. It is quite certain that the distrust of words and the questioning of language found in Gerz's works are rooted in this developmental stage, which would be considered retarded from a traditional point of view.

With his combinations of images and texts Gerz departs from the tradition established by John Heartfield and reaching up to Klaus Staeck. They created collages presenting social contradictions and power structures; staged dissonances, which focus on contradiction, providing rapid insights by means of paradoxes on the surface. One doesn't find these kinds of alienation or enlightenment strategies in Gerz's works. His works of art don't present didactics in an esthetic guise. The information content of Gerz's messages "keels" over, turning them into riddles when trying to understand them. Viewed from their expressive manner the riddles touch the sphere of the oracle, permitting reflection upon the potential category of an intellectual mandala. This enigmatic quality promotes a grasping of reality that goes beyond the type of communication which only conveys surrogates of reality with the bite-sized information tidbits of a fast info-food society.

Gerz's posters seem like windows cut into the foil of the information carriers that encompass us hermetically. They form visual lanes in the forest of the media's reality. They offer a place of repose to the restlessly reacting eye. Gerz's posting of placards illustrates the different potential meanings of the German word *Anschlag*. It means both public announcement and also attack, a radical form of counteracting which amounts to esthetic sabotage. His posters are "counter-notes" in the chorus of the information and promotion repertoire. Gerz is a wrong-way driver, traffic announcements broadcast warnings to beware of him, but he will note with firm certainty that wrong-way drivers are constantly coming towards him.

If these "wrong-way drivers" are viewed as loners by society and if they're offered a field of action by society, then Jochen Gerz and society definitely have a chance.

1 Heinz Bude, *Das Altern einer Generation. Die Jahrgänge 1938–1948*, Frankfurt/Main 1997, p. 36. **2** op. cit., p. 43. **3** Cited from Volker Rattemeyer, *Get Out of My Lies*, in: Catalog to the exhib. *Jochen Gerz. Get Out of My Lies*, Wiesbaden Museum, 1997, p. 7. **4** Jochen Gerz in a conversation with Jean-Francois Chevrier, 1989, in: *Jochen Gerz, Gegenwart der Kunst. Interviews (1970–1995)*, Statement-Series S 15, Regensburg 1995, p. 114. Gerz talks in greater detail about "1968" in an interview with Martin Kunz, in: Catalog to the exhib. *Jochen Gerz. Kulchur Piece # 5 Come on over to the Dark Side*, Museum of Art Lucerne 1979. **5** Jochen Gerz in a conversation with Bernard Ceysson and Jacques Beauffet, in: Catalog to the exhib. *Jochen Gerz. The French Wall*, Germanisches Nationalmuseum, Nuremberg, Kunstmuseum Düsseldorf im Ehrenhof, Musée d'Art Moderne de Saint Etienne, 1997, p. 221. **6** Ingrid Gilcher-Holtay, *"Die Phantasie an die Macht". Mai 68 in Frankreich*, Frankfurt am Main 1995, p. 240. **7** op. cit., p. 451. **8** Gerz later transformed the "reminder" into a poster. Posting comments on newly erected sculptures was common practice in 16th century Florence. **9** Catalog to the exhib. Jochen Gerz. "*Was sich beschreiben läßt, das kann auch geschehen,*" Kunsthalle zu Kiel and Schleswig-Holsteinischer Kunstverein, 1974, no page number. **10** Jochen Gerz in a conversation with Hubertus Amelunxen and Charles Grivel, 1988, in: Statement Series S 15 (footnote 4), p. 91. **11** Jochen Gerz in a conversation with Kevin Clark, 1977, in: Statement Series S 15 (footnote 4), p. 27. **12** Peter Sloterdijk, *Kopernikanische Mobilmachung und ptolemäische Abrüstung*, Frankfurt/Main 1987, p. 66. **13** Catalog to the exhib. *Jochen Gerz. Foto/Texte, The French Wall & Stücke*, Badischer Kunstverein Karlsruhe, Wilhelm-Lehmbruck-Museum Duisburg, Kunstverein Braunschweig 1975/76, p. 122. **14** ibid. **15** Louis F. Peters, *Kunst und Revolte, Das Politische Plakat und der Aufstand der französischen Studenten*, Cologne 1968. **16** Gilcher-Holtey (footnote 6), p. 244. **17** Bude (footnote 1), pp. 60 and 62. **18** Jochen Gerz in a conversation with Claire Gravel, 1978, in: Statement Series S 15 (footnote 4), pp. 32 and 33. **19** Jochen Gerz in a conversation with Michael Islinger and Tobias Nanz, Bauhaus-University Weimar, April 1999, no page. **20** ibid. **21** Gerz also addresses the demystification of the myth about the 1968 protest movement in his piece *Berkeley Oracle* which he places on a Web site. "Until now there were no political statements or verbal attacks. The tone of the questions is primarily of an individual, existential nature. This shows the amazing lack of interest in politics or social blueprints exhibited by users of the internet as a public media platform, particularly since Jochen Gerz's title refers directly to the student protests in the American university city of Berkeley in 1968." Angelika Beckmann. Jochen Gerz: "The Berkeley Oracle-Fragen ohne Antwort" (Zentrum für Kunst und Medientechnologie Karlsruhe 1999), in: Eikon, Internationale Zeitschrift für Philosophie und Medienkunst, No. 28, 1999, p. 52.

On the Principle of Dialog in Jochen Gerz's Works for Public Spaces

Andreas Hapkemeyer

"The only places in truly better condition than the peoples' homes were the numerous war cemeteries, where upkeep was entrusted to the governments of the various countries to which they belonged. They seemed doubly abandoned; their careful decorations resembled the defenses of a still-standing front against a forgetfulness which had long since taken place." These are the closing words of Jochen Gerz's short text "Den Medien den Rücken wenden" (Turning Your Back on the Media), of 1972. His criticism of conventional monuments already had grown quite clear, and this line of thought was finally to lead him to a new and different concept. This essay will attempt to explore this concept, and to show that in addition to his photo/text works–which up until the 1980s were generally understood to constitute the central feature of Jochen Gerz's *oeuvre*–there were various stages along the road to the establishment of the principle of dialog. (It remains quite clear, however, that the photo/text works as well, with their contrasts and juxtapositions of the media of writing and image, have always depended on the activation of dialog, and without it would been condemned to remain both mute and sightless.)

Something on the order of a prelude can be found in very early works for public spaces such as *Caution Art Corrupts* (Florence, 1968) and *The Book of Gestures* (Basel 1968). These are works in which stickers were pasted onto works of art (for example, Michelangelo's *David*) and other cultural monuments, or in which letters and handbills were mailed and distributed, and the artist's goal was to excite reactions from passers-by or recipients. The work, at this point, contains no feed-back principle, which of course is a constituent element of dialog. Reactions to an impulse which the artist sets in motion didn't become quantifiable until works like *Is There Life on Earth?*, which Gerz made in 1968–70 in Paris, or the *Art Questionnaire* which was directed to 600 workers at the Hoffman La Roche corporation (Basel, 1969): in the one case, the artist sent a message to various persons and asked them to reply by sending him an object; in the other, the persons addressed by the questionnaire were to fill it out and return it.

The group of works which are properly referred to as public monuments began with the *Monument against Fascism*, which Jochen Gerz and his wife Esther Shalev created in the years between 1986 and 1993. The *Monument against Fascism* is also the very first work which effectively functions on a principle of dialog, in the sense of a verbal exchange between two or more fundamentally equally-ranking partners, with the goal of reaching an understanding, a *rapprochement*, or the development of a debate with respect to a particular question. The simple fact that the work was constructed on commission contains, in itself, a moment of dialog: the artists had an interlocutor from the very beginning. The artists' exposition of their thoughts and points of view, and the process of involving the decision-making institutions in a fruitful discussion aren't to be understood as belonging simply to the work's preliminaries: they count already as one of the various forms in which the work achieved a manifestation, and the work's existence lies in the sum of such manifestations.

The stele erected in Harburg embodies the concept of a sculpture that consumes itself, or which gets worn out by its use: it was to sink into the earth at a speed determined by the public's interest in leaving marks on its surface. The surface of a column covered with a sheet of lead became the locus of an animated and sometimes aggressive discussion, primarily on the part of Harburg's citizens, on the theme of fascism: people inscribed their names in the lead, and made remarks; some wrote over the names and statements of those before them; there are also markings that have nothing to do with the theme, and which are simply graphic; someone even fired bullets against it. The pristine column which the artists originally left behind became a kind of social catalyst, in ways and to degrees that perplexed the artists themselves, showing them the limits of what had been intended as an educational, antifascist work. The structure of the work made it less a moral statement than a social seismograph.

Unlike the conventional monument which replies to the impermanence of life by setting up something static and apparently imperishable, Gerz attempts to make the monument and the human being more similar to one another, since the monument too is subject to the workings of time. He abandons the notion of the self-sufficient, "eternal" monument, and instead creates a work that lives and dies. Its physical manifestation is temporary, but accompanied by the progressive revelation of an immaterial dimension, which essentially comes to expression through language: in the artist's conversations with citizens and politicians, in the marks left behind by those who view and make use of it, in the citizens' discussions with one another, in newspaper articles and stories in magazines. The various forms of the dialog create and give expression to awareness, and human awareness is the work's true site. Finally, Gerz's monument was able to excite the spirits of the people of Hamburg-Harburg for a good seven years. And even after its final lowering into the ground, the work has not simply disappeared. A part of it still remains visible through a sheet of glass. Above all, it continues to live in the memory of those who contributed to it, or simply heard of it. There's also the fact–by no means negligible–of all the documentation, in the form of texts and photographs, which records its various phases and the various ways it looked in the course of time: this too assures its place in human memory. The work has traded its fixed, physical site for an always dynamic, immaterial site in the minds and emotions of human beings. In following years, Gerz was further to develop and explore this notion which first found realization in Hamburg: the notion of the work that achieves, augments and preserves its presence by way of the process of its physical disappearance.

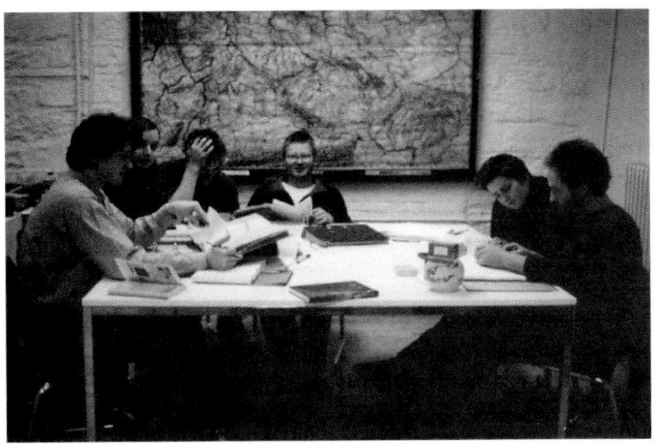

2146 Stones–Monument against Racism,
Saarbrücken 1990–93
Students at work

The invisible *Memorial against Racism*, realized in Saarbrücken in 1990–93, is one of the artist's best-known monuments, all throughout the world, and the process that created it was thoroughly imbued with the dimension of time which is always the hall-mark of a work rooted in dialog. It was based, first of all, on the compilation–in collaboration with a group of students at the academy–of a previously non-existent census of all the Jewish cemeteries which existed in Germany before 1933, and this task went on for years. Meanwhile, in secret, the students pried up paving stones from the square in front of Saarbrücker Schloss, inscribed the underside of each with the name of one of the cemeteries, and then put them back in place. Unlike the Hamburg monument, the work in Saarbrücken initially enjoyed no commission. It was only later that the on-going operations of Gerz and his collaborators forced Saarbrücken's political authorities to a reaction, and unleashed a hefty political debate: a retroactive commission was finally issued by the Provincial Parliament, under Minister President Lafontaine. The work–like its predecessor in Hamburg–is in many ways based on dialog: the elaboration of the concept derived from an exchange between Gerz and his students; discussions took place between Gerz's collaborators and the representatives of Germany's Jewish communities, and also with the political authorities; and finally the work was immersed in a large-scale public debate.

The work created relationships between groups and individuals who were previously unacquainted with one another. For most of the students who worked with Gerz, this undertaking was the occasion for their first encounter with their Jewish fellow citizens; and since the Jewish Communities, who were asked for the names of the Jewish cemeteries, were at first reserved and skeptical, the students had to muster considerable ability in the art of persuasion while drafting their letters and making their phone calls. Here too, the principle of dialog which Gerz built into the work resulted in a kind of collective authorship: the artist was responsible for the initial spark that set off a process which he guided and accompanied for a certain period of time, but the individual events that took place within that framework largely escaped his control. The artist created the mechanism, but the work would have gained no voice without the contribution of his countless co-authors. It is also highly important that the work again disappeared–after the public phase of the removal and replacement of the paving stones–and became invisible. It disappearance was a part of the very basis of its ability to set up and attribute value to dialog; dialog in fact takes the place of the visible work. The invisible monument will continue to exist for as long as the Square which bears its name exists: its existence lies in the way it survives in human memory. The physical duration of the work is far less important–and of far less interest to Gerz–than for the sphere of problems which the action addresses to remain alive in the minds of human beings.

Whereas the monuments in Hamburg and Saarbrücken are tangible material facts, even if invisible (at least from a certain point forward), this isn't true of *The Bremen Questionnaire–sine somno nihil*, of 1990–95. Even though the Smidt Bridge in the city of Bremen was subjected to a slight structural modification, the physical interventions involved can't be said to constitute the work itself, and are finally no more than an indication of something which in fact is absent. The monument finds its epicenter in a dream–in the sense of an act of utopian imagination–which expresses itself through language. The two hundred and forty-six people who collaborated with Gerz–as the result of an inquiry that reached some fifty thousand people, by way of questionnaires, television programs, and announcements in Bremen's daily paper, TAZ–presented their ideas as to the nature of a meaningful memorial, and finally agreed that a monument could also be entirely immaterial. Immateriality was seen as a metaphor for utopian aspirations, and an immaterial monument escaped the risk of a physical specificity that might rob it of the sense of openness and possibility. The monument consigned to the people of Bremen is synthesized in the text that's now found on the Smidt Bridge, where a sheet of glass allows passers-by to look down to the water flowing beneath it: "When you look at the water, you see yourself, and you yourself at the very same time are the image that rises up from you like a bird/ from a quivering bush. Perhaps forever. *The Bremen Questionnaire* is a sculpture which consists of the images in the minds of those/who imagine them. All who do so are its authors."

With the shift from monuments in urban spaces–where they continue to show a residual tangibility (if only in the form of a sheet of metal or glass on a bridge) even in spite of their substantial immateriality–to the use of the medium of the internet, Gerz took still another step forward in the process of dematerialization. Works like *Plural Sculpture* (1995) and *Berkeley Oracle* (1997–99) find their manifestation (at least in their initial phase) only in cyberspace, or on monitor screens. Their point of departure lies in a message that the artist makes available to the users of a web site, who represent a new group of potential interlocutors. The real substance from which the work is made consists of a fabric of questions and answers, expressed through language. Once again, one can speak of collective authorship; and we're dealing again with works that result from collaborations with art students. The artist himself is nothing more than the catalyst or point of departure for a complex process. The artist develops his concept by way of conversations with these collaborators, and he likewise engages discussion with the institutions that furnish financial and logistic supports. So, the organizational process on which the effort depends is an integral component of the work of art itself, which results from the interaction of any number of forces.

With *Plural Sculpture*, Gerz asks the question "If art had the power to change your times, what would you ask for?" It's also concerned, among other things, with the shape life seems to take in the era that follows the collapse of utopian thinking. In *Berkeley Oracle*, the people who visit the web site are invited to formulate questions which they consider to be highly important, but for which there are no answers. These works consist primarily of the verbal materials which come to be collected over the course of time. As well, the unanswerable questions of *Berkeley Oracle* can be seen as similar to Gerz's photo/texts, where all possibilities of clear interpretation are systematically avoided, so as to create situations where words and images are reciprocally irrelevant to one another, thus offering the viewer/reader an unencumbered space in a world that finds its principles in utilitarian thinking. Together, all of the answers–or rather, the questions–of those who contribute to the *Berkeley Oracle* create a constantly expanding utopian space. This space, which in fact is inherent in the concept of the work, finds articulation through the use of language and makes itself the work's true center.

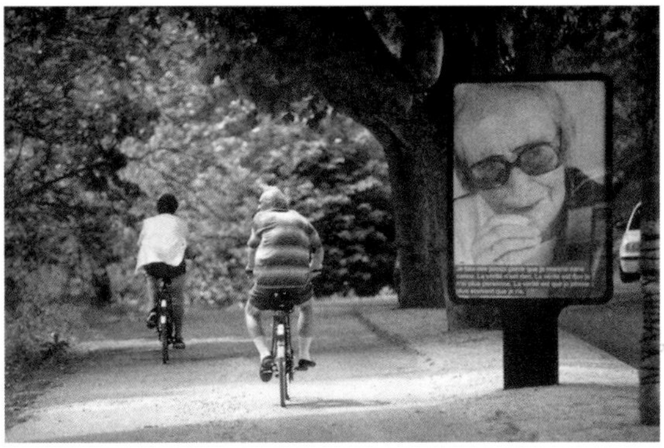

The Witnesses,
Cahors 1998

Still, however, the artist also chooses to materialize the work. Individual contributions to the *Berkeley Oracle* were printed on a photo that shows the steps of the Temple at Delphi; these photo/texts were then installed in unusual places in museum exhibition spaces: in the toilets, next to the telephones, in the corridors; they were likewise the subject of a special issue of the magazine *neue bildende kunst.* So, there is also a second phase in which Gerz continues the dialog on another level: the answers and questions are put into circulation, as a way of reaching out to a still greater number of people. Gerz opens up another, material system of circulation, which nonetheless flows finally back into the utopian space of imagination. All of this raises the question of the status of the work. An internet work can also make a new appearance on the walls of museums. Metamorphosis is a part of the identity of these works.

Two of the public works by Jochen Gerz which have received the most acclaim were occasioned by recent commissions in France. With both *The Living Monument* (Biron, 1995–96) and *The Witnesses* (Cahors, 1998), the first phase of the work (the immaterial phase) consisted of the artist's personal dialog with a limited number of persons who met certain formal criteria. A question posed by the artist became the point of departure for a process of memory and articulation on the part of his interlocutors, and the artist's further task was simply to record them. With both works, the process began as purely oral dialog and later found material form through writing, the inscription of panels of text, and the printing of posters with photo/texts. But these materialized works–or the objects which the works become–again lead those who view and read them to roads of reflection and dialog, and once again back into immateriality and the dimension of the flow of time.

Even if the monument in Biron makes use of a concrete physical presence, the obelisk itself is finally no more than a dead stone that finds its function in pointing to things which belong to life: to Gerz's conversations with all of the slightly more than one hundred inhabitants of this isolated village in Dordogne, and these conversations are a part of the work; to the effort of memory which each of these people undertook, performing it as best they could, and best saw fit; to the process of communication which came into play among these people as a result of affixing their statements to the monument, but with no indication of their names. And the many empty spaces which remain on the monument finally remind us that the process will continue, recording the statements of youngsters when they reach maturity, and of newcomers who move into the town; their statements too will find a place on the monument. A couple who lives in the town has been entrusted with the task of recording them, and of adding them to those already in place. So the monument is a totally open social sculpture: it condenses the villagers' thoughts on a fundamental question and makes those thoughts available for further encounters with those who view the monument and read its messages. Most of what has been said about the work in Biron also applies to the work in Cahors, where statements were taken from the women of the generation of Papon–a functionary of the Vichy regime who was responsible for the deportation of thousands of Jews, and who was tried in France in 1998 in a much-observed court proceeding. Here, however, the statements were coupled with the women's photo portraits and made public in the form of posters, projections, and appearances in newspapers. Gerz's question for the work in Cahors–as to what the "truth" might be–once again led to declarations that combine history and day-to-day existence, the political and the intimate. And women of an age that normally leaves them on the margins of society once again stood at the center of things, by way of the voicing of statements that have the power to stimulate reflection, and provoke both agreement and dissent.

The concept that Gerz developed on the occasion of the competition for the holocaust memorial for Berlin holds a special place in his work. Even though this monument has not been realized, the imaginative dimension that typifies Gerz's work allows us to speak of it as though it had been. The question as to why the holocaust happened encircles the designated space for the Berlin monument in honor of Europe's murdered Jews, and the monument itself is understood to consist of all the hundreds of thousands of replies which visitors give to that question, recorded in their various languages. The virtually endless number of replies itself becomes a metaphor for the incomprehensibility of the holocaust. The immense square holds thirty-nine light poles with the question "Why?" in all the languages of the Jews who were persecuted by the Nazis. The building where visitors offer their replies is an "Ear" designed by the Iranian architect Nasrine Seraji, and their preparation for doing so passes through three different phases, in three different rooms: visitors first take part in a viewing of a portion of the video documentation compiled by Steven Spielberg's Shoah Visual History Foundation, which has interviewed over fifty thousand survivors of the holocaust; in the next room, visitors converse with Jewish students who work as interns within the framework of another foundation that Gerz's project foresees; finally, they enter the Room of Silence where La Monte Young's "eternal e" resounds. The conversations with the interns bring visitors directly into contact with descendants of the victims of the holocaust. And these conversations are understood to be moments of true exchange, since the interns' task is more than a question of supplying information; no matter if from Germany or from other parts of the world, visitors should be confronted with the interns' personal points of view. The question "Why?" is ubiquitous and ever-present and throws visitors back upon themselves. The visitors record their replies in books preserved in the "Ear," and these replies are later inscribed on the floor of the Square. The true (immaterial) core of the work once again lies in the realm of reflection; but the concept also foresees its materialization by way of the inscription of the individual statements in the ground. The visitor (the hypothetical visitor) who treads across these writings while entering or leaving the area can hardly fail to feel the need to read them, and they offer a silent dialog with those who have been here before. Jochen Gerz remarked, on November 14, 1997, while addressing the jury for the monument in honor of Europe's murdered Jews, that "the history of the most radical imposition of silence allows for no reply that you do not furnish with your own individual voice." It is only through the exercise of the personal voice of every individual visitor that the memorial can take on life. Making certain that this takes place is what Jochen Gerz envisioned as the highest task of the monument he proposed for Berlin.

The project's most characteristic feature, as well as the feature that sets it apart from the other proposals, resides in its rejection of the notion that it could lie within the province of any single artist–as though personifying the conscience of a nation, or of all humanity–to attempt to offer an answer to this finally unanswerable question. In the course of addressing the Berlin jury, Gerz also asserted, "Just as in democracy, there is really no passive observer in this concept of art." Gerz sees the viewer as a partner of equal standing, just as all citizens should be partners of equal standing in political life. Unlike the spectator, the partner is vocal and contributes to a dialog. Gerz understands the democratization of the monument through the active participation of those who visit it to be the only way of bringing it to life. In any other case, the monument loses all validity. The subversive nature of the Berlin monument lies in the way it confronted its commissioners with the question as to whether or not they were prepared, while foreseeing a monument for the *tremendum*, to face the unusual challenges which such a process-oriented work would be destined to present for a number of decades to come.

The public works of recent years continue to find themselves at grips with the very same doubts which were already active in *Caution Art Corrupts*: Gerz has always understood that art as a vehicle of corruption or falsification has to be repulsed by life itself. Though it can't be denied that Gerz's public works belong to the realm of art, it must also be seen that their effectiveness largely derives from their allegiance to a discourse that centers on art as little as possible. Art quite easily bonds with rigid presuppositions, and can thereby lead to inappropriate expectations and results. Gerz, finally, is concerned with life, rather than with art; rather than with objects, he's concerned with events that occur in the human interior.

Jochen Gerz has continued over the years to develop the socially and process-oriented strategies that appeared in his work at the end of the 1960s: they are more pertinent now than ever before. In the course of the last twenty years, the inclusion of the public in the process of the work has achieved a critical detachment from what finally counts as a self-referential art that can only be of interest to insiders. Gerz's monuments seek encounters and confrontations with people who have nothing to do with the typical public of galleries and museums.

The extraordinary feature of Gerz's art lies in its highly effective use of words which are simple and never didactic, even while intent on moral edification. And they manage, with great conceptual clarity no less than with considerable intensity, to engage the interest of people with no particular predisposition to art, and to draw them into a process that also makes room for their own particular thoughts, inclusive of expressions of opposition and dissent. For Gerz's public works, life and dialog are finally synonymous with one another. Dialog and the enlargement of the notion of authorship are likewise functions of one another. And in all of this, the substantial difference between Gerz's works and the traditional monument is clearly to be found in the eminent role they attribute to the dimension of time. By relinquishing the visible object and allowing his works to make no claim to a place outside of time, Gerz augments their presence. Gerz's monument doesn't belong to the class of public works of which one of the most conspicuous features is that no one pays them any attention (Robert Musil). It's by daring to accept metamorphosis that it truly becomes a "living monument."

Biron–The Living Monument

White Memory on Red Glaze

Rosanna Albertini

Biron is a village in the south-west of France. A crumbled monument there, dedicated to the dead of World War I and to those deported in World War II, was pitiful to look at. It was easy to miss it even if Silvanie, seventy-eight years old, always remembered to put flowers on it. Silvanie was honoring her father, who had come back from the trenches in 1914 with asthma, and her husband, wounded after the 1939 call-up. But most of all she was taking care of the anxiety engraved into her own body by abandonment and fear. No one who lived in those years could avoid them; for those who were not there these are unimaginable feelings.

When yet another truck tire almost leveled the broken pieces of concrete on the way to the castle–the remains of the old monument–Biron's city council decided to rebuild it. The task was given to Jochen Gerz after consultation with the DRAC (the regional section of the French Ministry of Culture).

For Jochen Gerz no object in the world can replace memory, and real life makes art meaningful beyond clichés or visible appearance. To fulfill Biron's commission took him almost eight years. Inevitably, at the beginning, he was unpopular in the village. "It was embarrassing to be seen as an artist, almost as to be seen as a German. It's hard to be an image."

At the beginning Biron's citizens had no idea who Johen Gerz was or what he had done as an artist. Moreover, an unexpected outcome was created by the public commission. The contemporary "prince" asks the artist, "Give me an artwork to replace the commemorative monument," but the prince does not know what he or his voters might want. In this particular case the artist was convinced that Biron's citizens were the real authority, so he proceeded as if he were acting on their commission. The number of residents in Biron at the time was one hundred and thirty-four.

The living monument of Biron was unveiled on July 13, 1996, an exact replica of the old one in shape and size, the concrete having been replaced by a local stone the color of mustard. But the engraved names have not been abandoned this time. Gerz knocked at the door of everyone who lives in Biron, he listened to them one by one, and he took notes. He wanted to hear from their own mouths the words that tell what is worth living or dying for. This secret question, sculpted in his mind, was never voiced. He let them talk. Then, alone, Gerz condensed each meeting into a few lines, never more than nine. Etched on one-hundred-twenty-seven red tiles, these words have been affixed to the monument: forgetfulness is embodied in their white color. As the work progressed, Gerz also kept forgetting, and he became just one of many, just like everybody else. Art, for him, was a procedure that reshaped his own life–in the end, it was almost a pretext.

Nobody knew, not even Gerz, how deeply his idea–an artist's idea–was going to shake the community's life. Biron's citizens are no different from any other French citizens of our time. France is a country whose obsession with civilization extends into the smallest lost corners of the country, like Biron. On the railway tracks connecting Paris to Bergerac, the train's high velocity seems to be cutting and wounding the boring domestic sweetness of the hilly countryside. Everything that is produced by that soil ends up in bottles of wine and cans of *fois gras*. Up to a point, nature regenerates what is destroyed by history. The castle of Biron, viewed from afar, looks like the top of a mountain tracing an edge beneath the sky lowered by the rain. I knocked on the doors of the village one by one, repeating the ritual started by Johen Gerz.

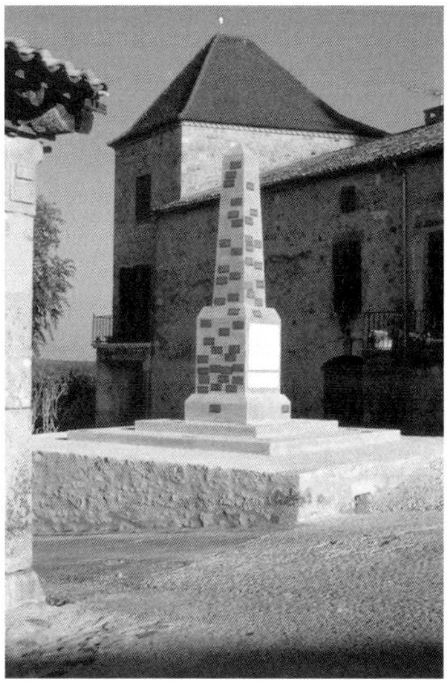

The Living Monument,
Biron 1995/96

"Mister Gerz? We learned from the newspapers that he was a German. I could not stand it; it made me so mad that I could not sleep. Then a letter arrived from the city council, inviting all of us to meet him and hear about his project. Mister Gerz is a gentle, cultivated man; we liked his idea. For us he was a foreigner, an unknown person who did a good thing: he forced us to re-create our memory. We were used to passing by the monument without paying attention, almost without seeing it. Now, that monument seems fantastic to me. I cried, as I read the other people's thoughts. I was so sure I knew the people who live around me, but I realized it wasn't true. It never happens that we really get close to one another–I don't know why. We can only miss what we didn't do. Our dead did not leave for nothing. They suddenly came back, among us."

"There are some of us, the ones who have been deported, for instance, who are still afraid to speak. It is too painful. I was scared myself: my heart was bumping before I met Mister Gerz. Rather than questioning us, he made us think."

"There are no signatures on the tiles, perhaps that's better. Anyway, the thoughts written on the monument are so personal, believe me, they are true. Mister Gerz pushed us to think about the war, about death. We had stopped doing that, because it's something that shakes the pit of your stomach."

In 1944 Julien had gone five days without eating or drinking: he hid in the cows' manure, to avoid being deported. At that time the *SS Totenkopf* squadron was perpetrating massacres: everybody had been deported from Lacapelle Biron; women and children had been burned alive in the church at Oradour sur Glane: houses were reduced to ashes, and no one survived. The very few who had escaped before the slaughter built a fence around the ruins–it has never been touched since then–and reconstructed the village slightly further away. In 1994 the Rwanda genocide happened in the same way. Whenever it appears, war seems to follow the same score. Julien remembers a German jeep exhibiting around the village the corpse of a member of the resistance, who had been beaten to death. An historical tale relates that in 1211 the citizens of Biron were forced to look at the corpse of Martin d'Algais, which had been tied to a horse and dragged around the village. "Father, what's history, what's it for?" a young boy asked his father, who was Marc Bloch, the famous historian.

"Mister Gerz has been able to talk with us. I'm proud of the monument. Is it art? Frankly, I didn't think about that. Our thoughts will be there when we are dead. Even if we can recognize each other, we are isolated and very selfish; not even for the grape harvest, we don't come together. This monument has altered the distances: we look at each other in a different way, surprised."

"We've been a part of making the new monument. Instead of our eyes, Mister Gerz has opened our hearts." "The words written on the monument are beautiful. Now I'm proud of the people who live here. It's our monument now. Is it true that the same kind of monument will be done in every French village?" "No, madam, sorry to disappoint you. This is your monument, unique and unrepeatable unless Mister Gerz opens a factory, but he doesn't seem to be that kind of person."

Bruno Desmaison, the vice-mayor, is in charge (during his lifetime) of gathering the thoughts of the future citizens of Biron, those boys and girls who have come of age. New tiles will be added to the stone, on the grass around the monument, everywhere where there is space. The monument will change and grow. What about the artist? Gerz, perhaps, would answer that the artist too belongs to a living time; the artist is only somebody bringing the unforeseen as a gift and transformation as a dream. The artist is a passing alien; his work is no less transitional.

As an artwork, the monument of Biron speaks in public about things that the public sphere usually rejects because they are intimately tied to feelings and personality. The artist made himself a human machine, a listening and recording medium that gives back the power of written words. I did not find one person in Biron who didn't fully recognize themselves in the few lines Gerz abstracted from hours of conversation, not even one who did not experience an awakening. Remaking the monument was an odd contingency, in which every single person shared either the work or destiny of the artist. Besides, special risks are implied by the public function of this monument: the citizens of Biron are hurt if a tourist laughs at the words attached to the stone. The art object, a small pillar clothed in thoughts, is simply exposed.

All the texts of the tiles have been published in a book, *The Secret Question*, published by Actes Sud in 1996. What the question is, exactly, is not transcribed. While talking with people in Biron, something instinctively prevented me from asking. Finally, at a kitchen table in a farmhouse, somebody told me, "There wasn't any question: we talked about life." Jochen Gerz confirmed this on the phone: "I had the question in my mind, but I never pronounced it." And yet they all answered.

Who is afraid of common sense?

"Though it helps to remove some problems, technology can lead us to bigger catastrophes, without any winners. But a person who takes no risks, either personal or social, doesn't accomplish big things. The place where we can express ourselves is in our desires; you do not learn courage: it's a gift. Let us not reproduce the same hatred we had in the past–whether against enemies or one of the same party. As we face the loss of memory, our choices disappear."

"To give birth to children, this seems normal to me. Everything else does not matter much. I only care about peace; a good agreement is better than shooting each other. In peace, more so than in war, the gift of life is necessary. To give his own life is a man's work; to give life is a woman's work."

"Do we need a massacre to save lives? Each of us has to find his/her own truth. I do not like it if somebody makes decisions for me. The Chief of State gives orders. To kill people you do not know–this is unimaginable. I suppose nowadays there are other ways to arrive at an agreement. Patriotism has gone to hell: young people today would not accept the experiences that we have experienced. But wars exist in other forms, economic, for instance. I do not like any of them."

"I hope our children and grandchildren will experience no more wars. Wars like that in Bosnia will always exist. I hope they will not touch us. When I was young, my parents refused to talk about war, so as not to scare us. I remember the defeat: we escaped by car; I did not suffer. Last year in Germany I saw Germans up close; I was surprised that they were friendly."

"Life is beautiful. To die for an idea? Never. It would contradict everything I believe. We won't kill each other if my idea is blue and his is red. I live in a thriving country, I rarely think about wars. Here we are privileged, far removed from almost everything unpleasant. I hope to be lucky enough to preserve this distance. People do not have to be forced; we must talk to each other. Will we be able to do it? And what about me? Will I be able to accept the monument?"

Please Think On

Helga Pakasaar

The idea that art can only be as good as its public is at the heart of Jochen Gerz's interactive works. From his early performance works to the recent public projects, he has assumed the role of artist as mediator between art and life. A provocateur whose strategies include humor, disguise, and subterfuge, Gerz teases the spectator into participating in a social exchange. Participation often involves becoming actively engaged in the artist's inquiries. As a producer absorbed into the work, the public is coerced into just noticing, solving a riddle, or contributing to a memory archive. Maker and receiver are thus on equal footing. Ever attentive to power relations, Gerz avoids the allure of visual spectacle by restricting himself to the sparest of aesthetic means. His visual modesty subverts expectation, turning passive reception of art into active reflection. For Jochen Gerz, art is above all about its ties to the social subject. His public works occupy what he calls a "no man's land," an interstitial zone between the real and its reproduction, between life and art.

Performance as an antidote to spectacle provides Gerz with tangible links to lived experience. While abandoning performance art per se in the early 1980s, he has sustained elements of the performative in the processes as well as content of his varied art production. Improvisation, for example, is important to his many tests, surveys and questionnaires. The artist's preferred method is to structure a work around methodical procedures that can accommodate random information and elements of chance. In order to be responsive to the contingencies of the particular context that each public piece evolves from, it is essential to be adaptable. Gerz's projects often start as collaborations that he eventually withdraws from as input from the communities involved increases, leaving them in the public realm.[1] In this sense, Gerz's public projects can be seen as extended performances.

Lengthy processes at times involving large numbers of people are an integral part of each project. The public pieces from the 1970s were provocative gestures for unwitting passers-by, or social actions documented in photographs. The complex operations of recent works are designed to galvanize willing participation. The *Monument against Fascism* (1986–93), for example, underwent daily changes for seven years as comments were scratched onto the lead surface of a column that was lowered into the ground until it disappeared. The clandestine operation of laying 2146 engraved cobblestones in the Saarbrücken city square for *Monument against Racism* (1990–93) took over a year of nocturnal work and several more years of bureaucratic procedures before the existence of this invisible piece was officially acknowledged. *The Living Monument* of Biron (1995–96) will always be incomplete as new generations add their reflections on war. The negotiations required to produce these works become absorbed as content. The performer/creator is nothing more than a vehicle for producing ideas and action, a type of troubadour who passes knowledge back to where it came from. The impulse towards non-material art without authors—what has been called "social sculpture"—is set up in Gerz's work to eventually dissolve into the public realm where it can slyly slip into cultural memory.

Throughout his career Gerz has adapted aspects of performance as a unique act that resists repetition and reproduction and in a sense becomes itself through disappearance. Always committed to "real time," he uses the temporal dimension of time-based media as a primary method. Like performance, his interactive works come into existence through social engagement, and live on in the imagination. The underlying premise of such ephemeral non-events is that memory can transform future events. Thus, the performative is used not only as a technique but also as a powerful metaphor. For example, *To Live* (1974) was a nine-hour writing performance of covering a floor with the word *leben* that became part of an interactive sculpture. Over the course of the installation, as curious viewers walked on the chalk words to read a plaque on the back wall, the artist's labor was erased. In the process of consuming the work it is destroyed. Traces of the words become a poetic expression of art as life.

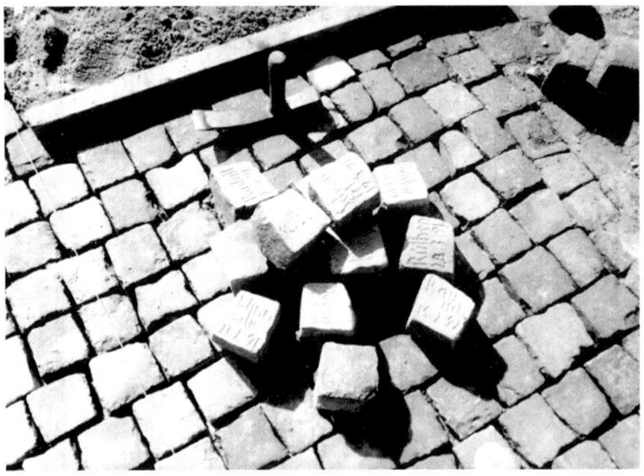

2146 Stones–Monument against Racism, Saarbrücken 1990–93

Constant and ever-changing public involvement can interrupt production and redirect the purpose of Gerz's works. The empowered viewer becomes embroiled in more than simply "completing the piece," as they say. There is a consistent rigor in the artist's unwillingness to succumb to the easy pleasures of aesthetic experience. He insists on an acceptance of absence and incompleteness, and allows for the ultimate art crime–an unresolved work. At the core of his overall project is the impulse to take this lack of synthesis, and the doubt and confusion it creates, and re-direct it towards discursive spaces of social interaction.

The vehicle of performance also allows the artist to confuse the boundaries of personal experience and social convention.. His performances often involved an enactment of extreme psychological and physical states that leveled public and private identity. For example, *To Cry until Exhaustion* (1972) and *Hand-Writing* (1972) were socially regressive endurance tests and pathetic attempts at communication that assaulted the maker as much as the witness. Typical of performance art at the time, the body had no character, yet the visceral intimacy of the activity provoked a subjective response.

Jochen Gerz has continued to articulate a space where distinctions between private and public collapse, a "no man's land" where spatial politics is most animated. Understanding that the public sphere is much more than officially designated, sanitized "public space"–administered urban zones of controlled civic interaction where most "public art" is actually housed–he takes into consideration the powerful impact of systems of information and knowledge on social identity. (Gerz was quick to investigate the immaterial public sphere of the internet.) Of greatest importance for the artist is the most ephemeral and unarticuled aspect of the public realm–that of collective memory.

In Gerz's interactive works, notions of the private as a place of differences and of the public as a unified, homogenous sphere of privilege get turned upside down. The early works presented urban experience as a fragile network of fleeting encounters, where personal thoughts intersect with communal ideals. The diverse and often contradictory voices that animate *The Witnesses* (1998), *The*

Living Monument and *The Bremen Questionnaire* (1990–95) suggest that individuals do not fit neatly into separated private and public identities. In this sense, the artist makes claims for a public space that is truly civic, like the discursive space of the commons that belonged to everyone and no one.

An urban site of transition and constant negotiation of territory where public and private overlap is the street. It is not surprising then that many of Gerz's performances of the 1970s took place on the street. In these subtle interventions that rely on chance encounters, pedestrians became both the subject and object of the work. In his first public intervention of 1968 the artist stuck labels saying "Caution Art Corrupts" on cultural monuments of Florence, tricking an unassuming public into questioning their personal beliefs in cultural value. In another simple gesture, *Exhibition of Jochen Gerz beside his Photographic Reproduction* (1972), the artist stood next to a photographic portrait of himself on a busy street. Aside from the joke about original and copy, this live sculpture/masterpiece reaches beyond semiotic games and art references precisely because of its public location. Activated by a glance from the casual passer-by rather than any authoritative gaze, this "exhibition" insinuates itself into the fabric of urban life. More than just a fleeting distraction, though, its absurdity was registered, briefly shifting the consciousness of those who witnessed it. Similarly, *329 Book of Gestures* (1969/73) was 5000 numbered cards saying "you are the missing part of a book [...] do not alter your behavior as a result of this information" scattered onto streets. The intimate tone of the joke punctures the personal space of the recipients who, turned into instant art, become accomplices in the piece simply by imagining a network of relationships. To suggest that the city is some vast dream, restores the personal to urban experience. As with the remaining element of the Bremen project dedicated to those who answered the artist's questionnaire–those who imagined an artwork–and to "all those who stand here and see something that does not exist," the ongoing piece continues because of the human capacity to imagine the unknown. In this sense, Gerz gives life to the claim that "the city is a book with 1,000,000 million poems" (Roland Barthes). Initially a concrete poet himself, he respects the limitations of words and simple manifestations of language.

Gerz's early interest in the workings of cities was part of critical inquiries (especially prevalent in Paris) that mapped the complexities of urban landscapes. As with the Situationists and Fluxus conceptualists, his interventions challenged the spectacle of post-war urbanism and shed light on the prosaic vagaries of everyday life. Transient, mundane sites and banal activities were the focus of Gerz's attention: working class neighborhoods (*Rue Mouffetard*, 1972), gardening (*Piece for 1, 2, 3, 4*, 1971), washing windows (*Piece for a Window Washer*, 1971). In Gerz's hands, civic systems of exchange like garbage collection (*Is There Life on Earth?*, 1968/1970) and telephone books (*The New Phonebook of Paris*, 1968/1971) became vehicles for imposing personal need on public "services", throwing off the social equilibrium such services are supposed to maintain. *Is There Life on Earth?* involved a call for personal garbage from the artist's friends and randomly selected persons in the Paris telephone book: garbage that was buried in cement in a Parisian construction site that transformed waste disposal into a perverse type of offering and act of communication. In *The Exhibition of 8 People Living in Rue Mouffetard* the artist displayed a poster of randomly selected names of inhabitants of that street. This cryptic announcement assumed the authority of public declarations, inciting reactions that ranged from fear of exposure to a desire to be a part of the publicity. A type of object lesson, it provoked a confusion of public and private needs that precipitated social interaction.

By simply recording a routine activity or through subtle manipulations of social behavior, the artist articulates the everyday. Assuming a decidedly anti-heroic stance, he offers reminders of what is already known. Working with materials and means common to public modes of address, he also draws attention to how quotidian experience is manipulated. Like the poster listing names on Rue Mouffetard that was reminiscent of commemorative plaques and wanted signs, Gerz exploited the commercial associations of billboards, his format of preference in the 1980s. *5 Billboards for Banff* (1984) were inverted arctic landscapes overlaid with text (each in a different language) declaring "those who know will say least." Playing off this Canadian resort town's promotion of wilderness consumption and snow culture, Gerz subverts its identity by invoking Inuit culture. The billboards function as warning signs that rupture the commercial environment with reminders of the social and political conditions that define place. Each location of *It's no Mystery* (1982)–another inverted landscape with the message "your knowledge will kill you"–whether in a modern German city or amongst military caravans in the Israeli desert, gave the piece a political meaning that the image and text alone could never have generated. Typical of the artist's restraint, the billboards have a political resonance that is not didactic. The "you" of Gerz's truisms is neither accusatory nor exclusive, but addresses everyone.

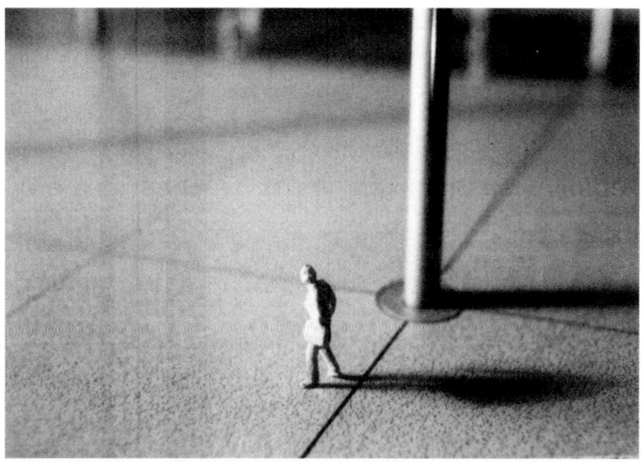

Why did it happen? Monument for the Murdered Jews of Europe, Berlin 1997/98 computer simulation

Always favoring black and white photographs, the ghostly presence of the billboards suggests that communication through representation is a flawed enterprise. These mysterious images inserted into civic order mark the "no man's land" that Gerz continues to explore.

The importance of giving expression to everyday culture remains at the core of Gerz's recent public projects that are shaped by input from diverse publics who rarely have a voice in official culture. Those who are powerless and without a voice become the substance of these works. Maintaining a performative intimacy, texts in these pieces are direct quotations that express the immediacy of spoken language. He makes evident that the acts of writing and the enunciation of speech are inextricably tied to the human body. Testimonials, opinions and confessions are strung together to form a puzzle of clues to a social map. Whether incomprehensibly idiosyncratic or utterly banal, the assemblage of voices, like any oral history, forms a fragmented picture of an historic moment. The intention driving Gerz's recent public projects is to literally make people speak, in as many languages as possible. The *Holocaust Memorial* (1997–98) in Berlin, for example, is designed to have people never be able to avoid asking why. In the process of deciphering different languages–modes of thinking–the relative nature of knowledge becomes apparent. In the reading of Gerz's work, one is lead into a field of declarations, opinions, fears, secrets, convictions, prejudices, and hopes. This is a place of uncertainty with no clear answers. Unlike the authoritative language maintained by the institutions that control human affairs, the stammering of beliefs represents the consciousness that comes from direct experience. Regarding these "open works," in Umberto Eco's sense of the term, the reader is a producer rather than a consumer whose interpretations expand the work. In the internet pieces *Plural Sculpture* (1995) or The *Berkeley Oracle* (1997–99), interpretation and apprehension become one. To navigate through these sites involves scanning for answers that make sense. This sifting process of identifying with or rejecting each speaker produces a web of fleeting social relations. The text-based works are performed as the participants, accomplices in an act of creative cooperation, actively build connections to belief. No longer spectators, interpreters or readers, they experience this wandering through text as an active collaboration in the making of meaning. Always wary of the narcotic effects of narrative, especially those imposed by the writing and making of history, Gerz leaves the idiosyncrasies of everyday speech to personal interpretation.

With the recent public project, *The Witnesses*, Gerz comes closest to producing a commemorative work, giving a temporary public face to those citizens who are usually the most invisible and silent. A series of posters hung in the streets of Cahors display portraits of local women together with their statements about life. Full of secrets and regrets, their confessions portray the ironies of existence in a way that their faces fail to communicate. The permeability of image and text that the artist often plays with, here is an unresolved tension between perceiving someone and knowing their thoughts, between representation and the real. As in other public pieces, the traumas of history are domesticated through the discourse of utterance. Verbal communication as an expression of cultural anxiety returns the political to lived social experience.

All of Gerz's public projects inexorably loop back to self-reflection and the imagination. Linking the fragility of art to that of life, he lives up to the claim that "the prerequisite for what I am doing is not art, it is life."[2] As the text piece of 1969 says: "Please Think On," Jochen Gerz continues to explore potentials for insight.

1 Many of the public pieces discussed are collaborative works with Esther Shalev-Gerz. Students often contributed to the development of works. **2** Stephen Snoddy, "25 May 1991 ...", in: Jochen Gerz, *Life after Humanism*, Manchester 1992, w/o p.

The Exhibition

Attenzione l'arte corrompe/Caution Art Corrupts/Achtung Kunst korrumpiert

Florence, 1968

Attenzione l'arte corrompe, poster, offset, 70 x 100 cm

The sticker *Attenzione l'arte corrompe* was employed in various places in the city of Florence, inclusive of being applied to the pedestal of Michelangelo's *David.* A year later, *Achtung Kunst korrumpiert* was plastered throughout the city of Basel during the exhibition "Für Veränderungen aller Art" (For Changes of Any and All Kinds). The text has been used in several public spaces, in three languages.

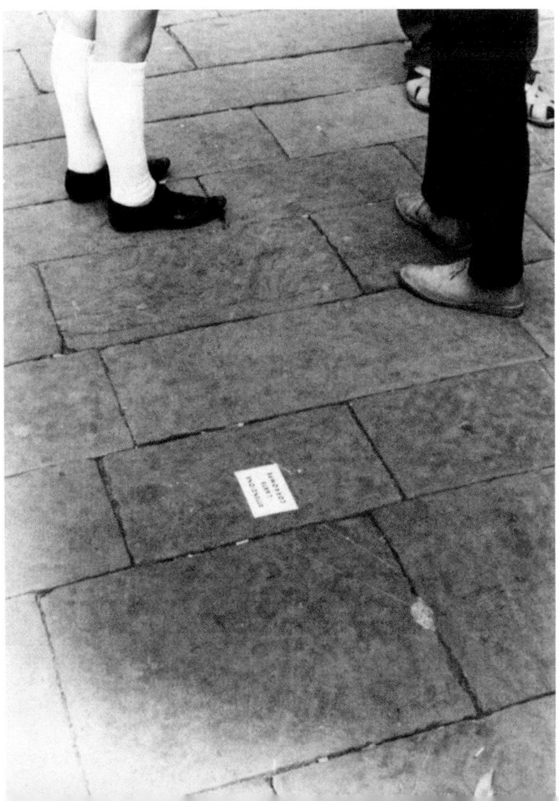

Florence, 1968

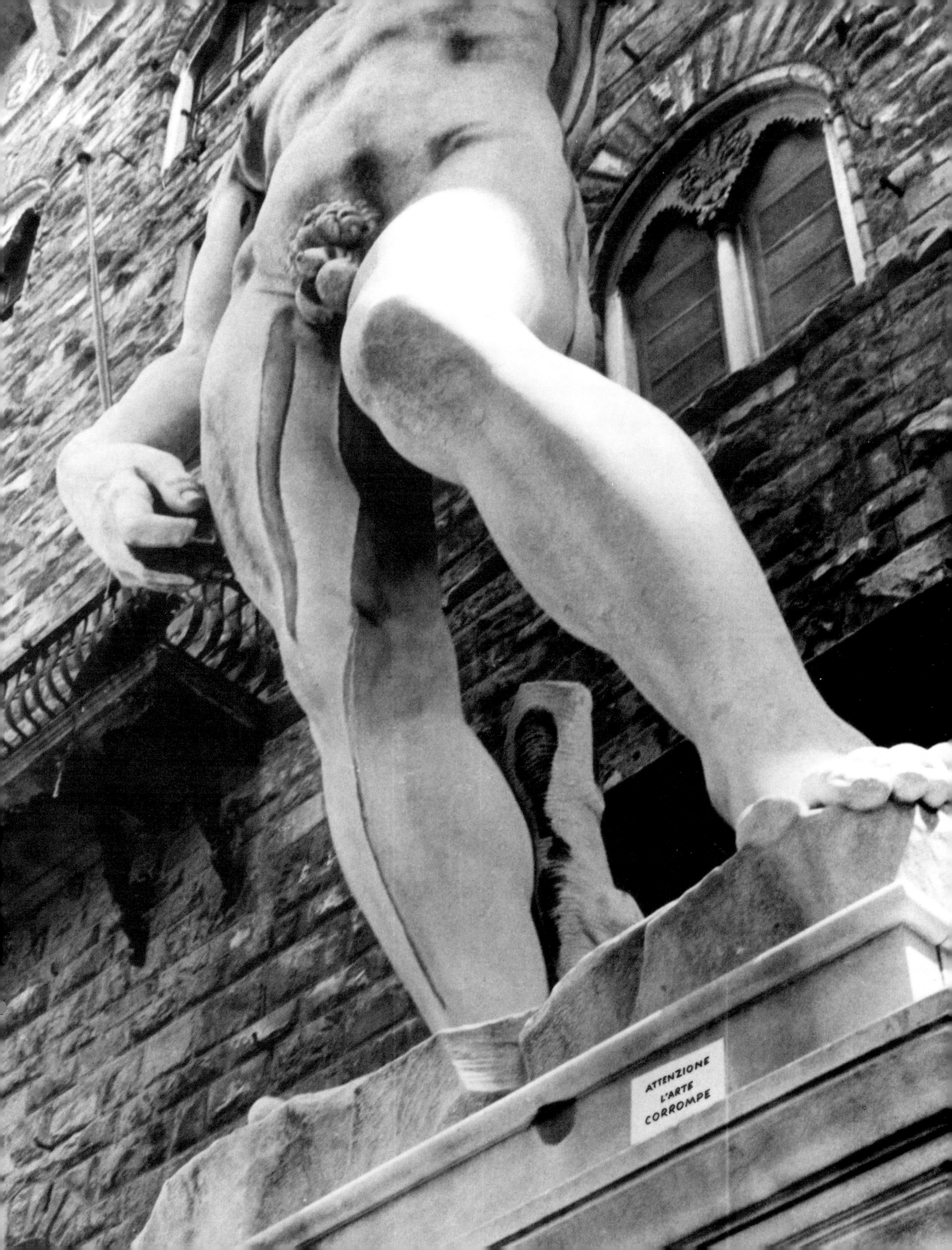
ATTENZIONE
L'ARTE
CORROMPE

ATTENZIONE L'ARTE CORROMPE

AGENTZIA AEP 8

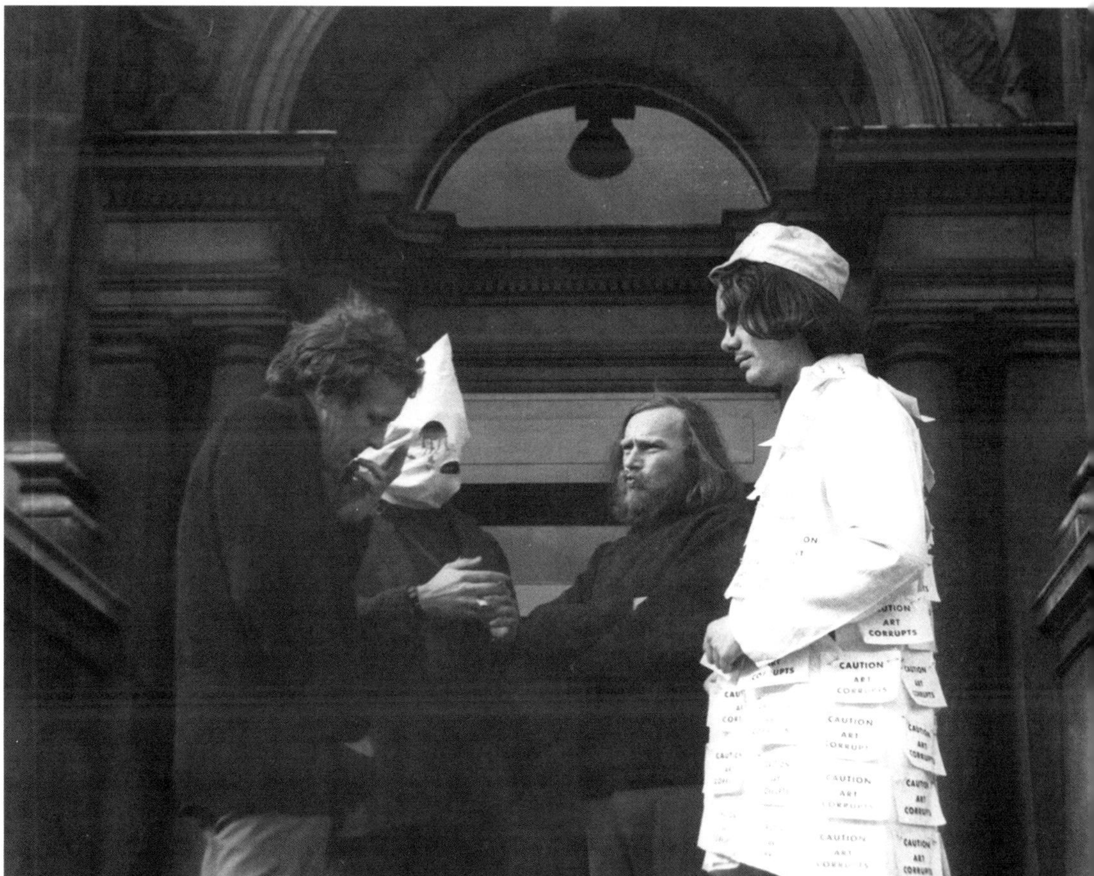

London, 1970

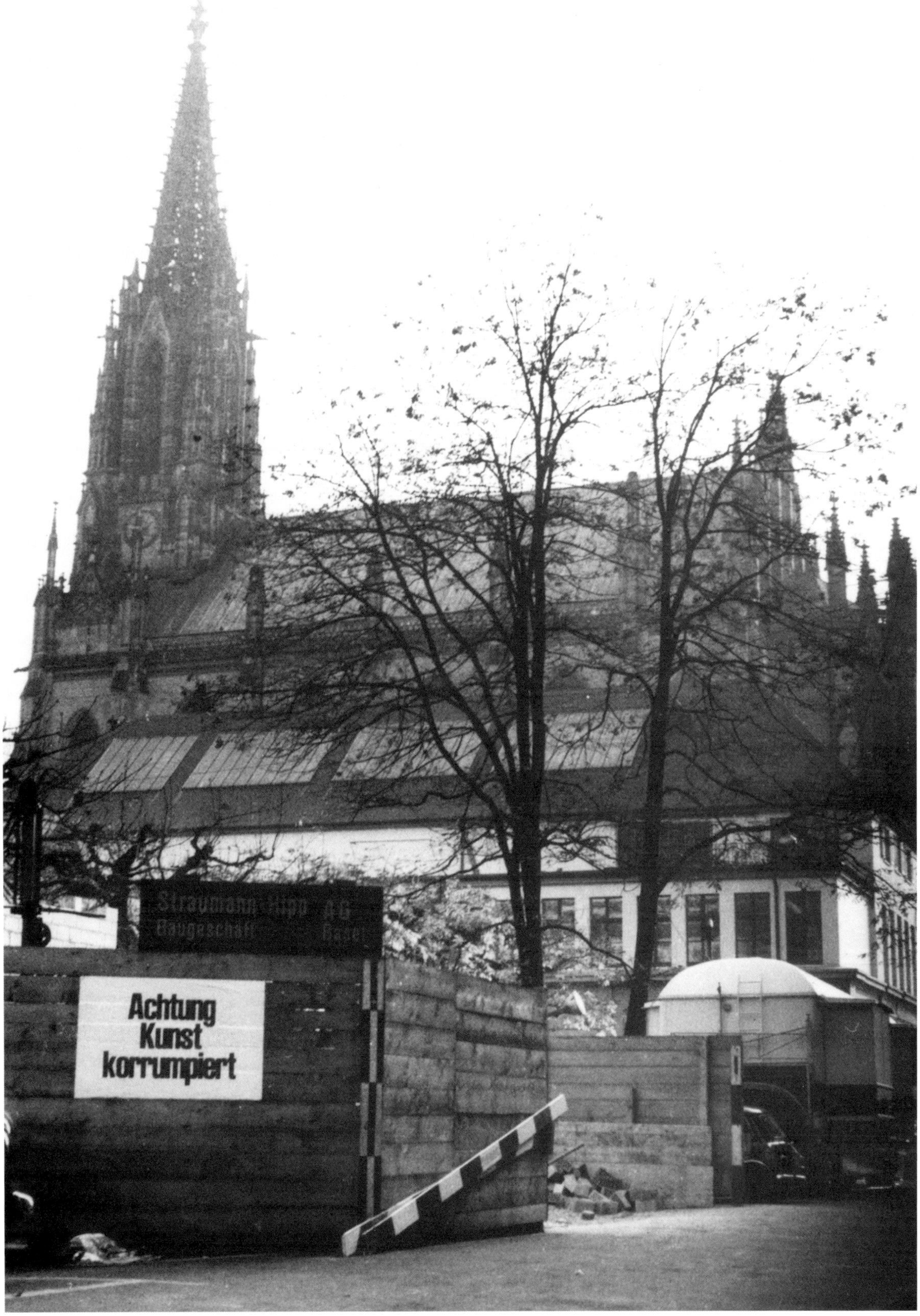

Basel, 1969

Exposition de 8 personnes habitant la rue Mouffetard, Paris, à travers leurs noms, sur les murs de leur rue même (The Exhibition of 8 People Living in Rue Mouffetard, Paris, by Way of Their Names, on the Walls of Their Street)

Paris, 1972

Die Entwicklung des Schreibens (The Development of Writing) # 5
Posters, printed with poster colors; 2 parts, 48 x 66.5 cm each
A collaboration with the students of the Ecole Nationale Supérieure des Arts Décoratifs, Paris
The names of eight persons residing in Rue Mouffetard, Paris, were printed on posters which were pasted up at various points along the same street. The work came to an end when the posters were papered over.

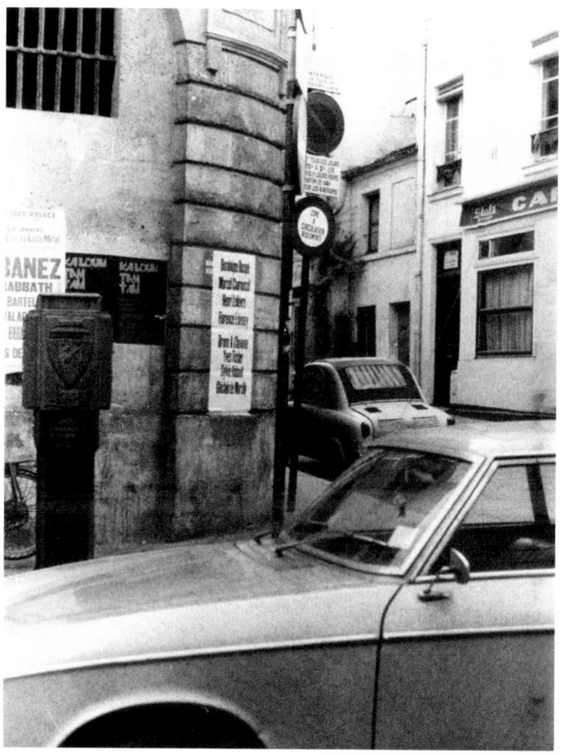

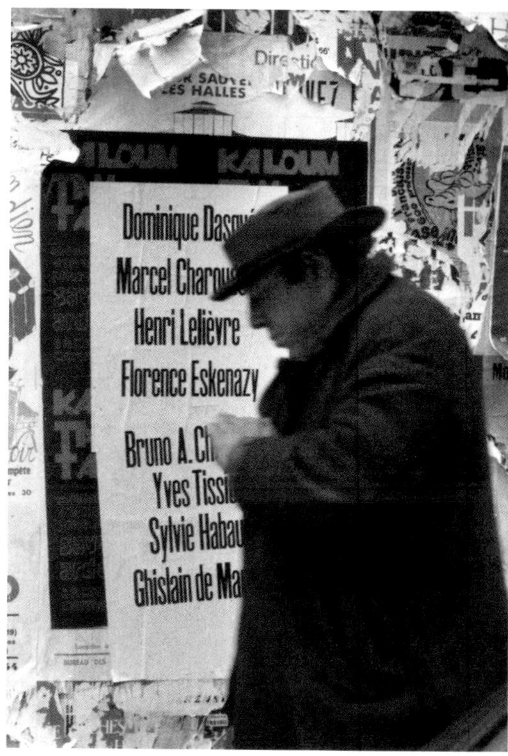

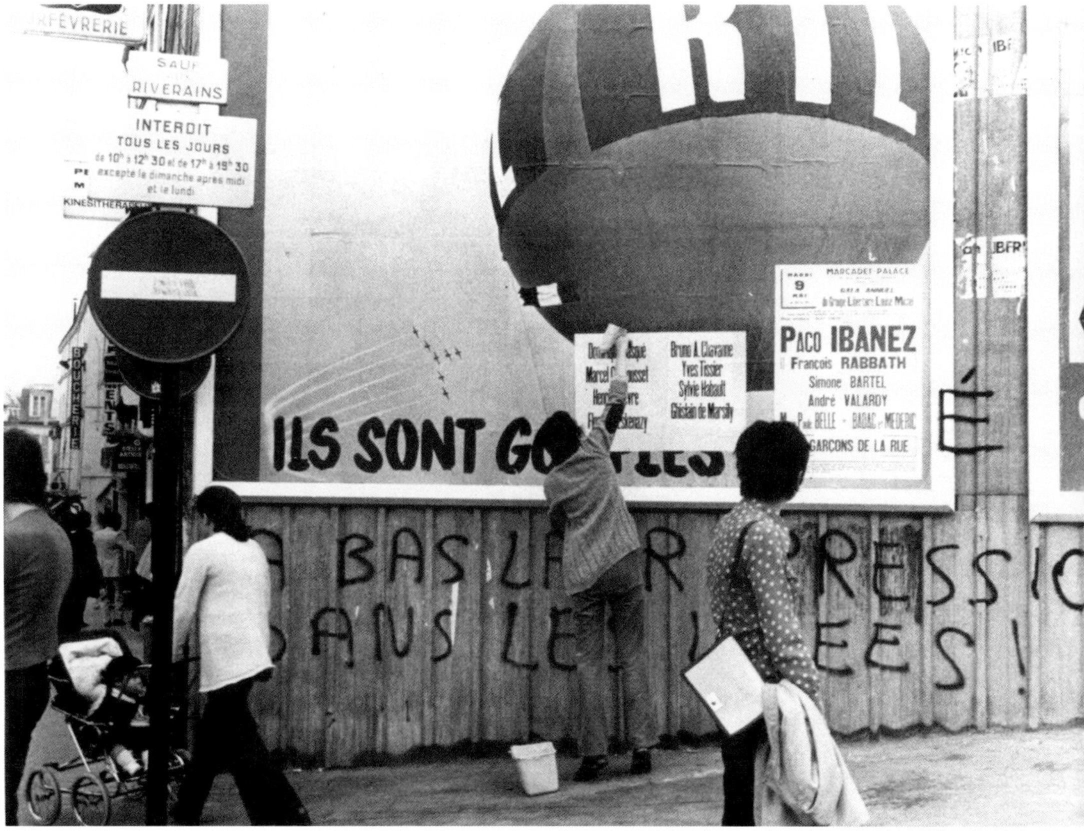
SAUF RIVERAINS
INTERDIT
TOUS LES JOURS
de 10h à 12h30 et de 17h à 19h30
excepté le dimanche après midi et le lundi
BOUCHERIE
Dominique Dasque
Bruno A. Chavanne
Yves Tissier
Sylvie Habault
Ghislain de Marsily
MARCADET-PALACE
PACO IBANEZ
Francois RABBATH
Simone BARTEL
André VALARDY
GARCONS DE LA RUE

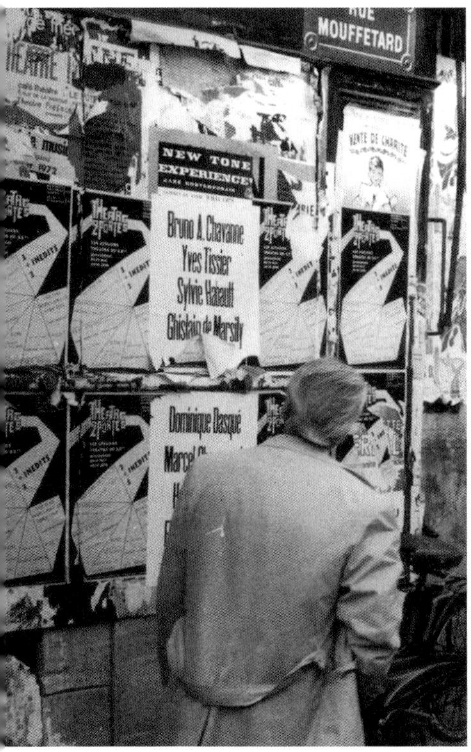
RUE MOUFFETARD
NEW TONE EXPERIENCE
Bruno A. Chavanne
Yves Tissier
Sylvie Habault
Ghislain de Marsily
Dominique Dasque

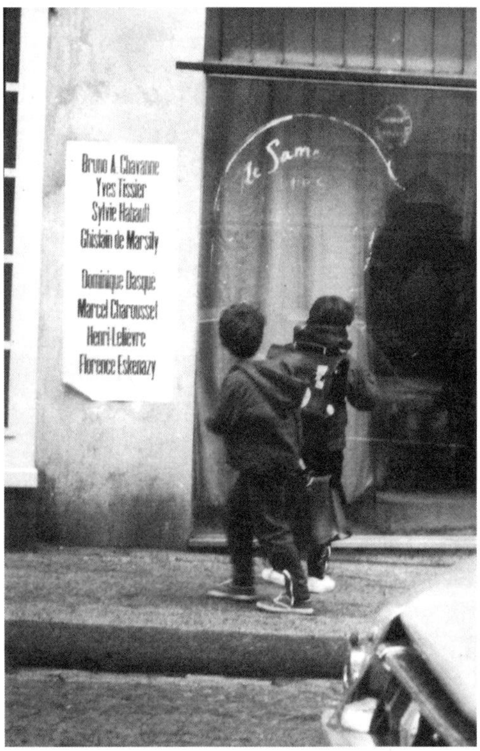
Bruno A. Chavanne
Yves Tissier
Sylvie Habault
Ghislain de Marsily
Dominique Dasque
Marcel Charousset
Henri Lelievre
Florence Eskenazy

Il n’y a pas de mystère (It’s no Mystery) **Chambéry, 1982**

Scannachrome, 260 x 360 cm

The poster shows the image of a night-time silhouette of a city, upside down, accompanied by the text: : *Il n'y a pas de mystère, c'est votre savoir qui vous tuera* (It is no mystery, your knowledge will kill you). The work was later presented with a German text in Kassel, and with a Hebrew text in Israel.

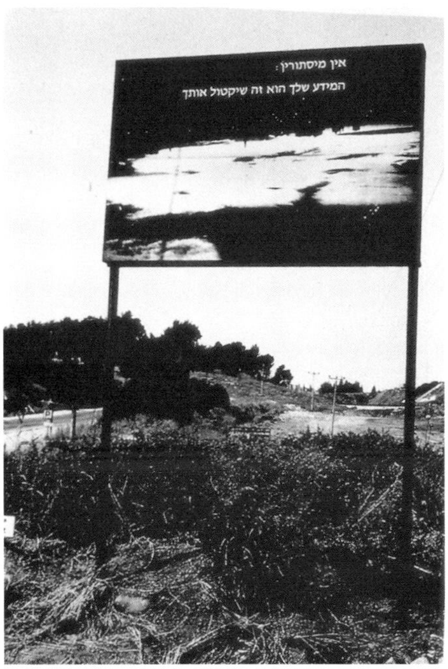

Israel, 1982

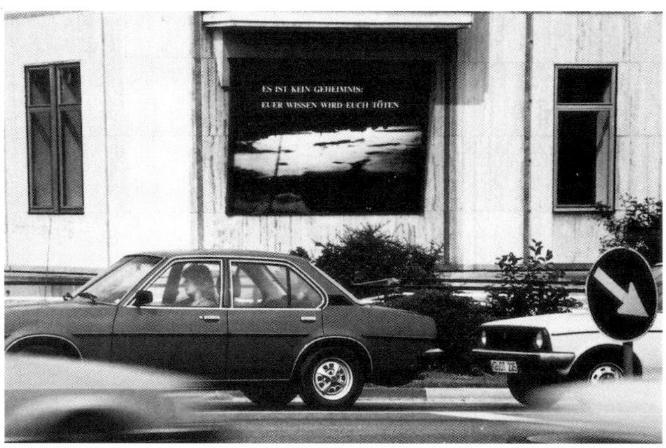

Kassel, 1982

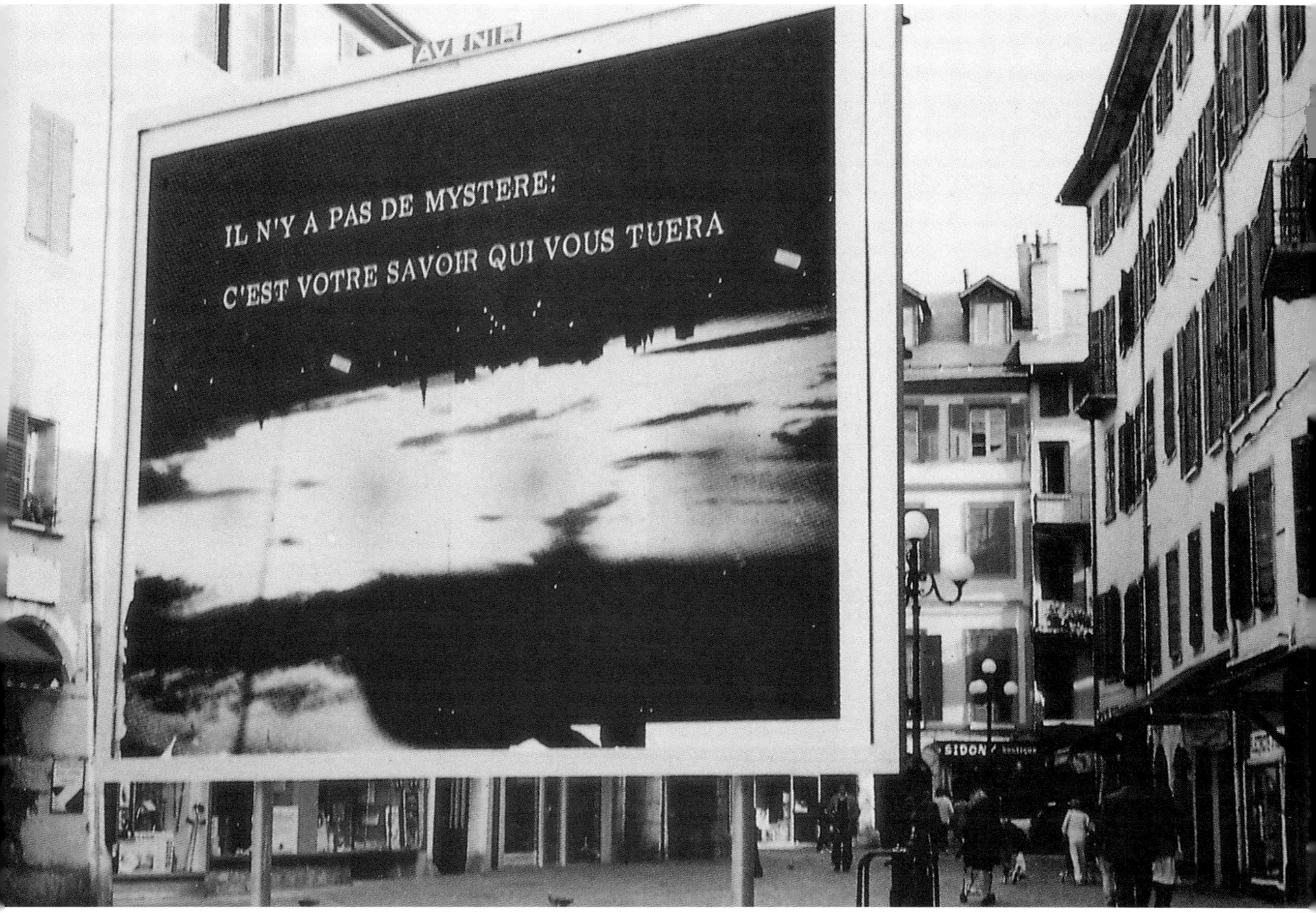

Chambéry, 1982

5 Billboards for Banff **Banff, 1984**

5 black and white photos on PVC; 120 x 210 cm each; The Banff Art Center, Banff, Alberta
The 5 posters show an image of a subpolar forest landscape, upside down, accompanied by the following text (in English, French, Hebrew, Russian and German): "Those who know will say least."
The posters were pasted up along Banff's main street.

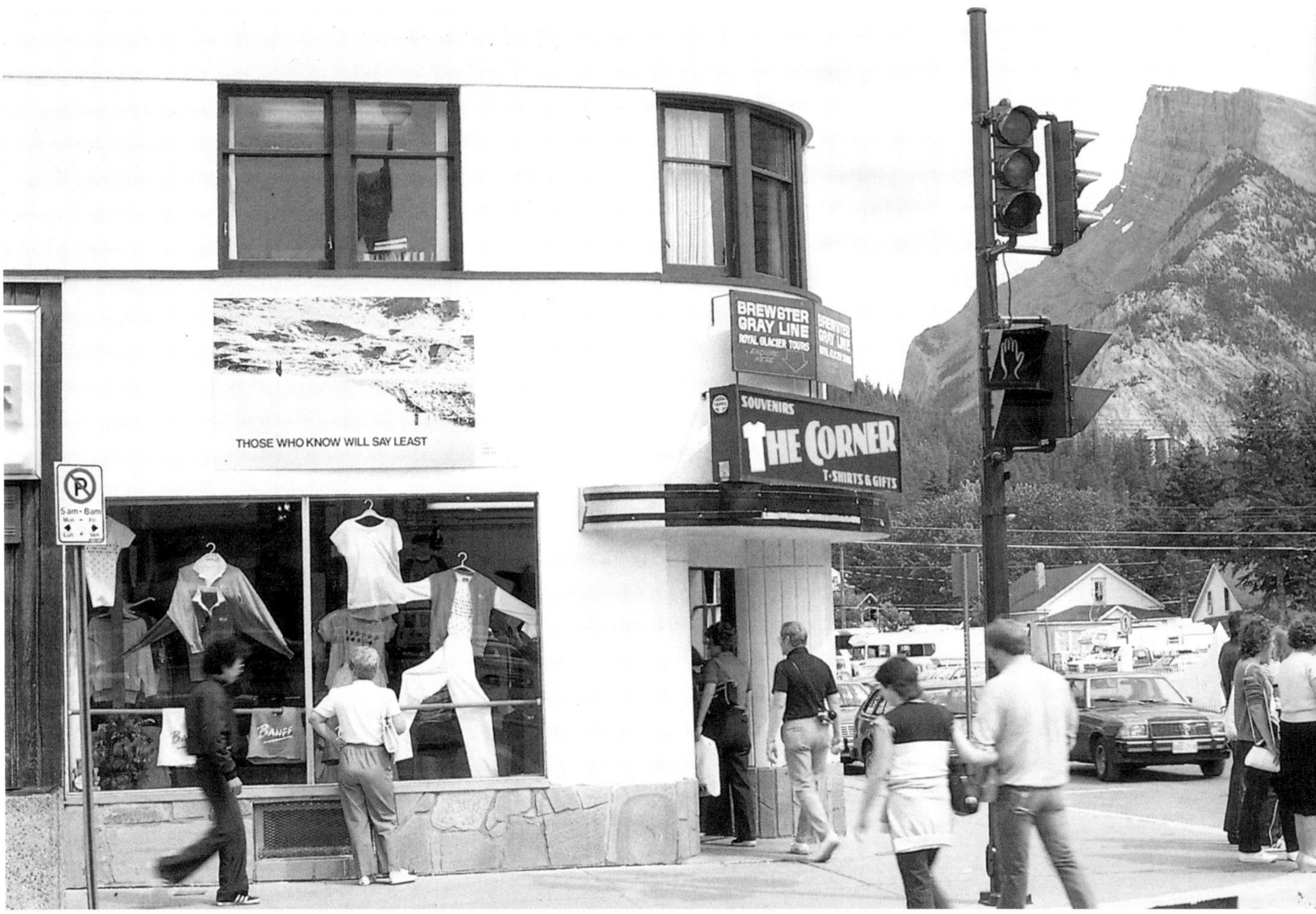

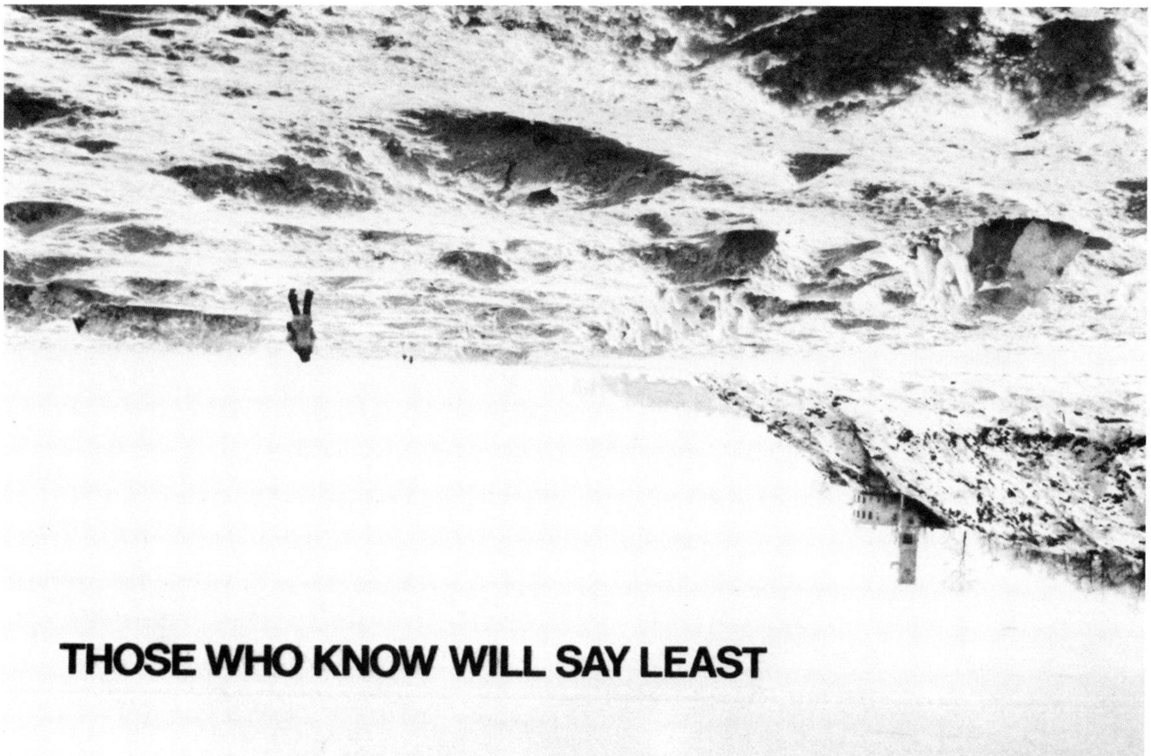
THOSE WHO KNOW WILL SAY LEAST

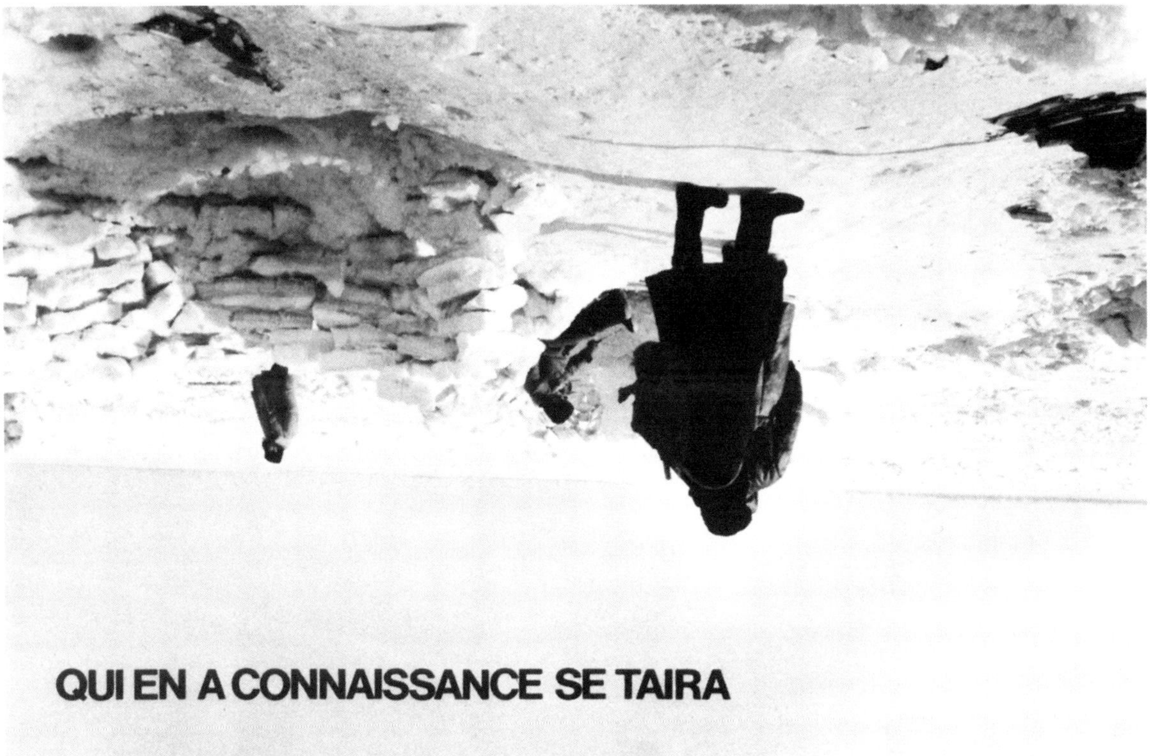
QUI EN A CONNAISSANCE SE TAIRA

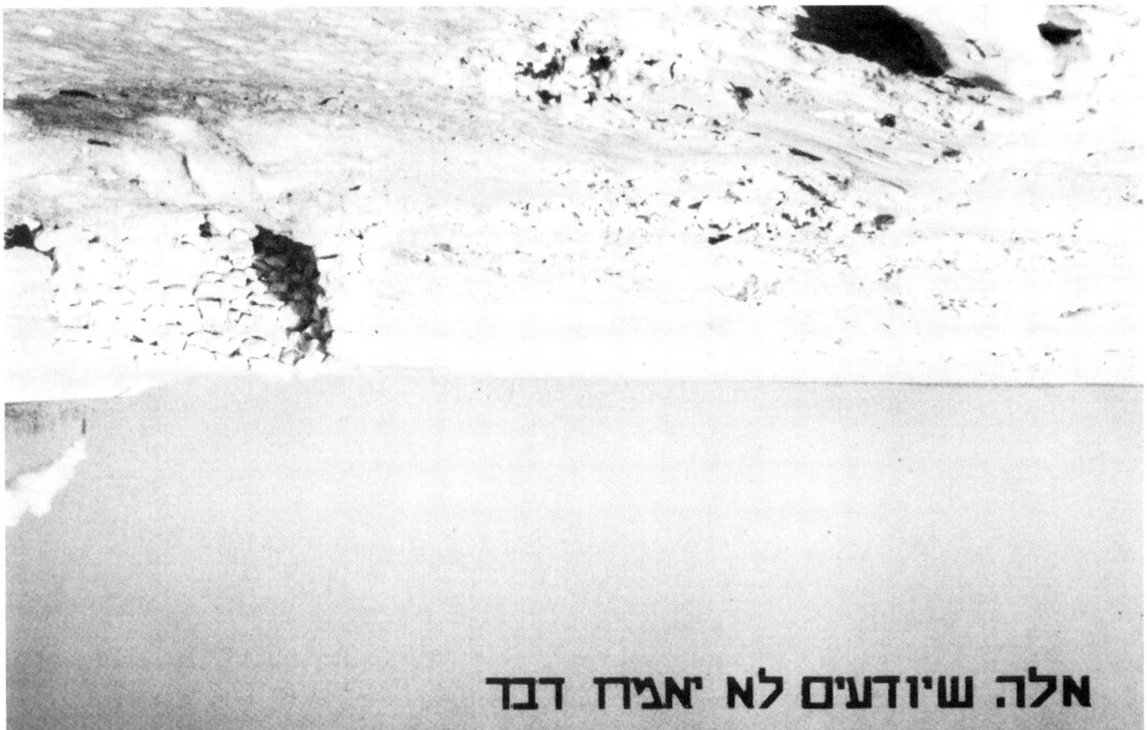
אלה. שיודעים לא יאמרו דבר

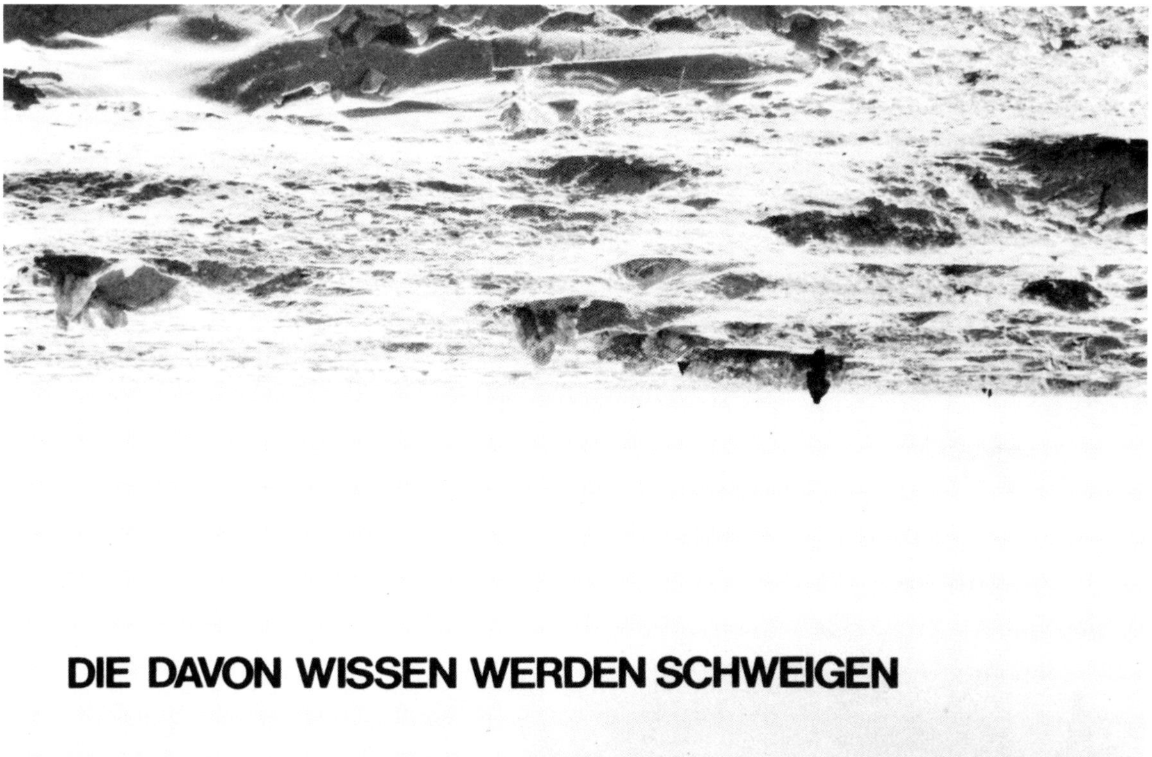
DIE DAVON WISSEN WERDEN SCHWEIGEN

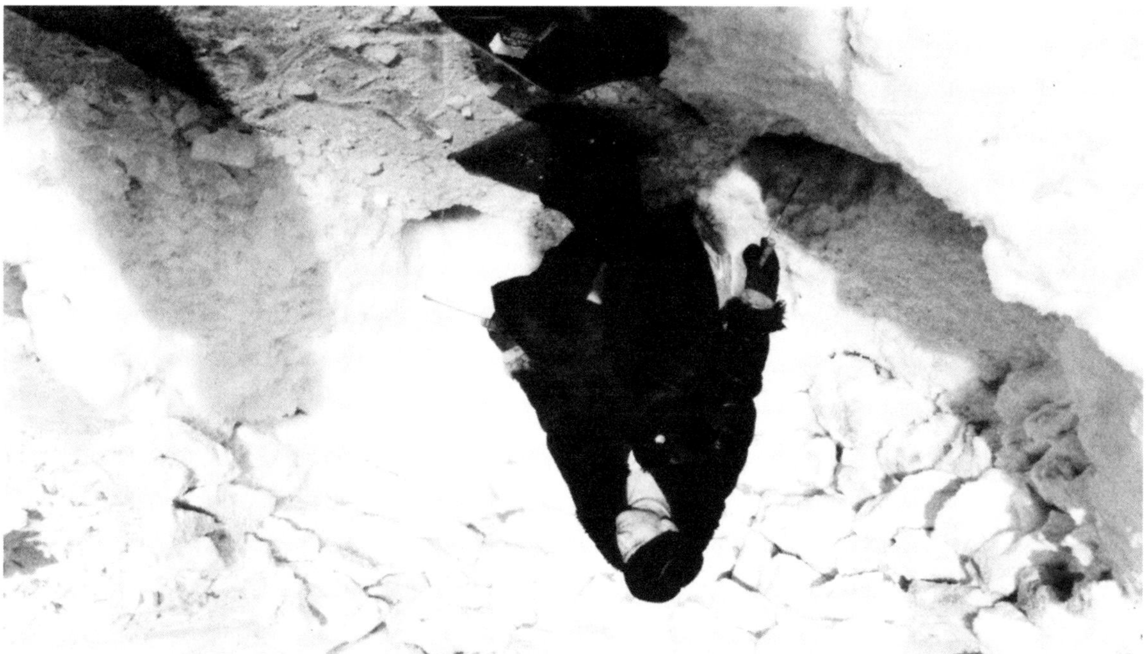
ТЕ КТО ЗНАЕТ СКАЖУТ МЕНЬШЕ ВСЕГО

Mahnmal gegen Faschismus (Monument against Fascism)

Hamburg-Harburg, 1986–93

Esther and Jochen Gerz; Installation
Stele in galvanized tubular steel with a lead coating, 1200 x 100 x 100 cm, weight ca. 7 tons, underground shaft of a depth of 14 m with an observation window, concrete foundation, 4 steel styluses for writing on the surface of the stele, tablet with text
Site: Hamburg-Harburg, Harburger Ring, at the corner of Hölertwiete/Sand, near the Harburg-Rathaus S-line train station
The Municipal Council of Hamburg-Harburg reached the decision in 1983, after several years of discussion, to erect a memorial against fascism. Under the aegis of the Municipal Cultural Commission, the competition for the memorial, in 1984, narrowed the field to five concepts. After further discussion and a public hearing, the commission was awarded on June 6, 1985 to the project proposed by Esther and Jochen Gerz. The project invited the city's citizens and visitors to use a steel stylus to engrave their names, as a sign of opposition to fascism, in the lead coating of a stele 12 m tall. As soon as the reachable part of the stele was covered with writing, it was to be sunk 140 cm. Between the dedication of the memorial on October 10, 1986 and its complete disappearance on November 10, 1993, the stele was lowered into the ground a total of eight times. Today a tablet inscribed with a text in seven languages records the process of the making of the monument, with a chronology of the erection, inscription, and sinking of the stele.

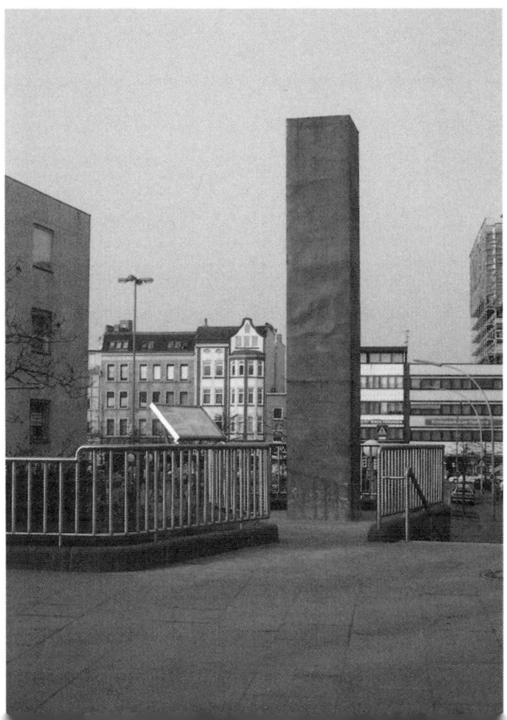

Monument against Fascism, Hamburg-Harburg, 1986–93

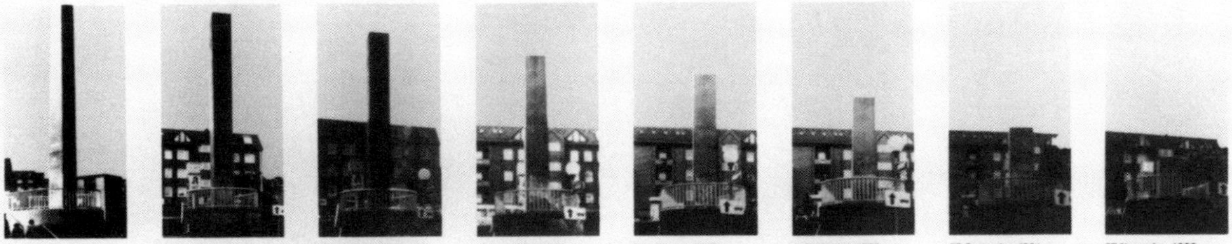

10. Oktober 1986	1. September 1987	23. Oktober 1988	6. September 1989	22. Februar 1990	4. Dezember 1990	27. September 1991	27. November 1992	10. November 1993
Einweihung	1. Absenkung	2. Absenkung	3. Absenkung	4. Absenkung	5. Absenkung	6. Absenkung	7. Absenkung	letzte Absenkung

Wir laden die Bürger von Harburg und die Besucher der Stadt ein, ihren Namen hier unseren eigenen anzufügen. Es soll uns verpflichten, wachsam zu sein und zu bleiben. Je mehr Unterschriften der zwölf Meter hohe Stab aus Blei trägt, um so mehr von ihm wird in den Boden eingelassen. Solange, bis er nach unbestimmter Zeit restlos versenkt und die Stelle des Harburger Mahnmals gegen Faschismus leer sein wird.

Denn nichts kann auf Dauer an unserer Stelle sich gegen das Unrecht erheben.

Harburg'da yaşayan ve bu kenti ziyaret edenleri isimlerini bizim isimlerimize ekleyerek katılmaya çağrıyoruz. Bu, bizi uyanık olmaya ve uyanık kalmaya mecbur etsin. 12 metre boyundaki kurşun sütunda imza ne kadar çoğaldıkça o kadar yere gömülecektir. Günün birinde sütun tamamen yere gömülerek kayboluncaya ve faşizme karşı uyanı anıtının yeri boş kalıncaya kadar bu devam edecektir.

Çünkü, bizden başka hiçbir şey haksızlığa karşı kalıcı olarak direnemez.

We invite the citizens of Harburg, and visitors to the town, to add their names here to ours. In doing so we commit ourselves to remain vigilant. As more and more names cover this 12 metre tall lead column, it will gradually be lowered into the ground. One day it will have disappeared completely, and the site of the Harburg monument against fascism will be empty.

In the end it is only we ourselves who can rise up against injustice.

Nous invitons les citoyens de Harbourg et les visiteurs de cette ville à joindre ici leurs noms aux nôtres. Cela pour nous engager à être vigilants et à le demeurer. Plus les signatures seront nombreuses sur cette barre de plomb haute de douze mètres, plus elle s'enfoncera dans le sol. Et un jour, elle disparaîtra entièrement et la place de ce monument contre le fascisme sera vide.

Car à la longue, nul ne pourra s'élever à notre place contre l'injustice.

אנו מזמינים את תושבי הרבורג ומבקרי העיר להוסיף שמם לשמנו. בעשותנו זאת אנו מתחייבים להשאר על המשמר. כמה שיותר שמות יכסו את עמוד העופרת בן 12 מטרים, הוא יורד לאיטו לתוך האדמה. יום אחד הוא יעלם לחלוטין ורחבת האנדרטה נגד פשיזם תהייה ריקה.

שהרי רק אנו עצמנו יכולים לקום נגד אי־צדק.

Мы приглашаем жителей и гостей города Гарбурга присоединить свои имена к нашим. Это обяжет нас всех быть бдительными и оставаться таковыми и впредь. Чем больше подписей будет набираться на свинцовом столбе 12-метровой высоты, тем глубже он будет опускаться в землю, пока однажды полностью не исчезнет, оставляя место Гарбургского монумента против фашизма пустым.

Ибо только мы сами можем противостоять несправедливости.

إننا نهيب بمواطني مدينة هاربورغ وزوارها إلى تسجيل أسمائهم على هذا النصب التذكاري. ليأخذوا على أنفسهم عهدا بالحذر من الفاشية. لقد صمم هذا النصب التذكاري المغلف بالرصاص، والمنتصب على ارتفاع ١٢ مترا، على أن ينزل في الأرض تدريجيا إلى أن يتوارى يوما ما عن الأنظار، ويغدو المكان المخصص له في مدينة هاربورغ كرمز لمناهضة الفاشية خاليا. وهكذا، فكلما ارتفع عدد الأسماء عليه ازداد انخفاضه في الأرض.

إذن، لا يمكن لأحد أن يحل محلنا دواما واستمرارا في مناهضة الظلم.

Harburgs Mahnmal gegen Faschismus, Krieg, Gewalt – für Frieden und Menschenrechte wurde nach einstimmigem Beschluß der Bezirksversammlung Harburg im Auftrag der Kulturbehörde Hamburg nach dem Konzept von Esther und Jochen Gerz realisiert.

The plaque beside the monument

An excerpt from the text for the project (1983):

Monuments against fascism... almost always show no daring or energy or artistic meaning; and, all the same, they arouse no sense of identification among the broader public. The content and spirituality of a memorial—even when perceived as a provocation—don't derive from the free choice of the commissioner or the artist, and instead are an echo of the human vitality of which the memorial is supposed to remind us. The inconceivability of the social developments of the twentieth century (National Socialism, and so forth) stands in crass contrast to the memorials that refer to them.
[...]
As opposed to the notion of the achievement of permanence by way of the memorial (by way of culture) we deploy the idea of a different function on the part of the monument: permanence is "sacrificed." The "sacrifice" of permanence is a social and religious act. The population of Harburg and those who visit the city cause to the monument to disappear. The visible becomes invisible, the memorial turns into memory (recycling). The non-cyclical object becomes a part of the cycle of time.
[...]
Either the monument "works"—which is to say that the initiative of the population renders it superfluous—or it remains a monument to its not having worked, as a meaningless ornament.

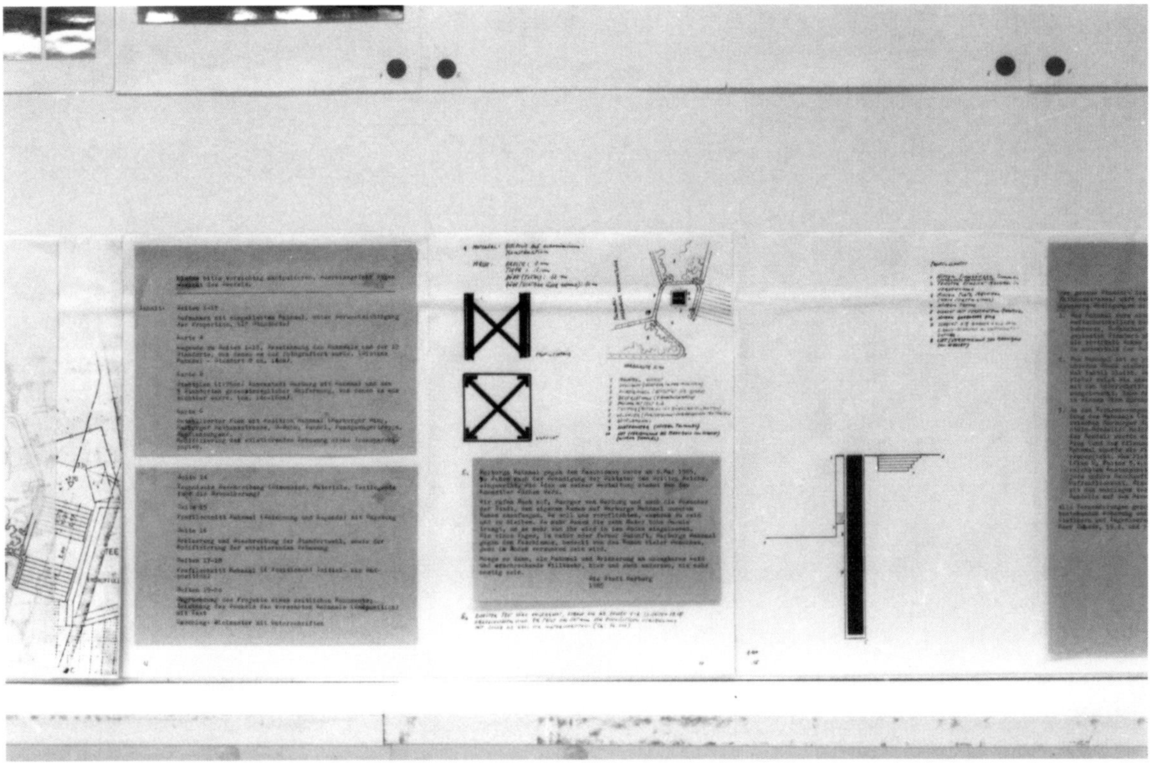

Project, detail

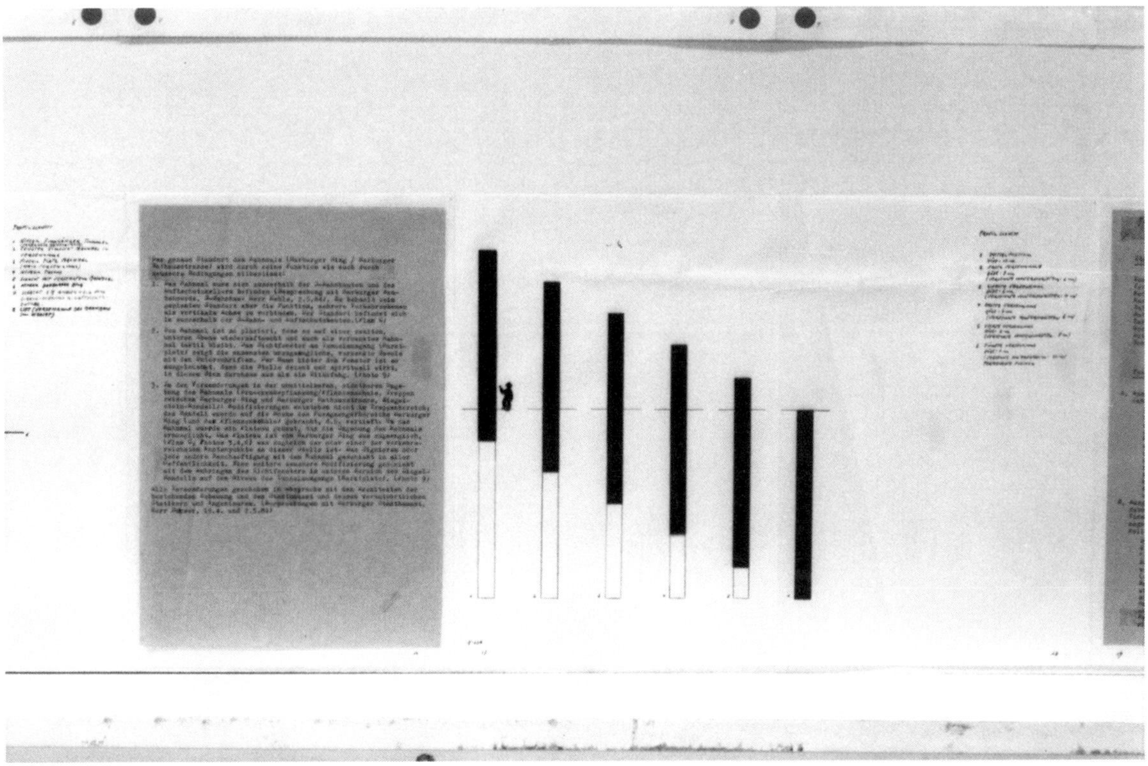

Project, detail

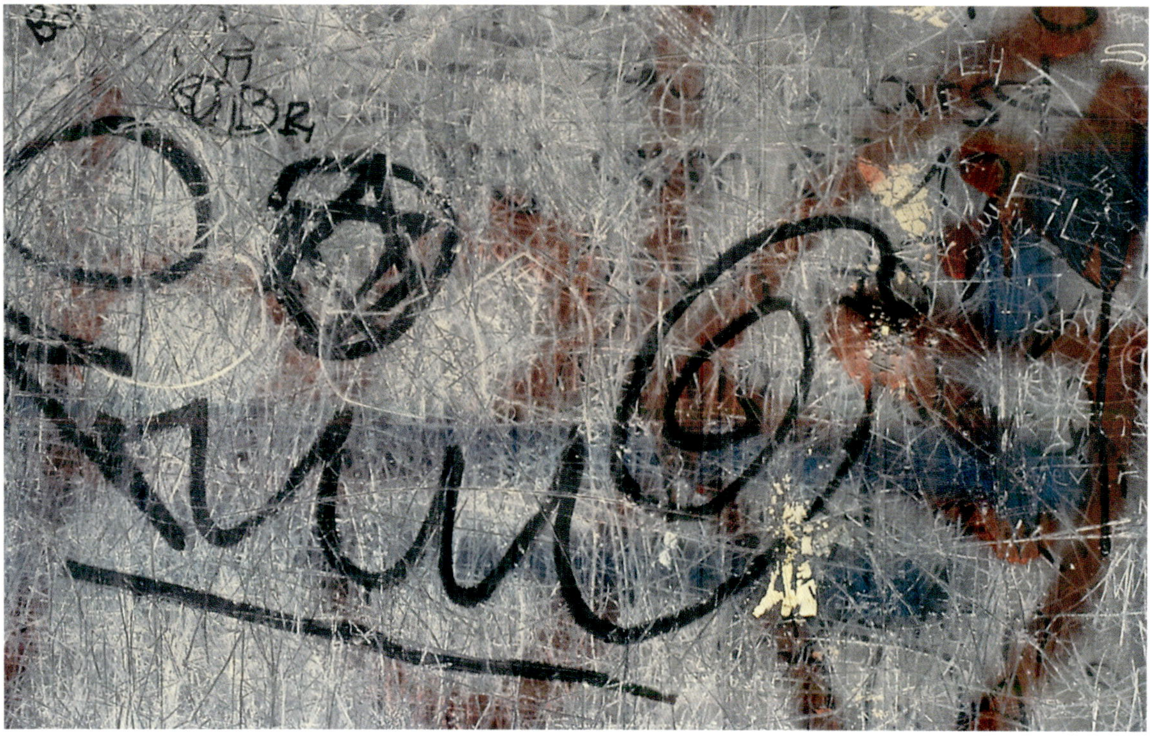

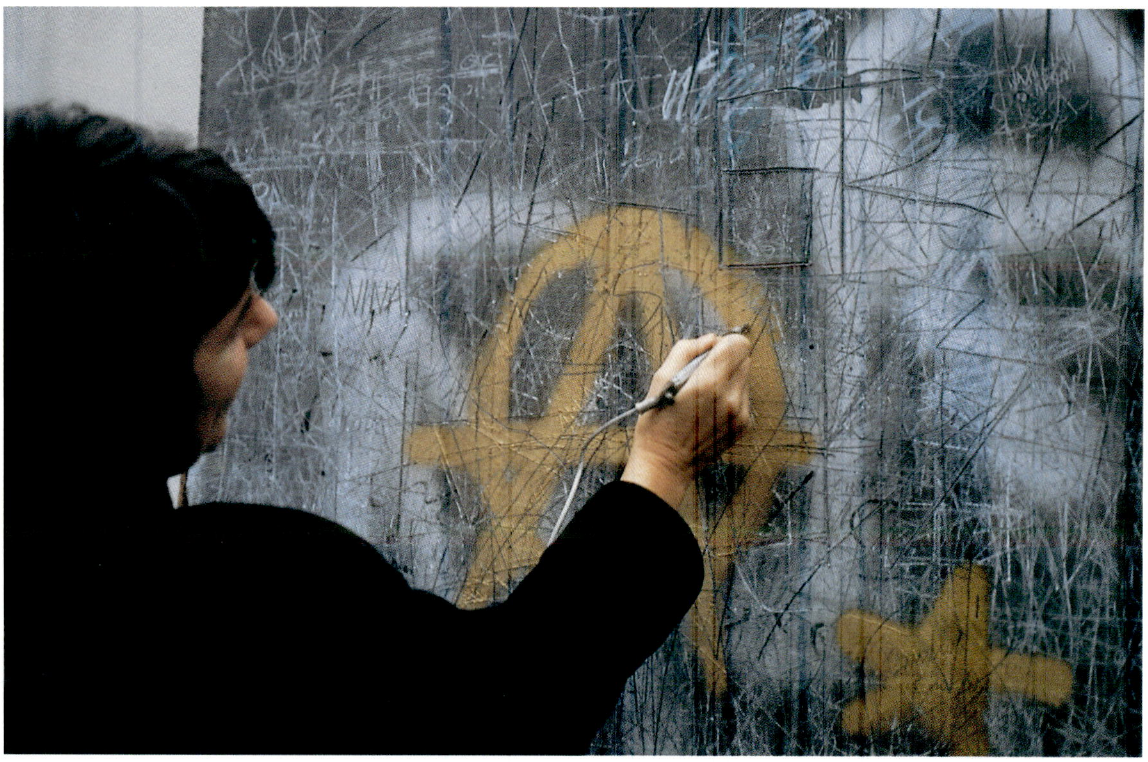

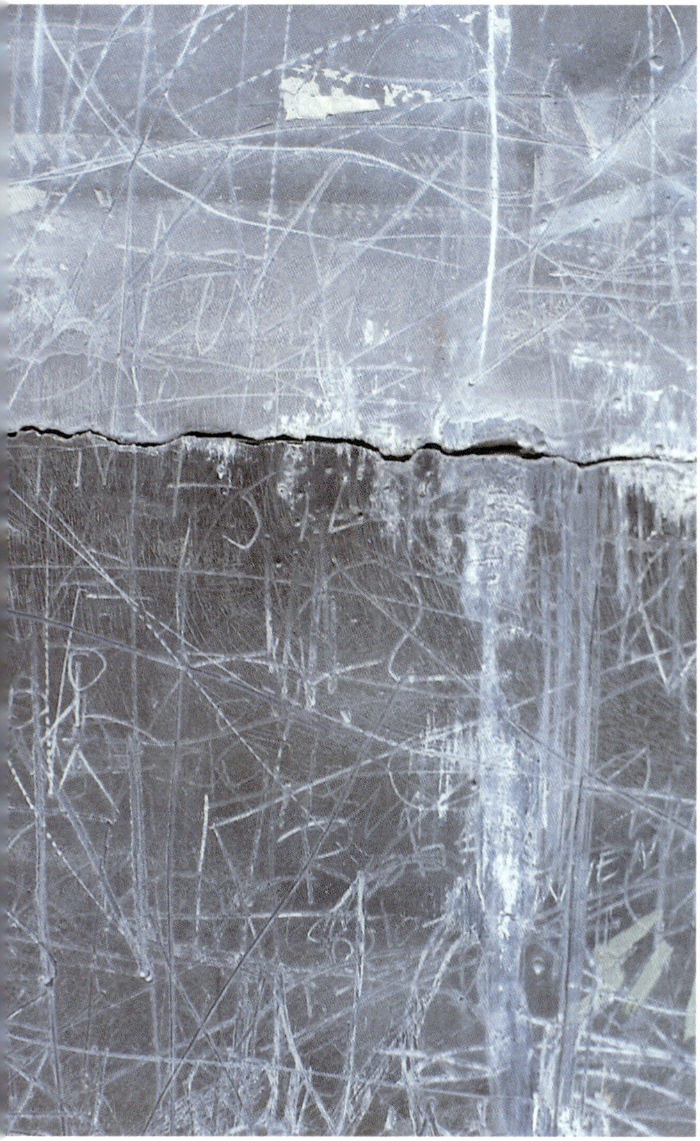

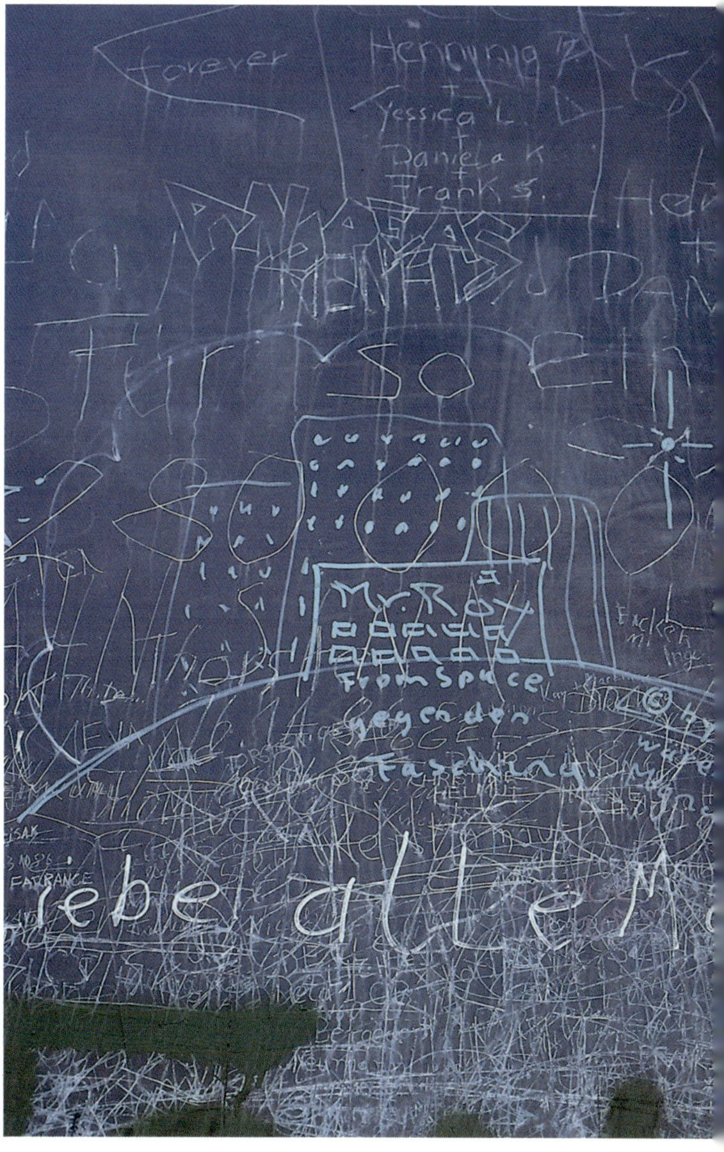

Inscriptions on the stele

2146 Steine–Mahnmal gegen Rassismus (2146 Stones–Monument against Racism)

Saarbrücken, 1990–93

Installation

2146 engraved paving stones; site: Square of the Invisible Monument, Saarbrücken

In collaboration with the students of the Hochschule für Bildende Kunst, Saarbrücken

With the help of Germany's Jewish Communities, a list was compiled of all the Jewish cemeteries which existed in Germany before the second world war. The names of these 2146 cemeteries were engraved on the bottoms of paving stones which were removed from the square at the end of the avenue that leads to Saarbrücker Schloß, the seat of the Provincial Parliament. At first there was no commission for the work, and it was only by night that the stones were removed from the plaza in front of the castle and replaced with engraved ones. In the course of the project, the work was approved and retroactively commissioned by the Provincial Parliament. What once was known as "Schloßplatz Saarbrücken" was renamed "Platz des unsichtbaren Mahnmals," or Square of the Invisible Monument.

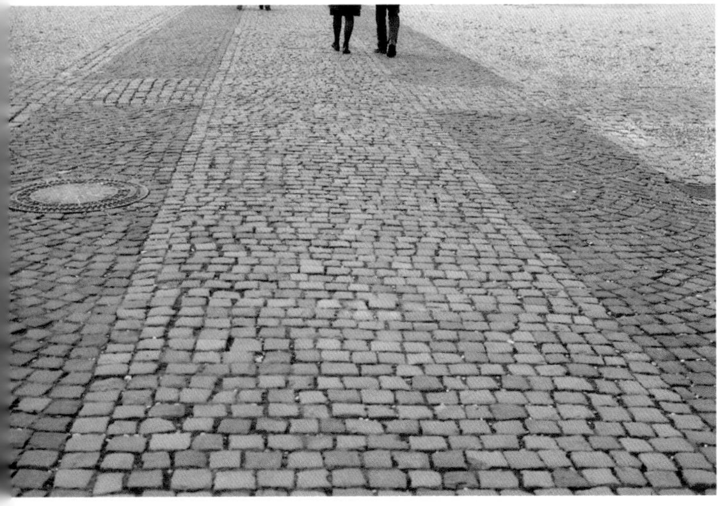

Square of the Invisible Monument   Replacement of the stones

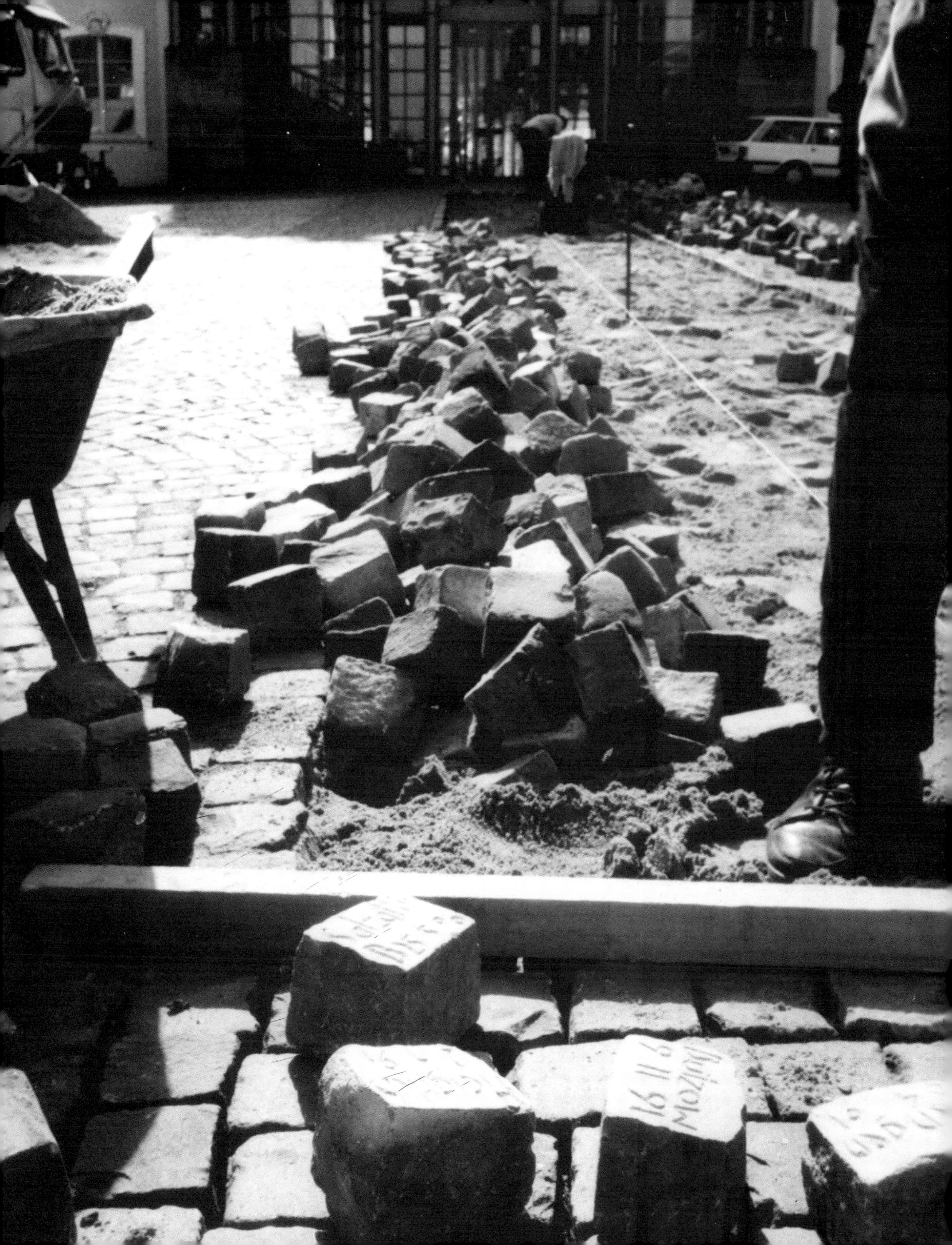

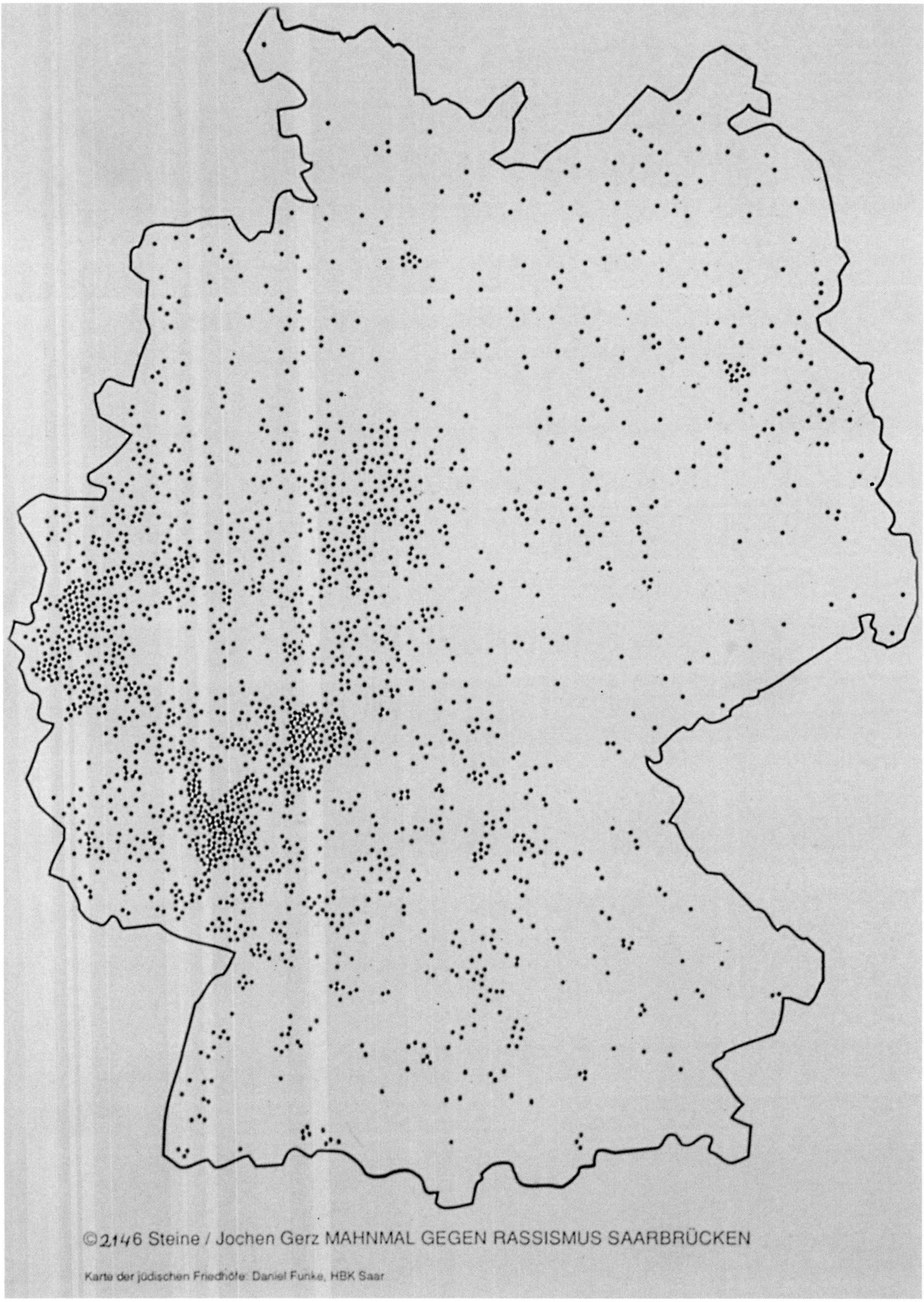

The map of Germany, marked with the 2146 cemeteries

Aach		5501	RP
Aachen	I, Lütticherstr. 39, Ecke Körnerstr.	5100	NW
Aachen	II, Binsfelder Str.	5100	NW
Abenberg		8549	BY
Abensberg		8423	BY
Abterode		3447	HE
Achim		2807	NI
Adelebsen		3404	NI
Adelsdorf		3101	BY
Adorf		3543	HE
Aerzen		3258	NI
Affaltrach		7104	BW
Ahaus		4422	NW
Ahlden		3031	NI
Ahlen	Beckumer Str.	4730	NW
Ahrensburg		2070	SH
Ahsen	Der Heidegarten	4354	NW
Albisheim		6719	RP
Aldenhofen		5173	NW
Alfeld	Ot. Wettensen	3220	NI
Alikendorf	Richtung Hadmerste	0-3231	ST
Allendorf		6301	HE
Allersheim		8701	BY
Allmannshofen		8851	BY
Alme	Vorm Buchenberg	5790	NW
Alpen	Ulrichstr.	4234	NW
Alsbach		6146	HE
Alsdorf	Ot. Begau, Alter Römerweg	5110	NW
Alsdorf	Böcker Viehweide	5110	NW
Alsenz	I	6762	RP
Alsenz	II, Judenbegräbnis	6762	RP
Alsfeld		6320	HE
Alsheim		6526	RP
Alt-Landsberg		0-1274	BB
Altdorf		8300	BY
Altena		5990	NW

The list of Germany's Jewish cemeteries, before 1933 (excerpt)

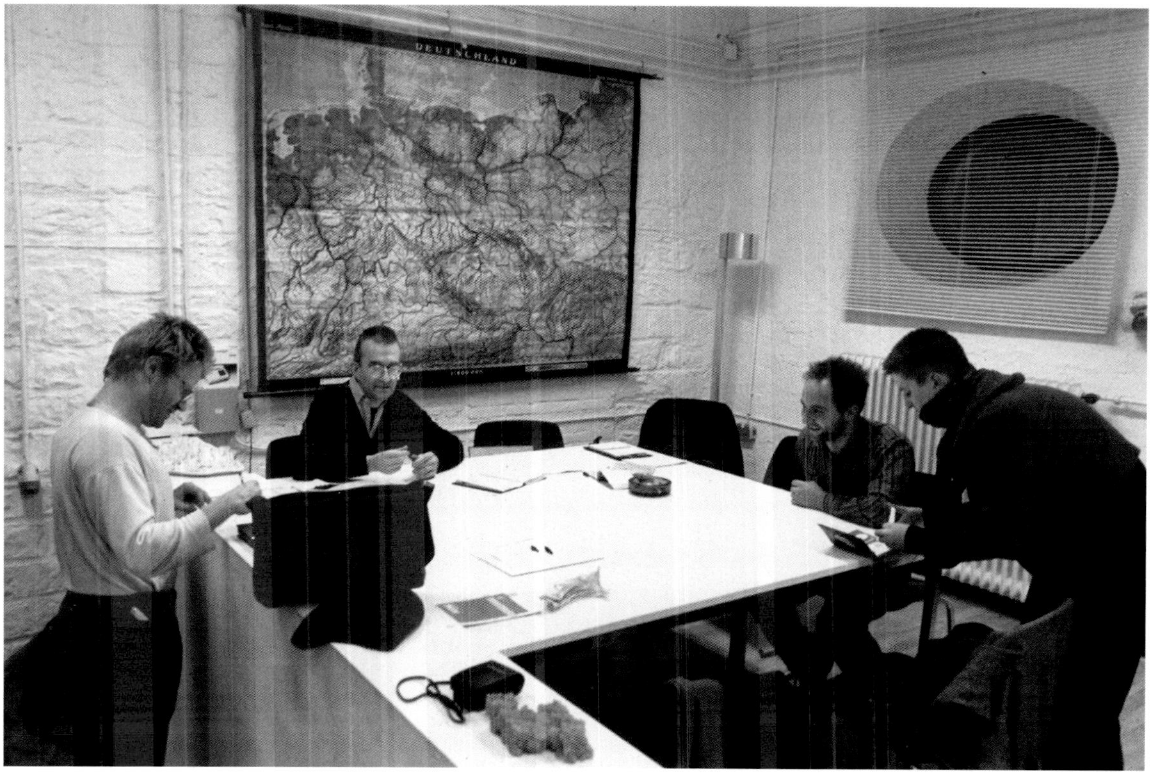

Jochen Gerz and students at work

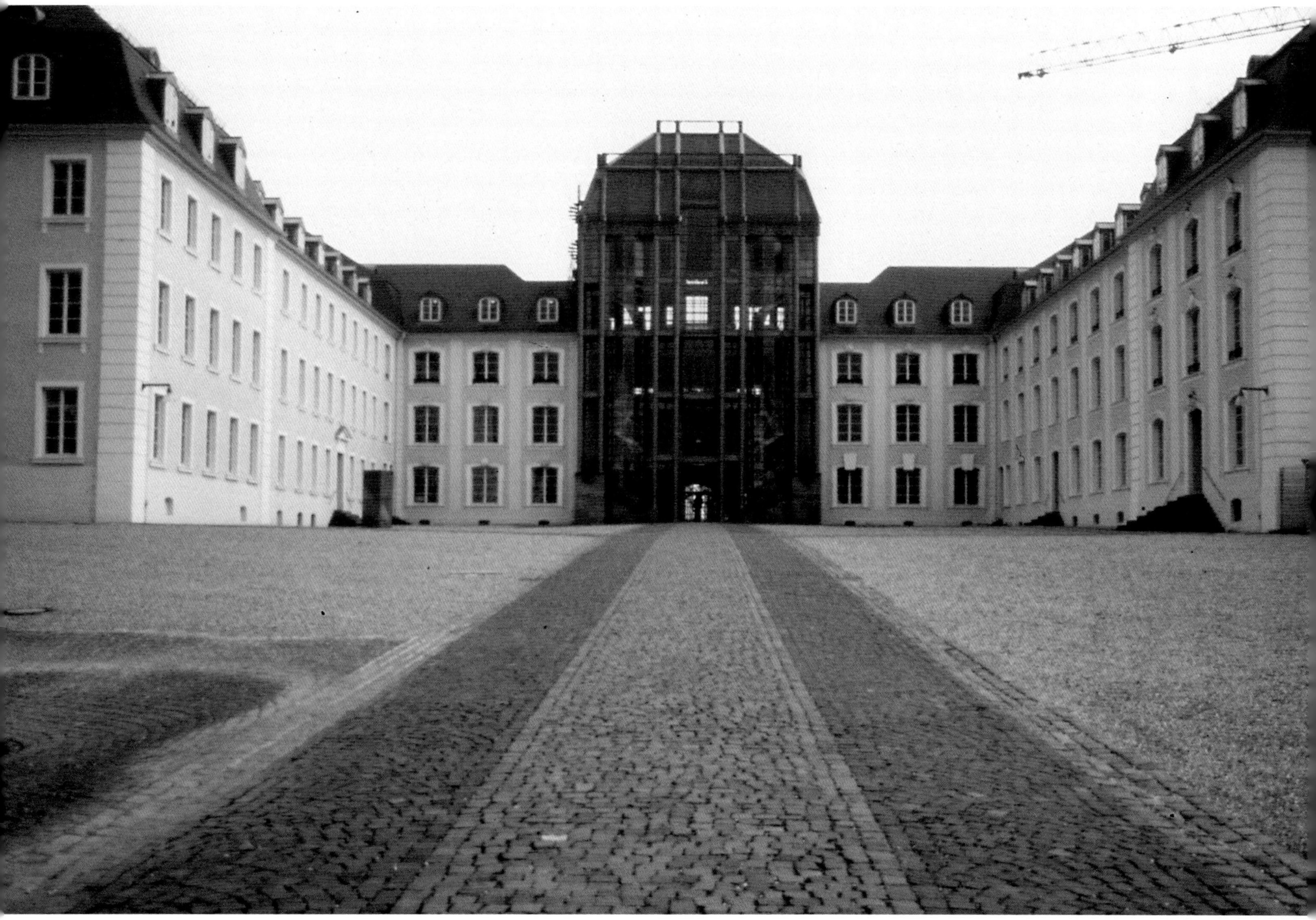

Square of the Invisible Monument

Die Bremer Befragung–sine somno nihil
(The Bremen Questionnaire–sine somno nihil)
Bremen, 1990–95

Questionnaire and installation
Steel frame construction; triangular V4A steel plate with engraving, of a thickness of 1 cm; triangular sheet of glass, of a thickness of 4.5 cm.; length of sides, 115 x 200 x 230.7 cm
In collaboration with the students of the Bremen Hochschule für Bildende Kunst
On November 29, 1990, the City of Bremen awarded the Roland Prize for Art in Public Spaces to Jochen Gerz. The prize was connected to the commission to realize a work in a public space in Bremen. Since the commission established no guide-lines for the form of the work, the artist decided to undertake an inquiry, starting in 1991, among the city's inhabitants, asking for their notions and opinions on art in public spaces. In the course of the inquiry, some fifty thousand persons were reached by questionnaires in the press, as well as by television and handbills, and were able to take a position on the following points: What do you see as sufficiently important to constitute a theme for a public work? Do you think that your ideas could be realized by a work of contemporary art? Would you like to take part in the realization of the work? The 246 people who in six public seminars took part in the realization of the project all agreed that a sculpture in a public space doesn't necessarily have to take the form of a material object. A rectangular plate consisting of a steel and a glass triangle were subsequently inserted into the Bürgermeister Smidt Bridge in such a way that the sheet of glass projects out over the Weser. The railing of the bridge was modified, and made to follow its contour. The gaze of passers-by falls through the sheet of glass to the water of the Weser below. The metal plate is engraved with a text on *The Bremen Questionnaire* and lists the names of the participants.

Bridge text:
When you look at the water, you see yourself, and you yourself at the very same are the image that rises up from you like the bird/from its quivering bush. Perhaps forever. *The Bremen Questionnaire* is a sculpture which consists of the images in the minds of those/who imagine them. All who do so are its authors.

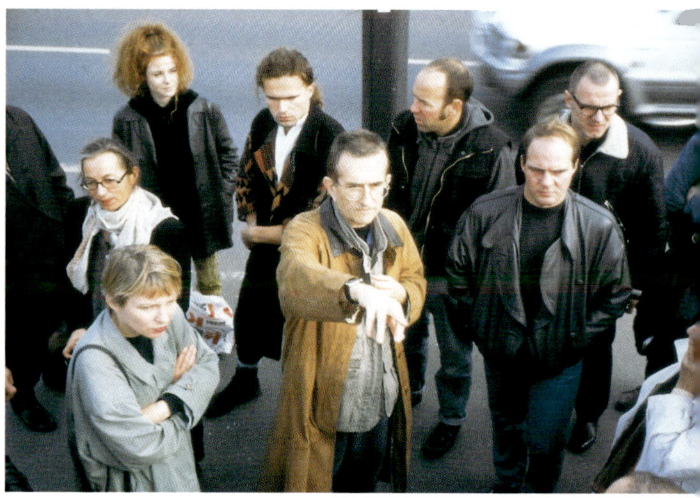

Participants in the seminar with Jochen Gerz

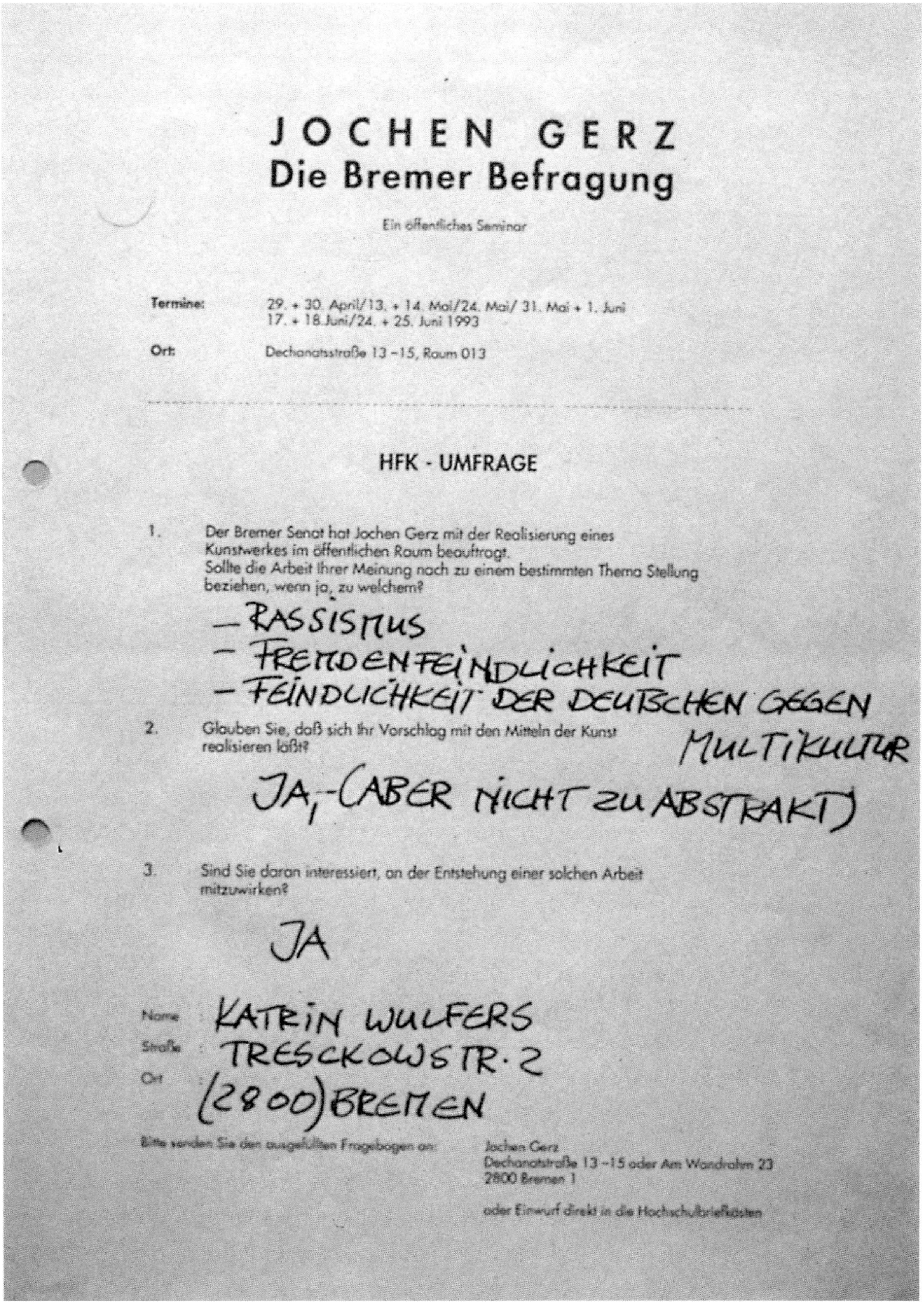

JOCHEN GERZ

Die Bremer Befragung

Ein öffentliches Seminar

Termine: 29. + 30. April/13. + 14. Mai/24. Mai/ 31. Mai + 1. Juni 17. + 18.Juni/24. + 25. Juni 1993

Ort: Dechanatsstraße 13 –15, Raum 013

HFK - UMFRAGE

1. Der Bremer Senat hat Jochen Gerz mit der Realisierung eines Kunstwerkes im öffentlichen Raum beauftragt. Sollte die Arbeit Ihrer Meinung nach zu einem bestimmten Thema Stellung beziehen, wenn ja, zu welchem?

– RASSISMUS
– FREMDENFEINDLICHKEIT
– FEINDLICHKEIT DER DEUTSCHEN GEGEN MULTIKULTUR

2. Glauben Sie, daß sich Ihr Vorschlag mit den Mitteln der Kunst realisieren läßt?

JA, (ABER NICHT ZU ABSTRAKT)

3. Sind Sie daran interessiert, an der Entstehung einer solchen Arbeit mitzuwirken?

JA

Name: KATRIN WULFERS
Straße: TRESCKOWSTR. 2
Ort: (2800) BREMEN

Bitte senden Sie den ausgefüllten Fragebogen an: Jochen Gerz
Dechanatstraße 13 –15 oder Am Wandrahm 23
2800 Bremen 1

oder Einwurf direkt in die Hochschulbriefkästen

Questionnaire card, Bremen

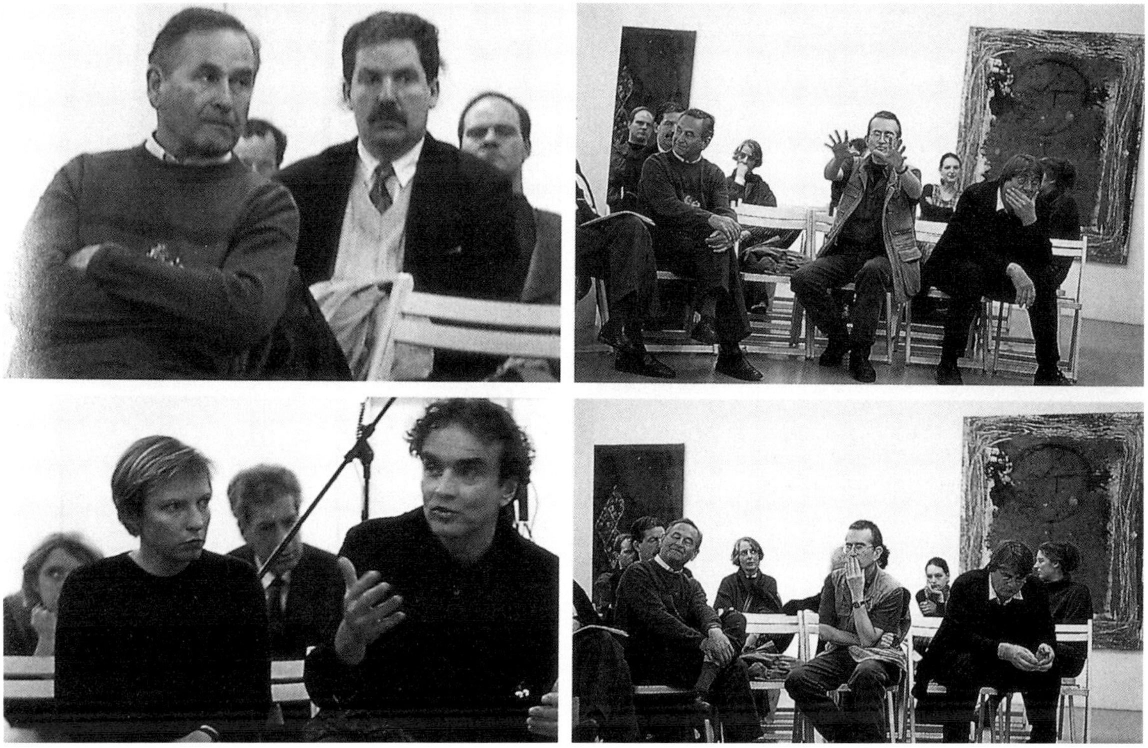

Participants in the seminar with Jochen Gerz

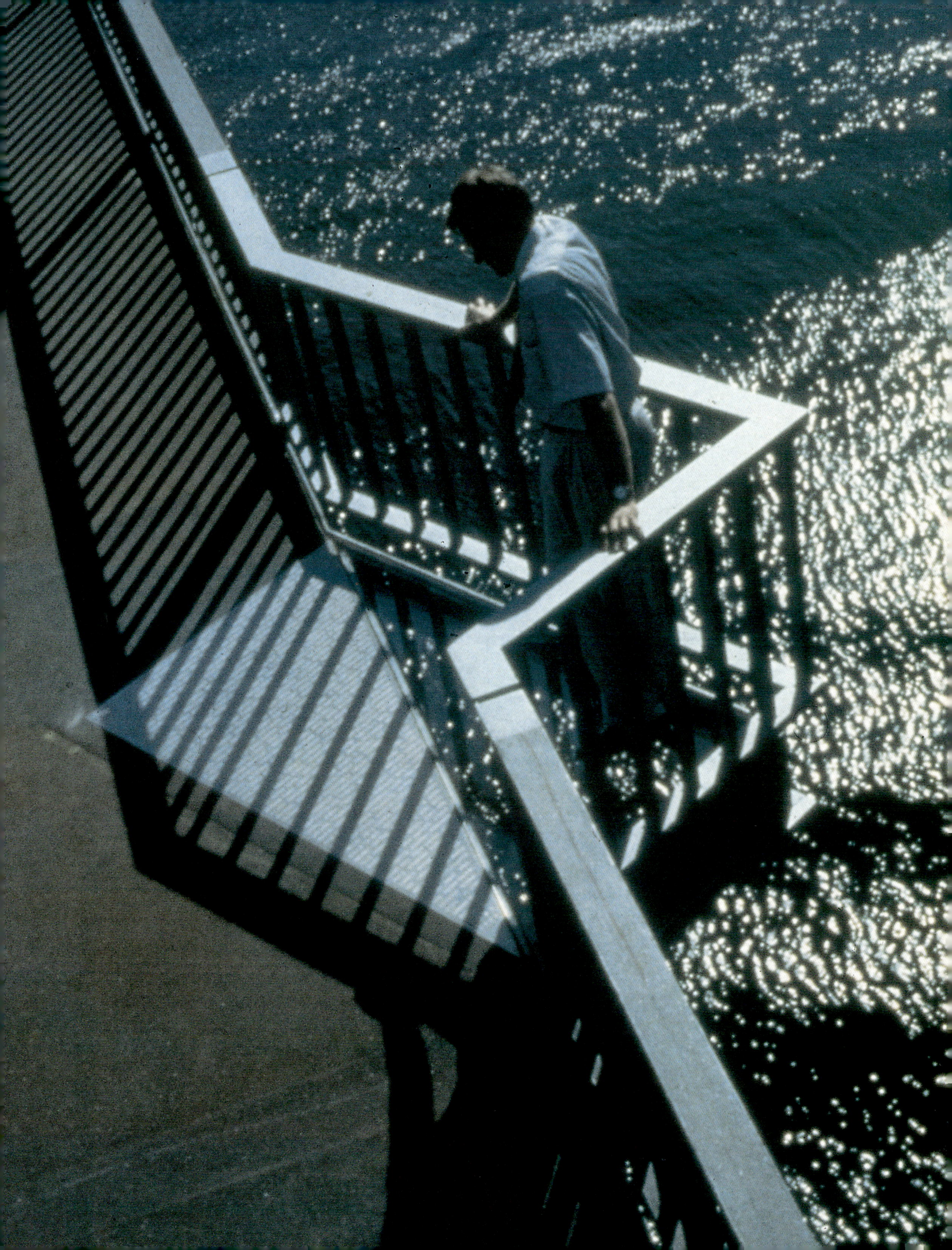

Free 1990

Poster with various texts, 240 x 360 cm

The image of the photo work *Free* was used in several cities as a poster, with glued-on or printed additions, for the traveling exhibition *Jochen Gerz. Life after Humanism*, 1993-94. "The Senator for Culture and the Integration of Foreign Immigrants warns: Art is incomprehensible." In Altenburg, a square sticker was used, with the text "And for whom does freedom lie?" In Karlsruhe, the poster was emblazoned with the phrase: "Art lovers, the asylums for foreign immigrants are full of Documenta artists."

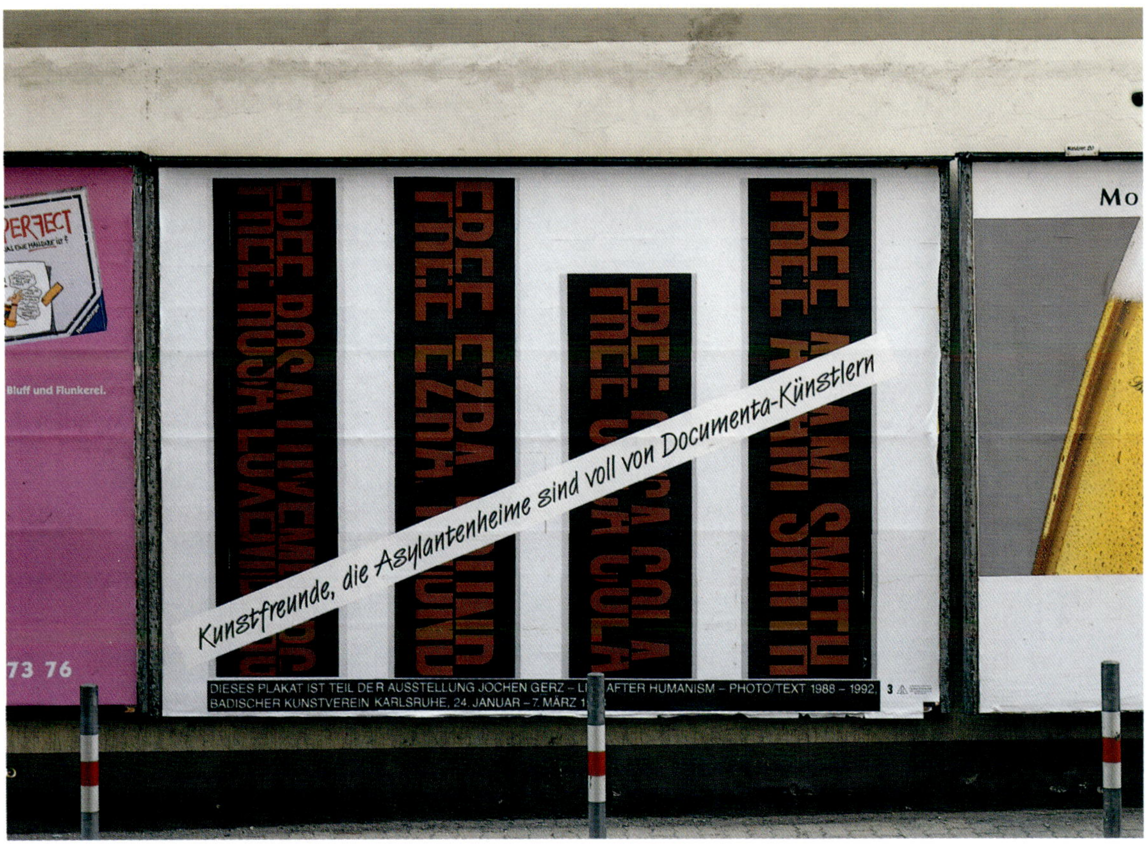

Karlsruhe, 1993

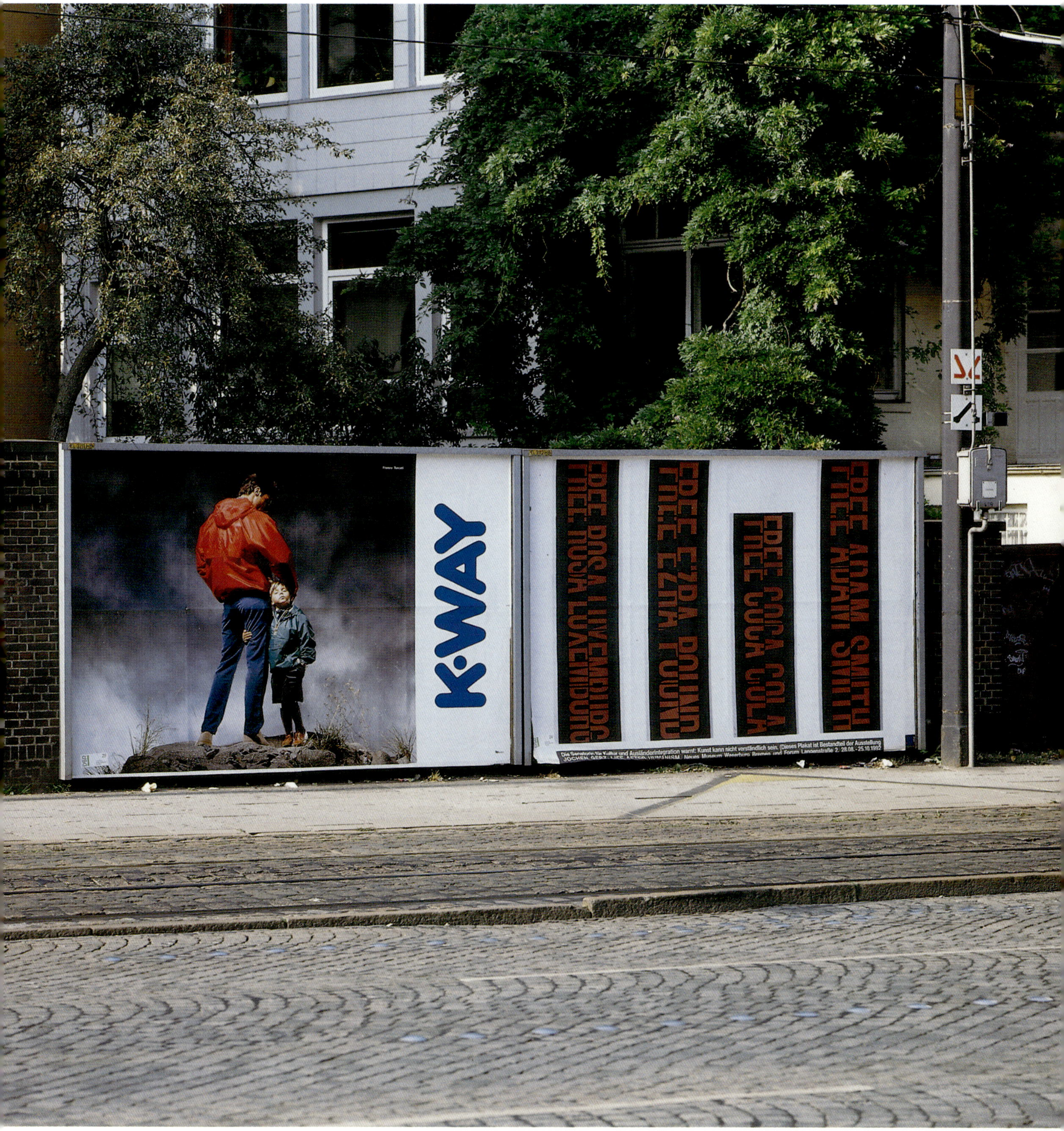
K·WAY
FREE ROSA LUXEMBURG
FREE EZRA POUND
FREE COCA COLA
FREE ADAM SMITH
Die Senatorin für Kultur und Ausländerintegration warnt: Kunst kann nicht verständlich sein. (Dieses Plakat ist Bestandteil der Ausstellung

Bremen, 1992

People Speak **Odessa, 1993**

Poster, offset, 240 x 360 cm

The occasion for the creation of the poster was the action "I am You–Artists against Violence," which was organized by the Munich branch of the Goethe Institut. After Odessa, Antwerp and Munich, in 1993, the work was shown in more than ninety cities on four continents.

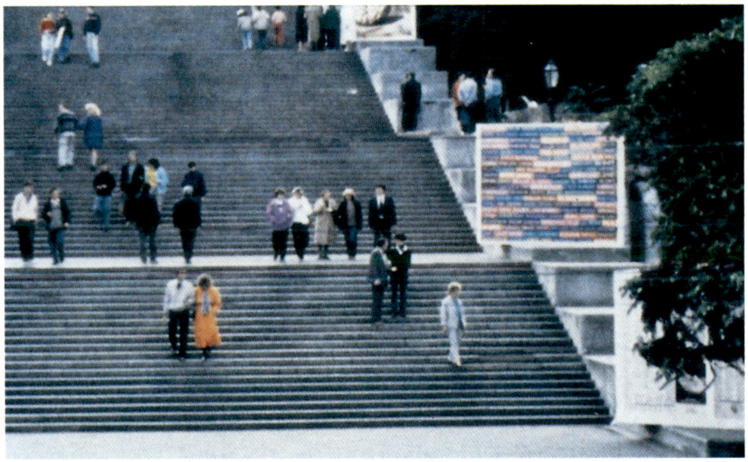

Odessa, 1993

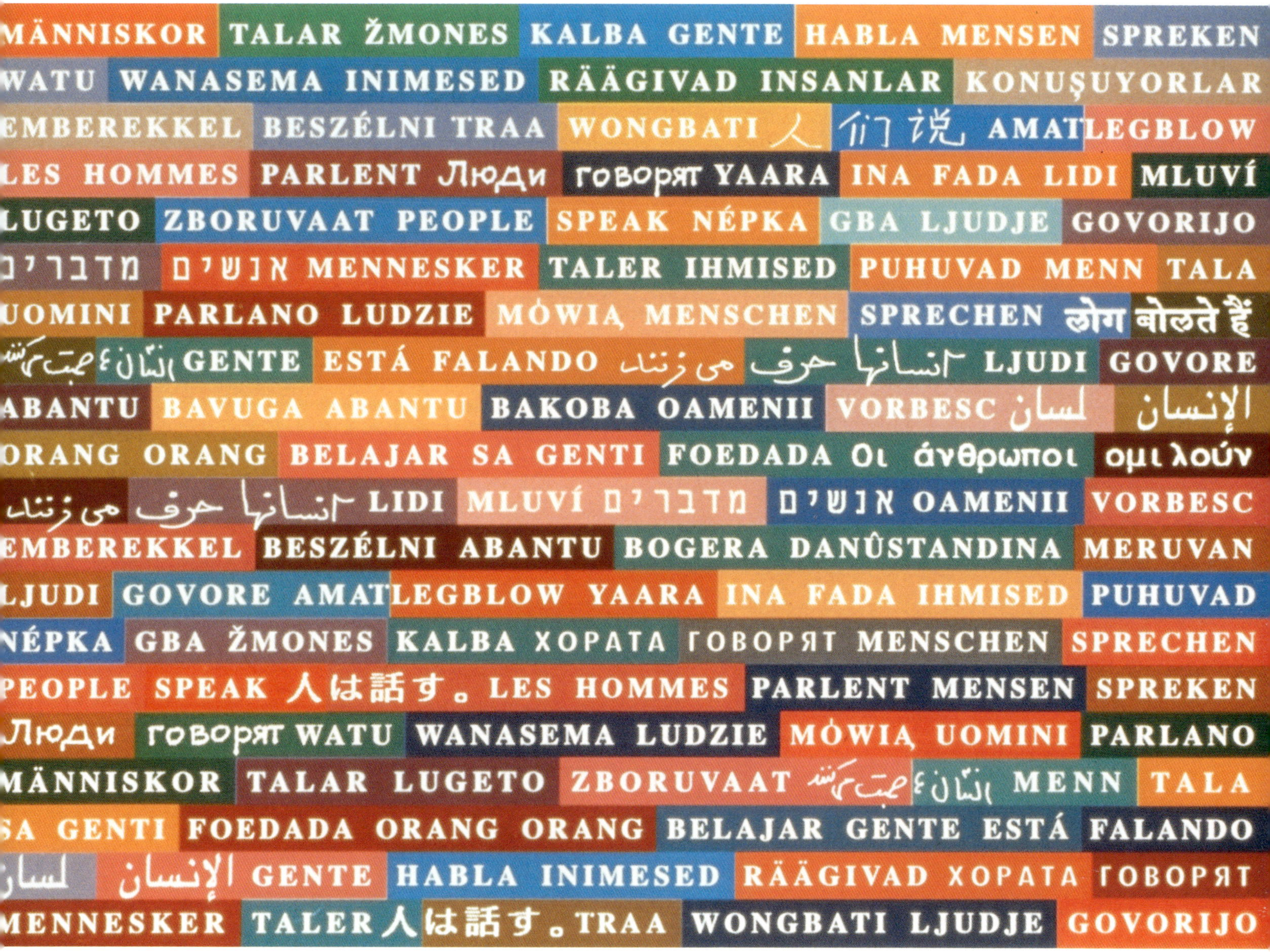
MÄNNISKOR TALAR ŽMONES KALBA GENTE HABLA MENSEN SPREKEN
WATU WANASEMA INIMESED RÄÄGIVAD INSANLAR KONUŞUYORLAR
EMBEREKKEL BESZÉLNI TRAA WONGBATI 人们说 AMATLEGBLOW
LES HOMMES PARLENT Люди говорят YAARA INA FADA LIDI MLUVÍ
LUGETO ZBORUVAAT PEOPLE SPEAK NÉPKA GBA LJUDJE GOVORIJO
מדברים אנשים MENNESKER TALER IHMISED PUHUVAD MENN TALA
UOMINI PARLANO LUDZIE MÓWIĄ MENSCHEN SPRECHEN लोग बोलते हैं
GENTE ESTÁ FALANDO LJUDI GOVORE
ABANTU BAVUGA ABANTU BAKOBA OAMENII VORBESC لسان الإنسان
ORANG ORANG BELAJAR SA GENTI FOEDADA Οι άνθρωποι ομιλούν
LIDI MLUVÍ מדברים אנשים OAMENII VORBESC
EMBEREKKEL BESZÉLNI ABANTU BOGERA DANÛSTANDINA MERUVAN
LJUDI GOVORE AMATLEGBLOW YAARA INA FADA IHMISED PUHUVAD
NÉPKA GBA ŽMONES KALBA ХОРАТА ГОВОРЯТ MENSCHEN SPRECHEN
PEOPLE SPEAK 人は話す。LES HOMMES PARLENT MENSEN SPREKEN
Люди говорят WATU WANASEMA LUDZIE MÓWIĄ UOMINI PARLANO
MÄNNISKOR TALAR LUGETO ZBORUVAAT MENN TALA
SA GENTI FOEDADA ORANG ORANG BELAJAR GENTE ESTÁ FALANDO
لسان الإنسان GENTE HABLA INIMESED RÄÄGIVAD ХОРАТА ГОВОРЯТ
MENNESKER TALER 人は話す。TRAA WONGBATI LJUDJE GOVORIJO

The Plural Sculpture 1995

Internet

In collaboration with art students at the State University, New York, with Purchase College of Art, with the Public Art Fund, New York, Ada Web, New York, and also the New York Kunsthalle

The question "If art had the power to change your times, what would you ask for?" was placed on the internet. There were over 230 replies, which were presented in September 1995 at the New York Kunsthalle.

A few of the answers:

If art had the power to change our time, it would become an instrument of power. Power corrupts. Art can reflect on our time, criticize it. Art can create links between different people and different fields. No more, no less.

More time.

That art would awaken people to truth through science and technology rather than lies through mythology and religion.

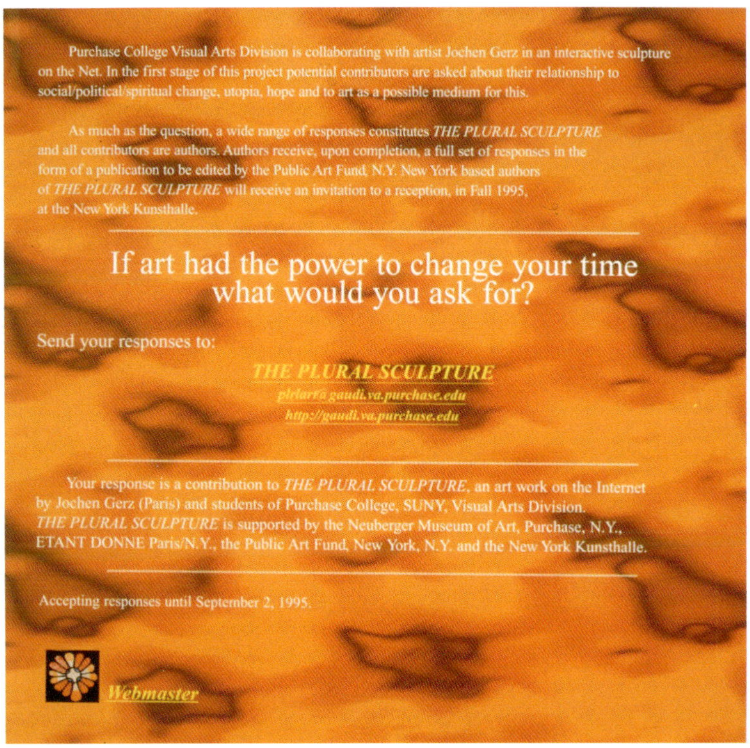

Website

Website

THE PLURAL SCULPTURE

If art had the power to change your time, what would you ask for?

Your answer is a contribution to ***THE PLURAL SCULPTURE,*** an art work on the internet by Jochen Gerz and students of Purchase College, SUNY, Visual Arts Division.

Your answer is:

(extendable)

All contributions will be collected for six weeks on the America On-Line system. After completion, ***THE PLURAL SCULPTURE*** will be redistributed on system to random mailboxes. ***THE PLURAL SCULPTURE*** is supported by the Neuberger Museum of Art, Purchase, New York, the Public Art Fund, New York, The New York Kunsthalle and Etant Donne Paris/NY.

Le Monument vivant (The Living Monument) **Biron, 1995/96**

Work in progress
Sand-stone obelisk on a two-level base; reddish-brown enameled plaques with white, silk-screened writing, 10 x 17.5 x 1 cm each
Total measurements: 360 x 316 x 316 cm
Site: Place Jean Poussou, Biron
In collaboration with students at the Ecole municipale des Beaux-Arts, Bordeaux
On commission from the French Ministry of Culture, the old monument to the fallen, *Le Monument aux morts*, in the village of Biron was to be refurbished. The inhabitants of the village were asked to reply to an unpublished question, and thus to make a statement on the subject. Their 127 replies were then silk-screened onto red brass plaques and attached to the monument's newly erected obelisk. Since the dedication of *The Living Monument* on July 13, 1996, a village couple poses the question to all new residents and to youngsters who reach the age of adulthood. Their answers are then added to the monument.

A few of the answers:

When you are twenty years old, it seems impossible to die. Perhaps for freedom. You thank those who died for you. Freedom always comes first, but you never knows what the future will bring. There have always been wars. Among us Europeans as well. I lived through the 1940s, and in spite of all the dead and the horrors, we were nonetheless very very happy.

We're being called to Yugoslavia, to fight with a battle unit. It's clear, that we're not going there to defend French territory, but the poor people who are surrounded by war. They used to send us for training to Poland. The goal is to put an end to war. We're not fighting against an enemy, but against war. It's no longer enough to defend your country, you must also defend its values.

I volunteered, but the war was practically over. Then I wanted to go to North Africa; but since the country was occupied, they asked me to stay in Toulouse, which I didn't want to do. I was declared unfit for service. With the Germans, I think that's all over by now. One's happy now to live here in peace.

Place Jean Poussou

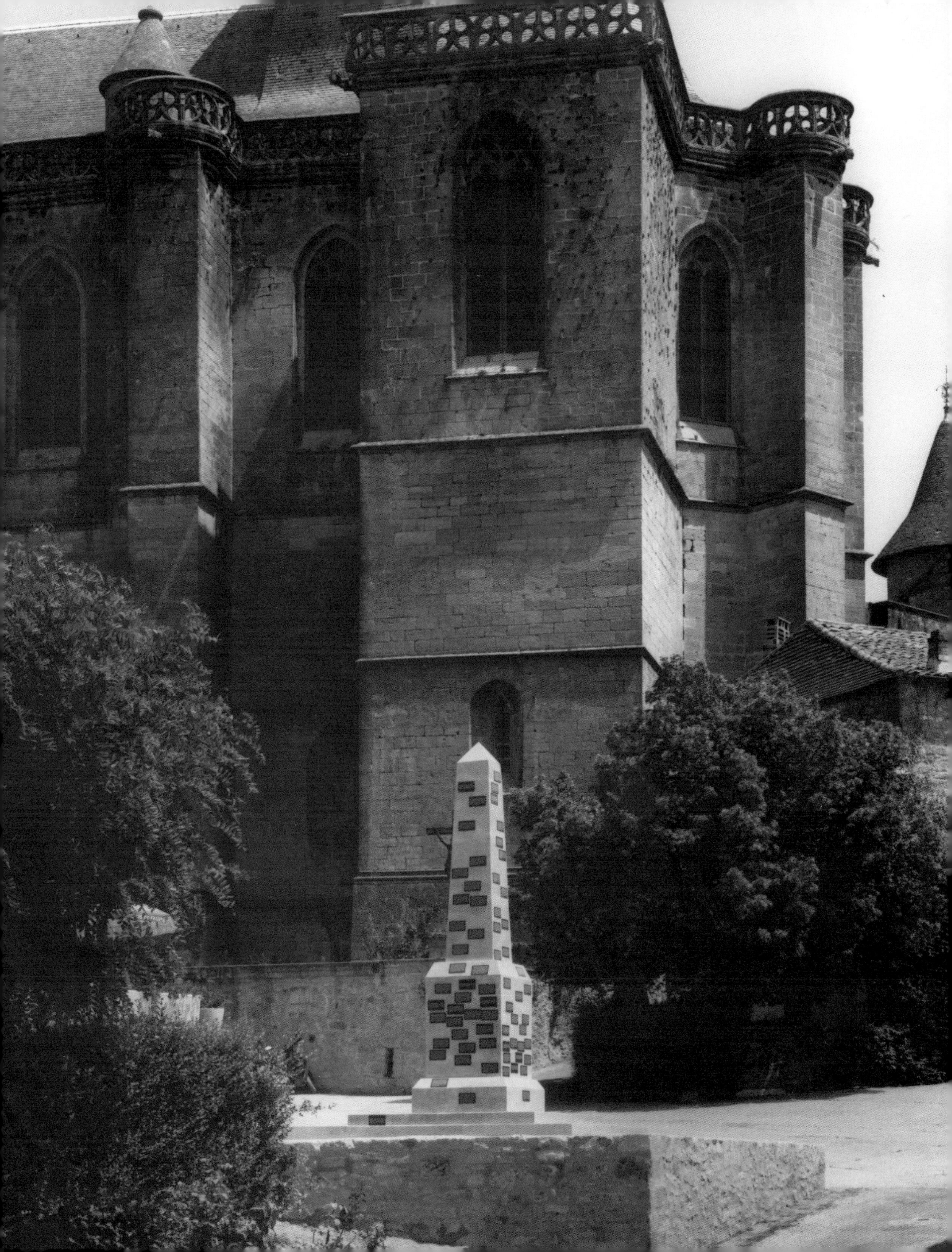

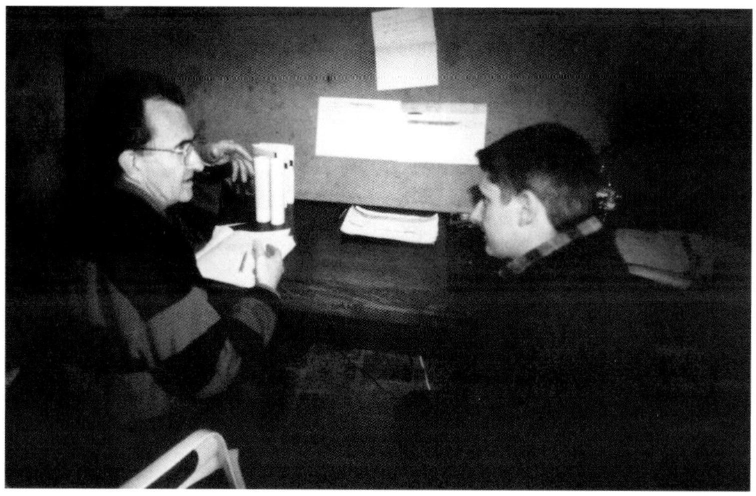

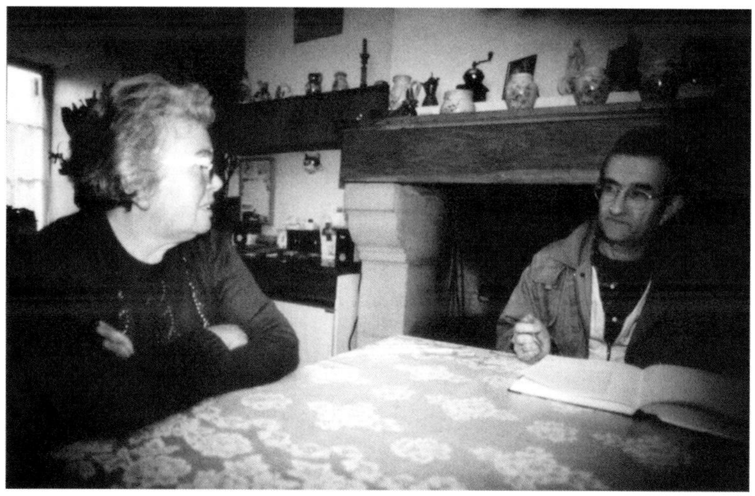

Jochen Gerz conversing with the town's inhabitants

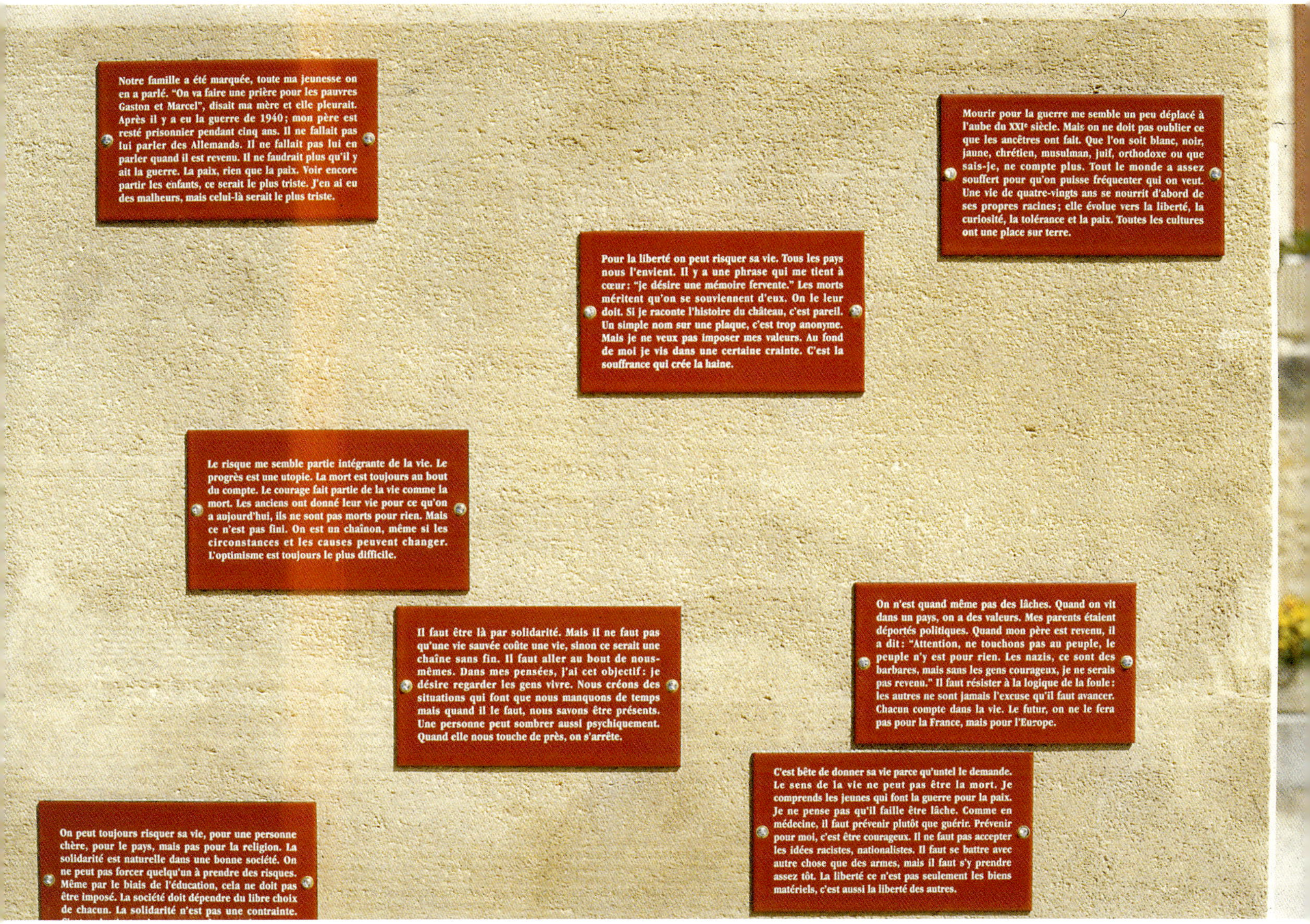
Notre famille a été marquée, toute ma jeunesse on en a parlé. "On va faire une prière pour les pauvres Gaston et Marcel", disait ma mère et elle pleurait. Après il y a eu la guerre de 1940; mon père est resté prisonnier pendant cinq ans. Il ne fallait pas lui parler des Allemands. Il ne fallait pas lui en parler quand il est revenu. Il ne faudrait plus qu'il y ait la guerre. La paix, rien que la paix. Voir encore partir les enfants, ce serait le plus triste. J'en ai eu des malheurs, mais celui-là serait le plus triste.
Mourir pour la guerre me semble un peu déplacé à l'aube du XXIe siècle. Mais on ne doit pas oublier ce que les ancêtres ont fait. Que l'on soit blanc, noir, jaune, chrétien, musulman, juif, orthodoxe ou que sais-je, ne compte plus. Tout le monde a assez souffert pour qu'on puisse fréquenter qui on veut. Une vie de quatre-vingts ans se nourrit d'abord de ses propres racines; elle évolue vers la liberté, la curiosité, la tolérance et la paix. Toutes les cultures ont une place sur terre.
Pour la liberté on peut risquer sa vie. Tous les pays nous l'envient. Il y a une phrase qui me tient à cœur: "je désire une mémoire fervente." Les morts méritent qu'on se souviennent d'eux. On le leur doit. Si je raconte l'histoire du château, c'est pareil. Un simple nom sur une plaque, c'est trop anonyme. Mais je ne veux pas imposer mes valeurs. Au fond de moi je vis dans une certaine crainte. C'est la souffrance qui crée la haine.
Le risque me semble partie intégrante de la vie. Le progrès est une utopie. La mort est toujours au bout du compte. Le courage fait partie de la vie comme la mort. Les anciens ont donné leur vie pour ce qu'on a aujourd'hui, ils ne sont pas morts pour rien. Mais ce n'est pas fini. On est un chaînon, même si les circonstances et les causes peuvent changer. L'optimisme est toujours le plus difficile.
Il faut être là par solidarité. Mais il ne faut pas qu'une vie sauvée coûte une vie, sinon ce serait une chaîne sans fin. Il faut aller au bout de nous-mêmes. Dans mes pensées, j'ai cet objectif: je désire regarder les gens vivre. Nous créons des situations qui font que nous manquons de temps mais quand il le faut, nous savons être présents. Une personne peut sombrer aussi psychiquement. Quand elle nous touche de près, on s'arrête.
On n'est quand même pas des lâches. Quand on vit dans un pays, on a des valeurs. Mes parents étaient déportés politiques. Quand mon père est revenu, il a dit: "Attention, ne touchons pas au peuple, le peuple n'y est pour rien. Les nazis, ce sont des barbares, mais sans les gens courageux, je ne serais pas revenu." Il faut résister à la logique de la foule: les autres ne sont jamais l'excuse qu'il faut avancer. Chacun compte dans la vie. Le futur, on ne le fera pas pour la France, mais pour l'Europe.
On peut toujours risquer sa vie, pour une personne chère, pour le pays, mais pas pour la religion. La solidarité est naturelle dans une bonne société. On ne peut pas forcer quelqu'un à prendre des risques. Même par le biais de l'éducation, cela ne doit pas être imposé. La société doit dépendre du libre choix de chacun. La solidarité n'est pas une contrainte.
C'est bête de donner sa vie parce qu'untel le demande. Le sens de la vie ne peut pas être la mort. Je comprends les jeunes qui font la guerre pour la paix. Je ne pense pas qu'il faille être lâche. Comme en médecine, il faut prévenir plutôt que guérir. Prévenir pour moi, c'est être courageux. Il ne faut pas accepter les idées racistes, nationalistes. Il faut se battre avec autre chose que des armes, mais il faut s'y prendre assez tôt. La liberté ce n'est pas seulement les biens matériels, c'est aussi la liberté des autres.

Detail

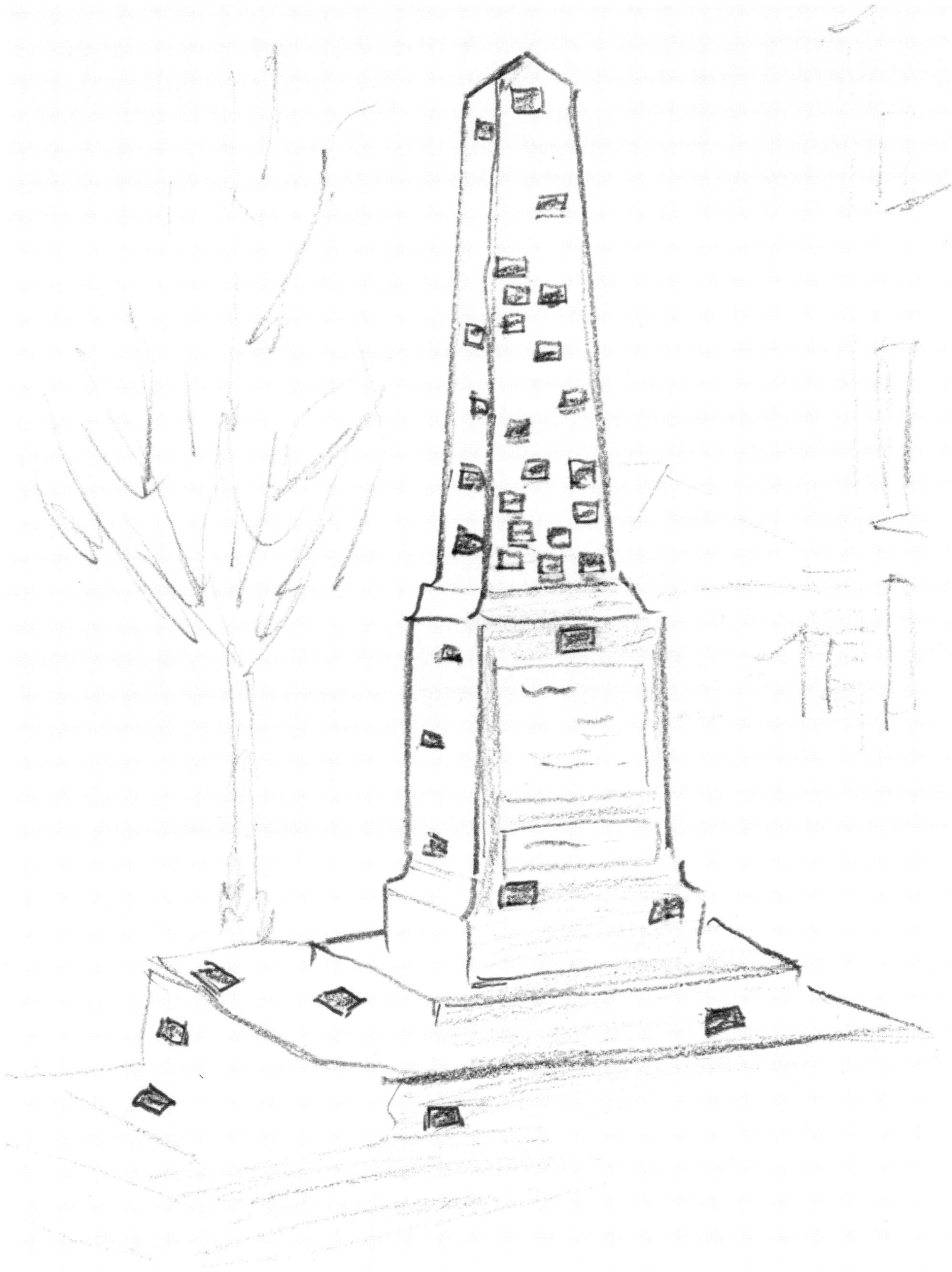

Study for the project

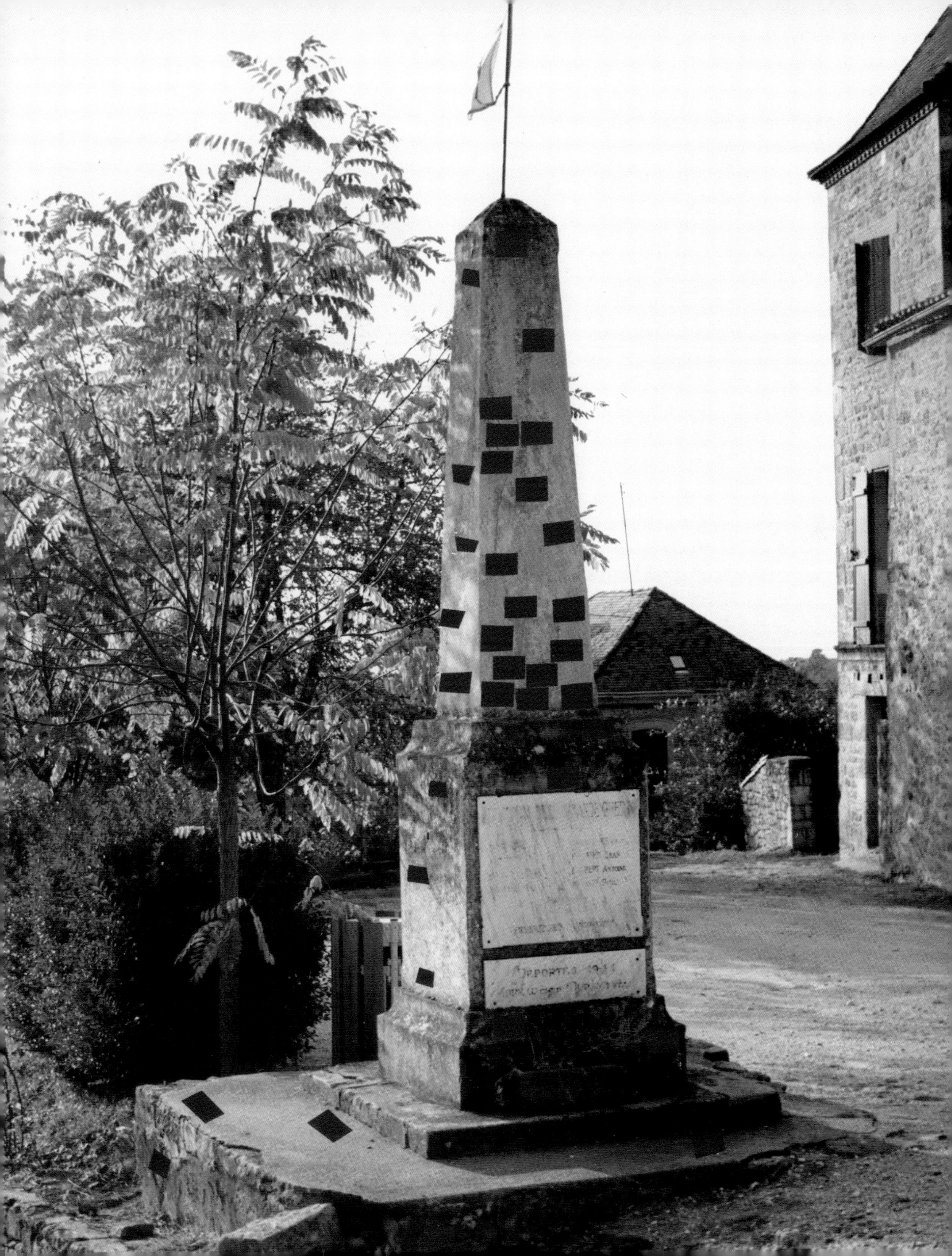

Warum ist es geschehen? Denkmal für die ermordeten Juden Europas (Why Did It Happen? Monument for the Murdered Jews of Europe)

Berlin, 1997/98

Model

In February 1997, after ten years of discussion, the city of Berlin opened a second competition for a *Monument for the Murdered Jews of Europe*. The designated plot of land for the monument measures some 20,000 square meters, and Gerz's plan was to turn it over to the visitors. They were to be invited to give an answer to the always repeated question, "Why did it happen?" Their answers will be collected by interns who worked with a Monument Foundation, and whose task was to function as receptionists, in a building that formed a part of the memorial. This "Ear" building was designed by the Iranian architect Nasrine Seraji, and was to consist of three rooms: the Room of Memory, the Room of Replies, and the Room of Silence. The Room of Memory was to be one of the collection centers of the Shoah Foundation of the American film director Steven Spielberg, which records the memories of Jewish survivors of the concentration camps. In the Room of Replies, visitors were to record their answers in books that were to line the building's glass walls. In the last room, the Room of Silence, visitors were to hear "the eternal e" of the American composer La Monte Young. In addition to being collected in the books preserved in the "Ear," the visitors answers were progressively to be engraved into the floor of the square, up until the time, after several decades, of covering it entirely. The square was to hold thirty-nine lamp poles bearing neon lights that spelled out the word "Why?" in all the languages of Europe's persecuted Jews.

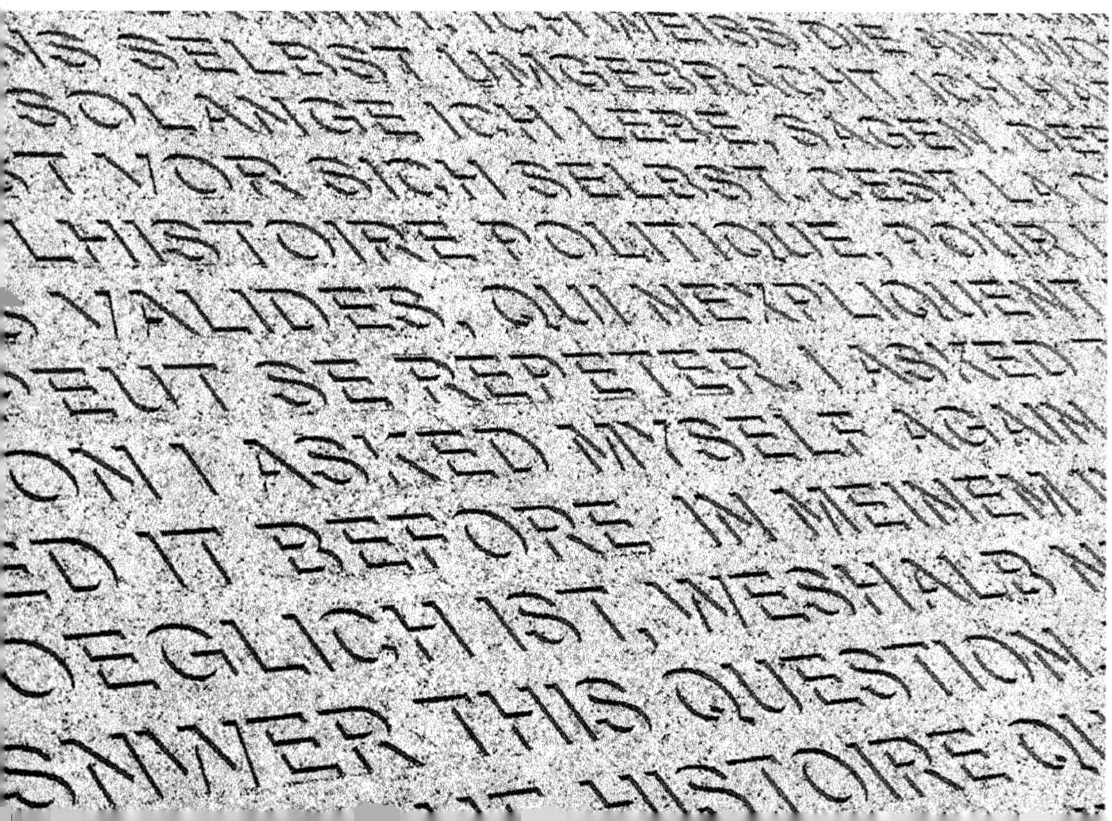

The engraved floor, computer simulation

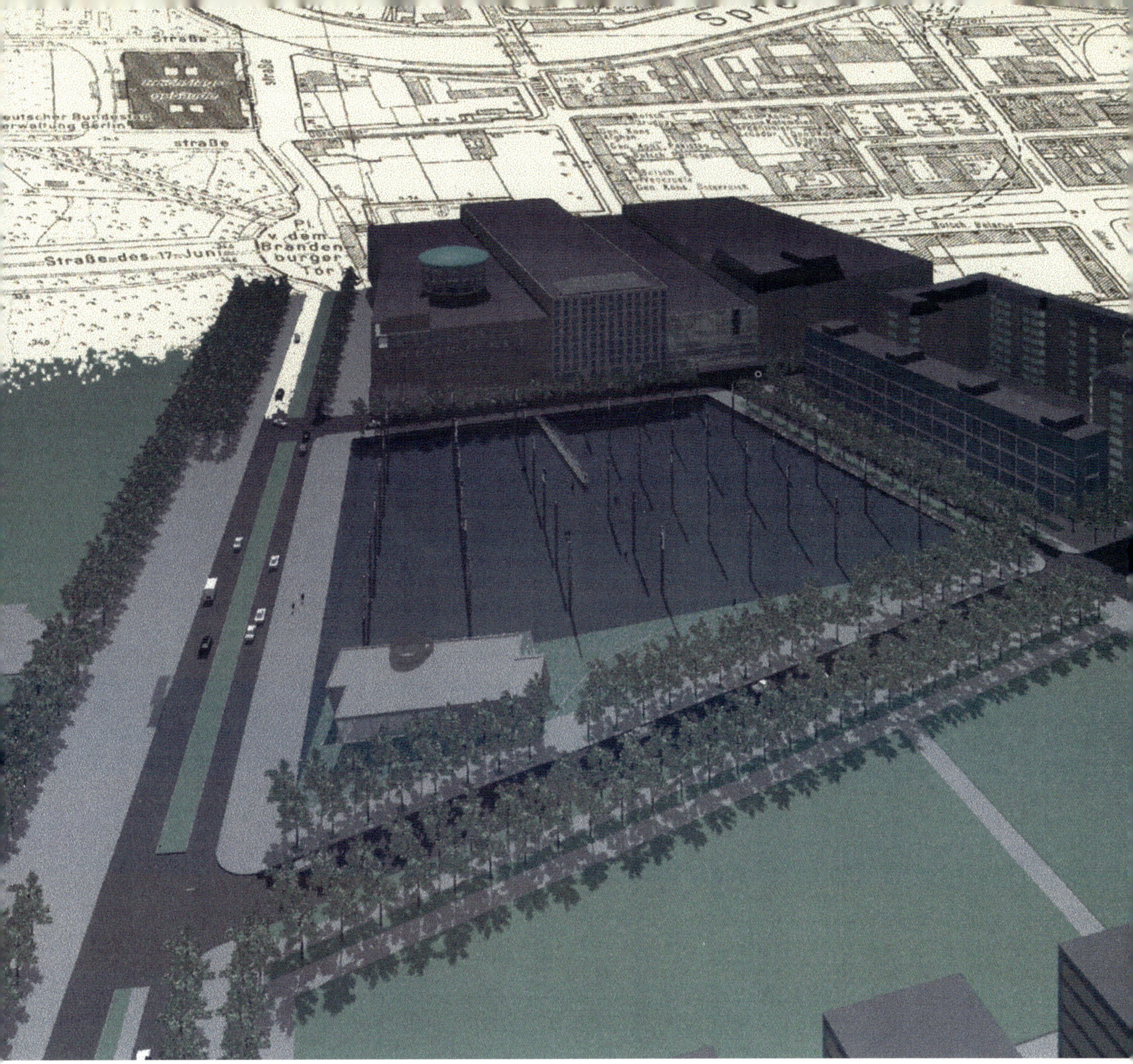

Overall view, computer simulation

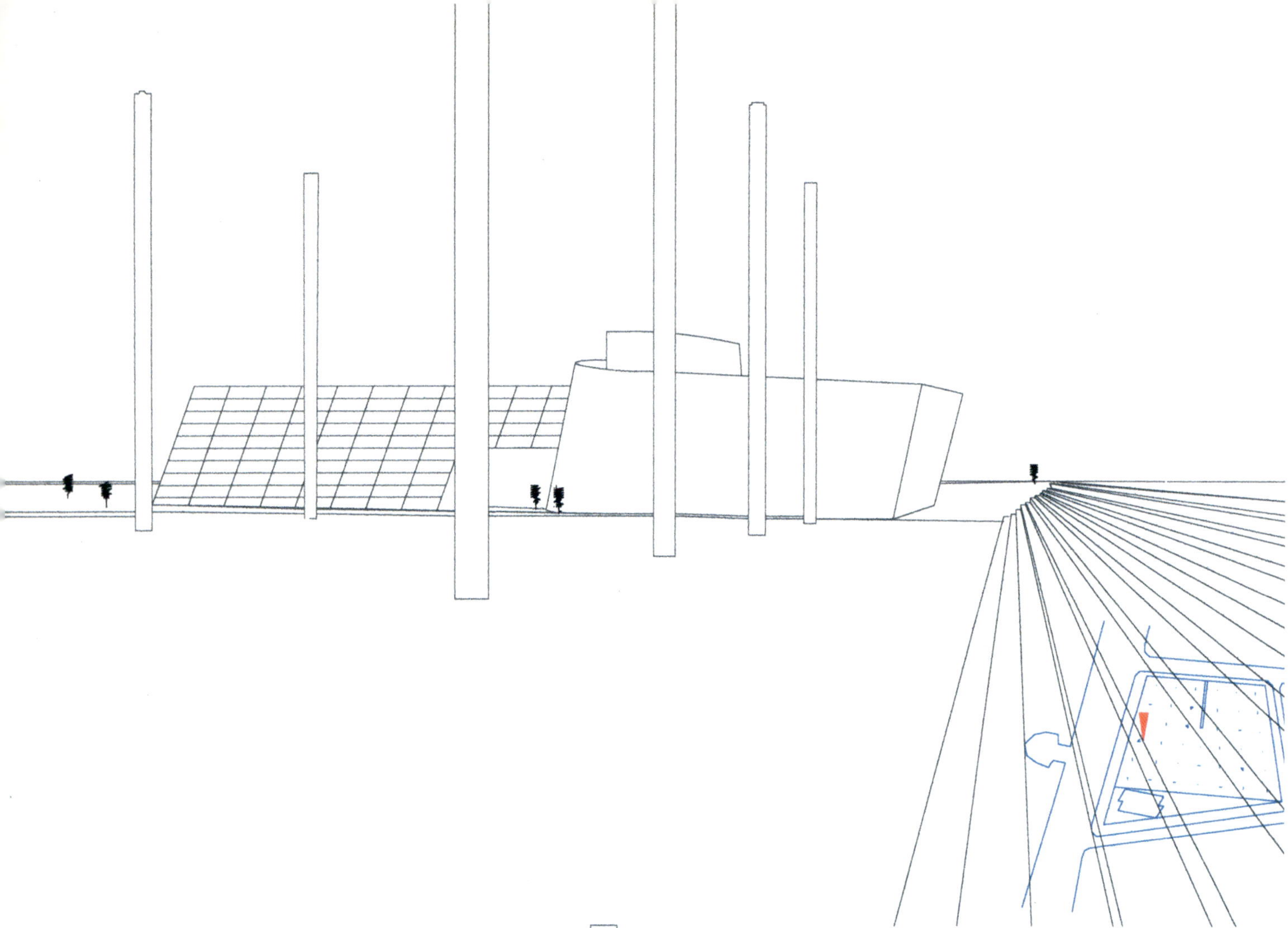

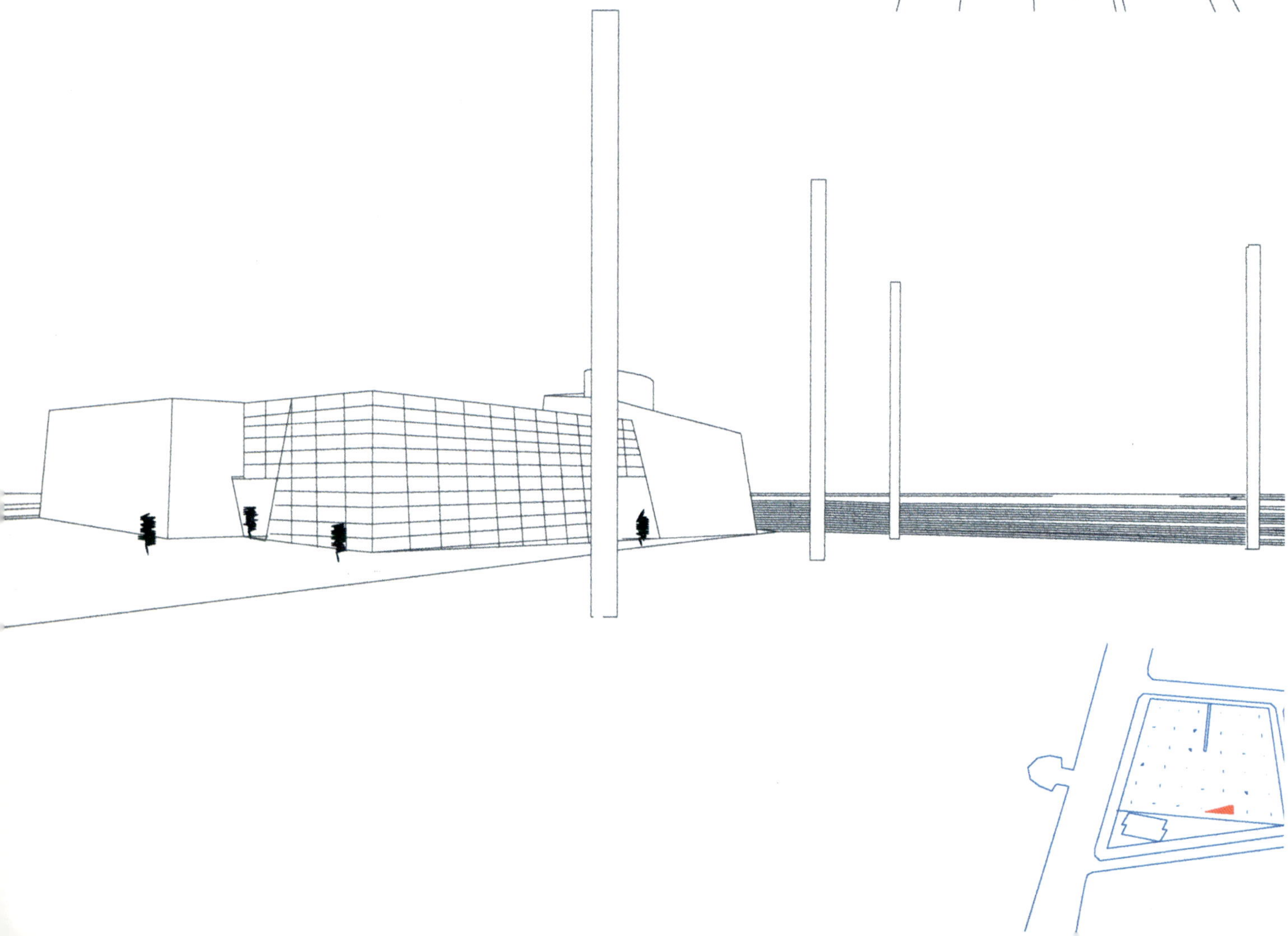

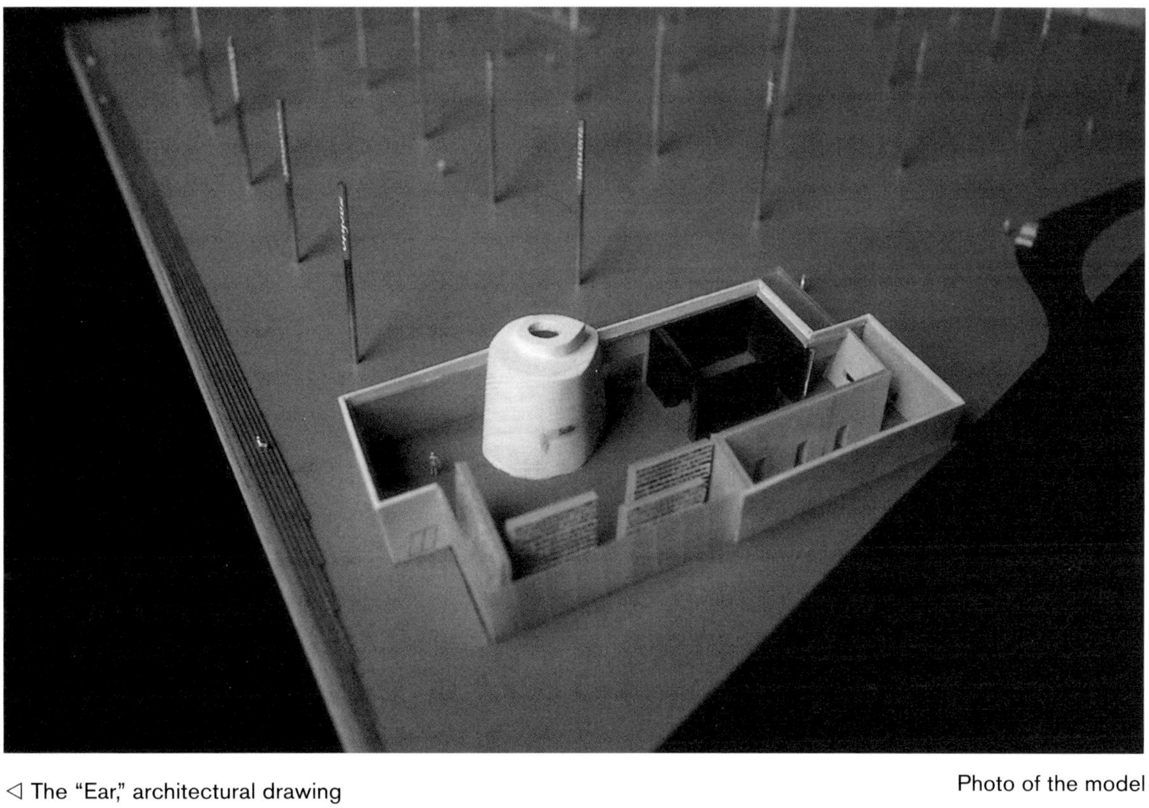

◁ The "Ear," architectural drawing

Photo of the model

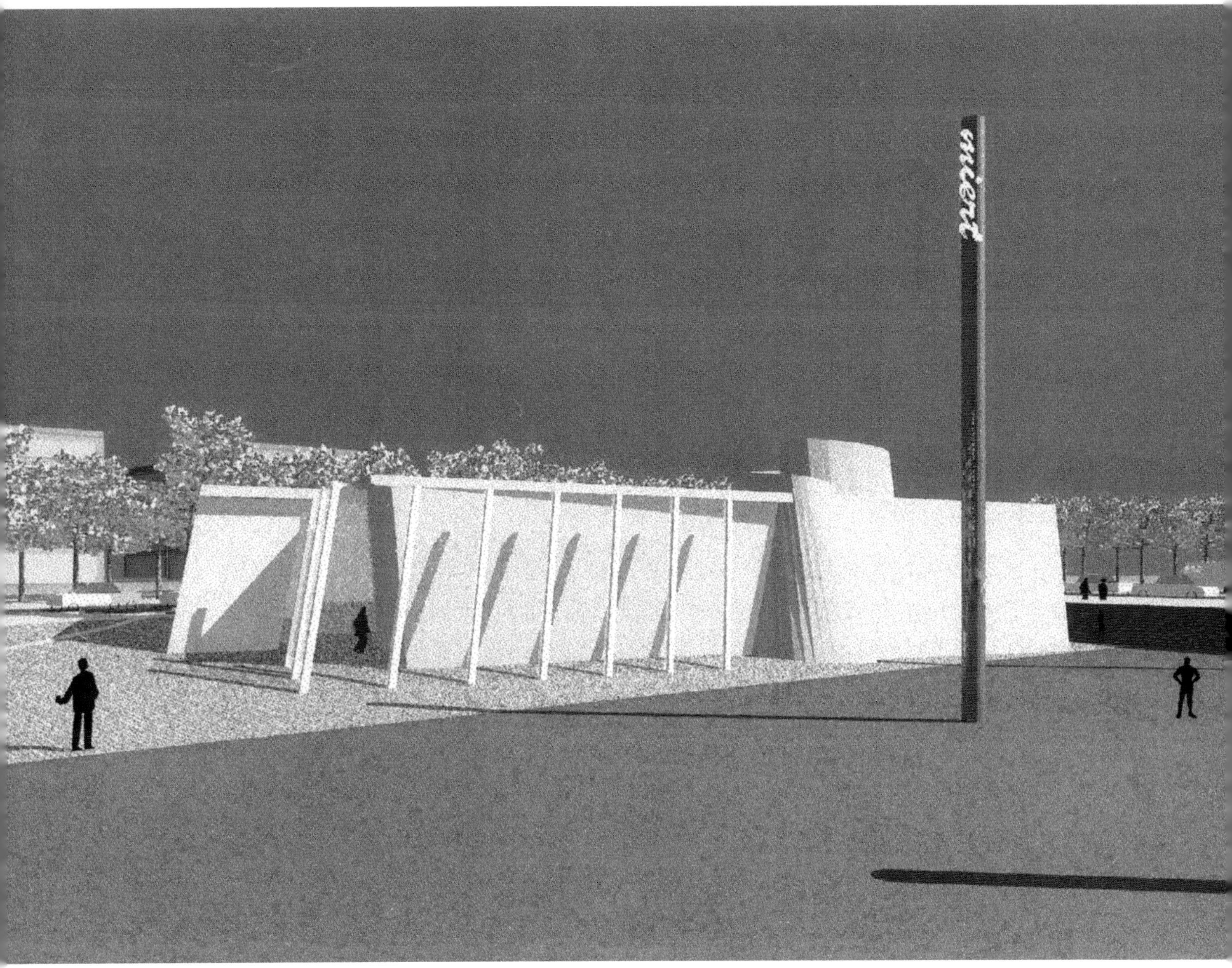

The "Ear," computer simulation

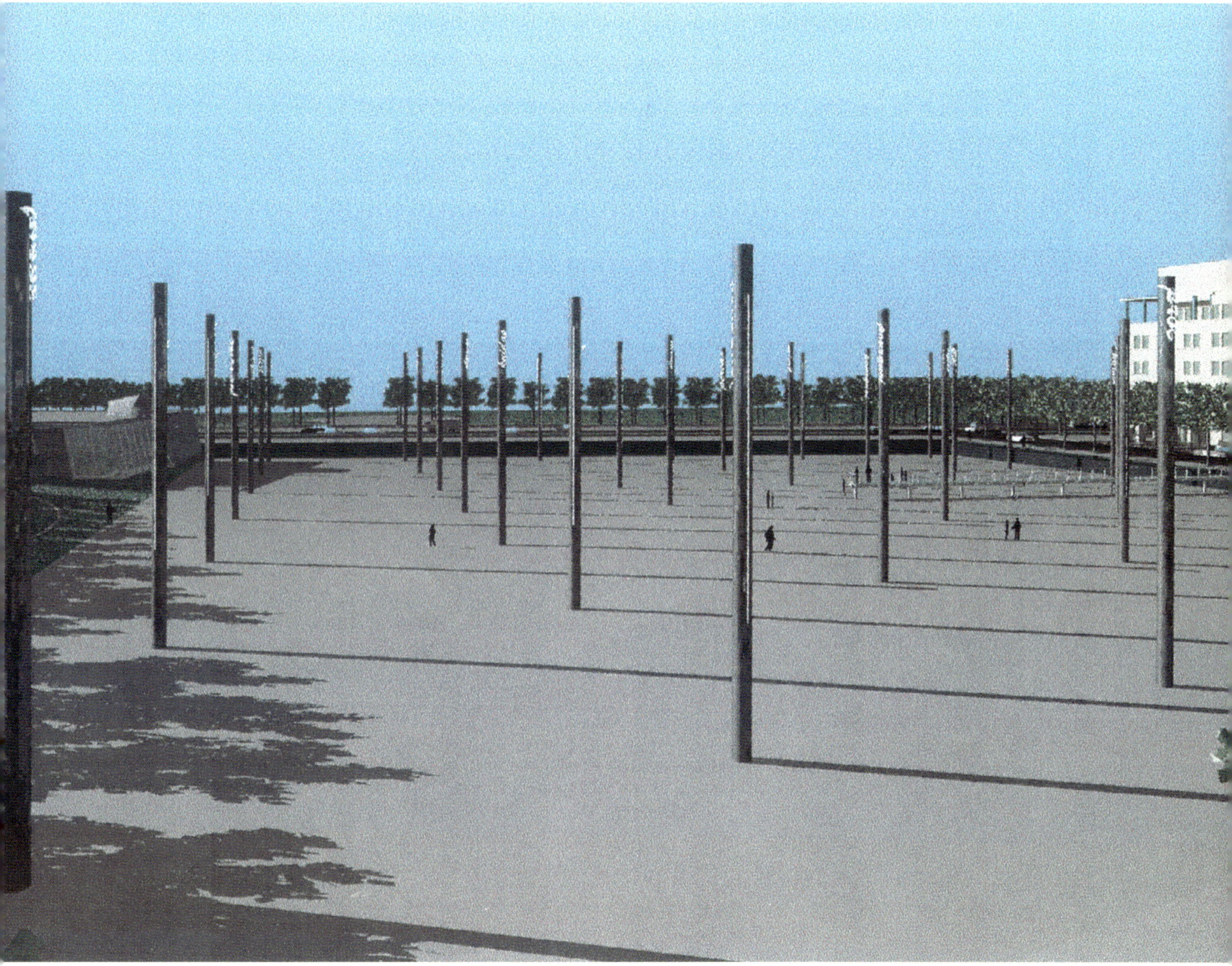

The square, computer simulation

The Berkeley Oracle. Questions Unanswered **Berkeley/Karlsruhe, 1997/98**

Internet/installation
In collaboration with the University of California, the Berkeley Art Museum, the Pacific Film Archive, Ada Web, New York, the Staatlichen Hochschule für Gestaltung, Karlsruhe, the Zentrum für Kunst und Medientechnologie at the Medienmuseum, Karlsruhe, and the magazine *neue bildende kunst*, Berlin
40 photo panels, 18 x 24 cm each
The *Berkeley Oracle* invites the visitors to its web site, in five languages, to ask questions which have never been asked before, or which always have recurred and remained unanswered. These questions are to be collected for a number of years. Berkeley is a symbol for questions which fired new thoughts, passions and protests in 1968, and it thus takes up the heritage of setting off ever new doubts and discussions. A series of chosen questions will be recorded on plaques and installed in unexpected places in the Berkeley Art Museum and in the Zentrum für Kunst und Medientechnologie at the Medienmuseum in Karlsruhe, where visitors will encounter them without preparation. They will also be published in an issue of the magazine *neue bildende kunst*.

A few of the questions:

Would art exist if time and death did not exist?
Where does God spend his vacations?
Is it true that true desires only arise in the mind?
What is beauty?
How many children will I have?
Is it time to stop caring?

Installation at the Berkeley Art Museum, Berkeley

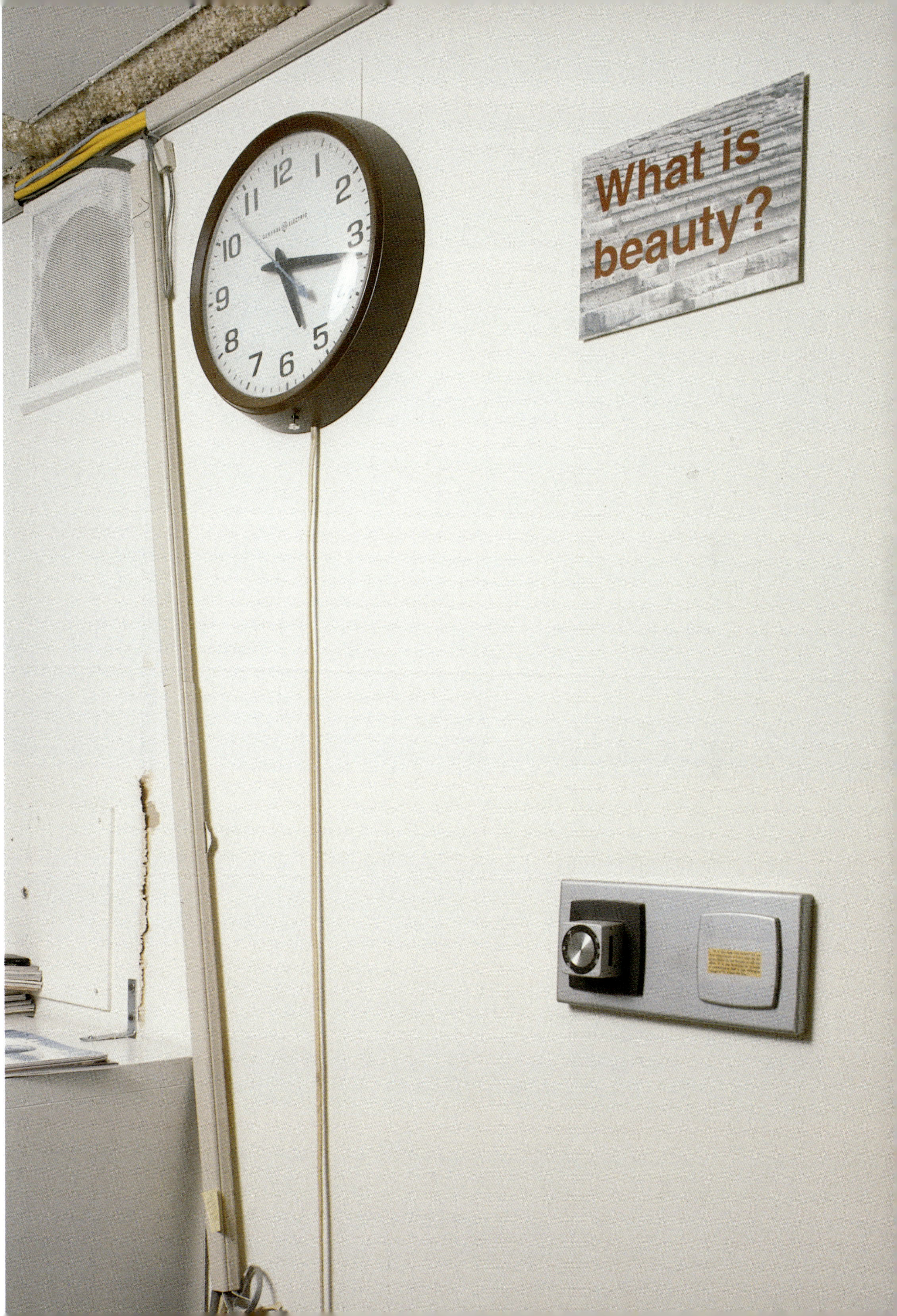
What is
beauty?

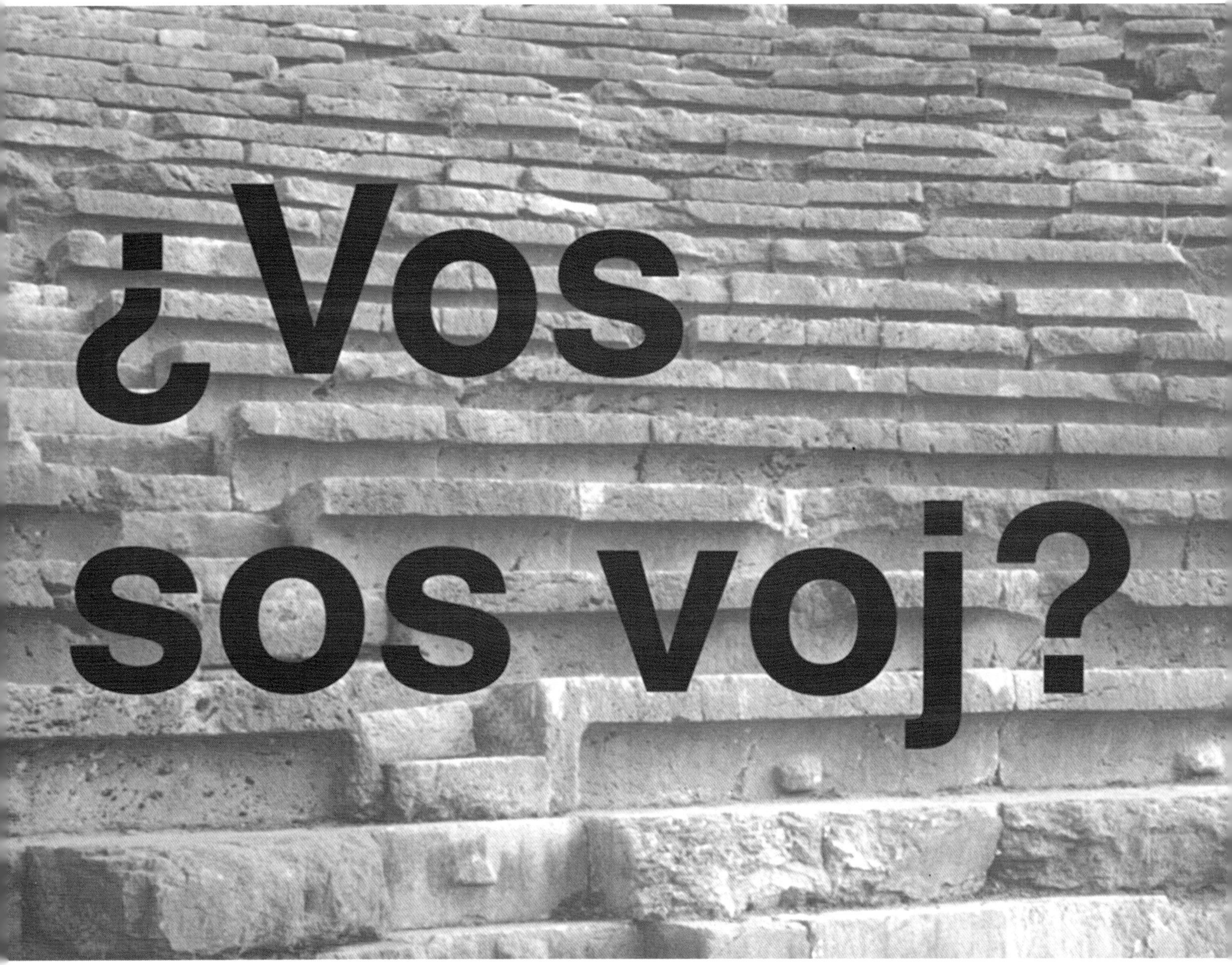
¿Vos
sos voj?

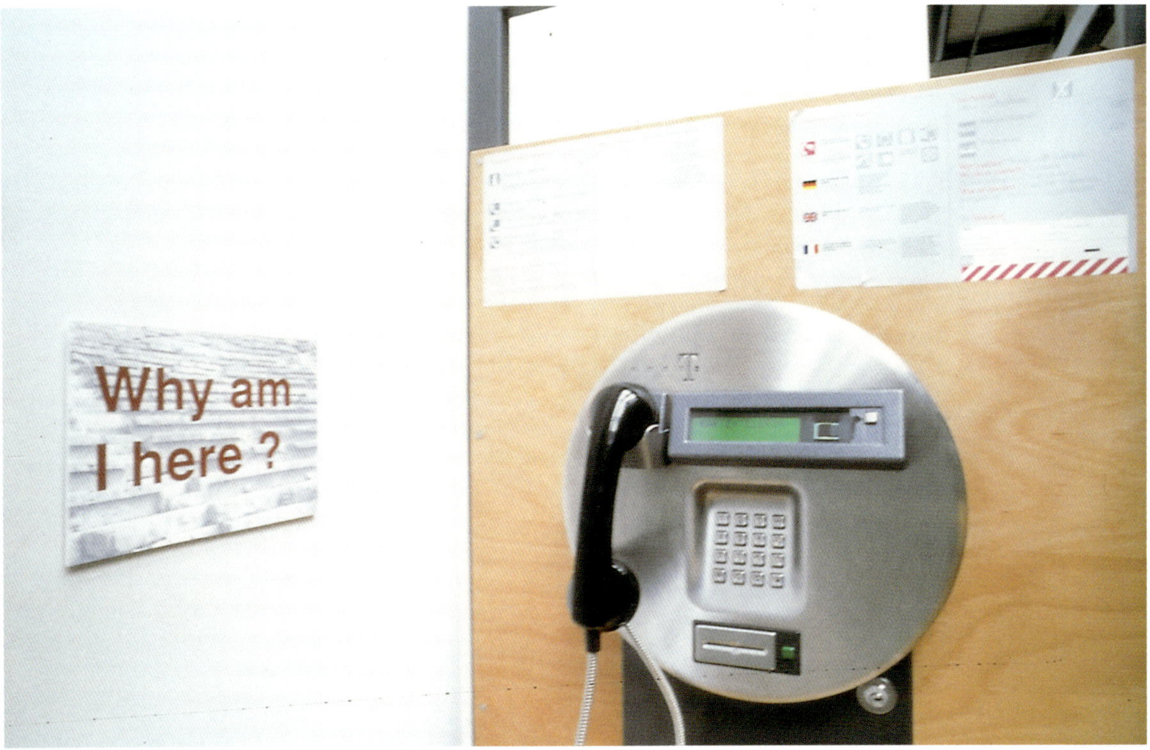

Installation at the Zentrum für Kunst und Medientechnologie, Karlsruhe

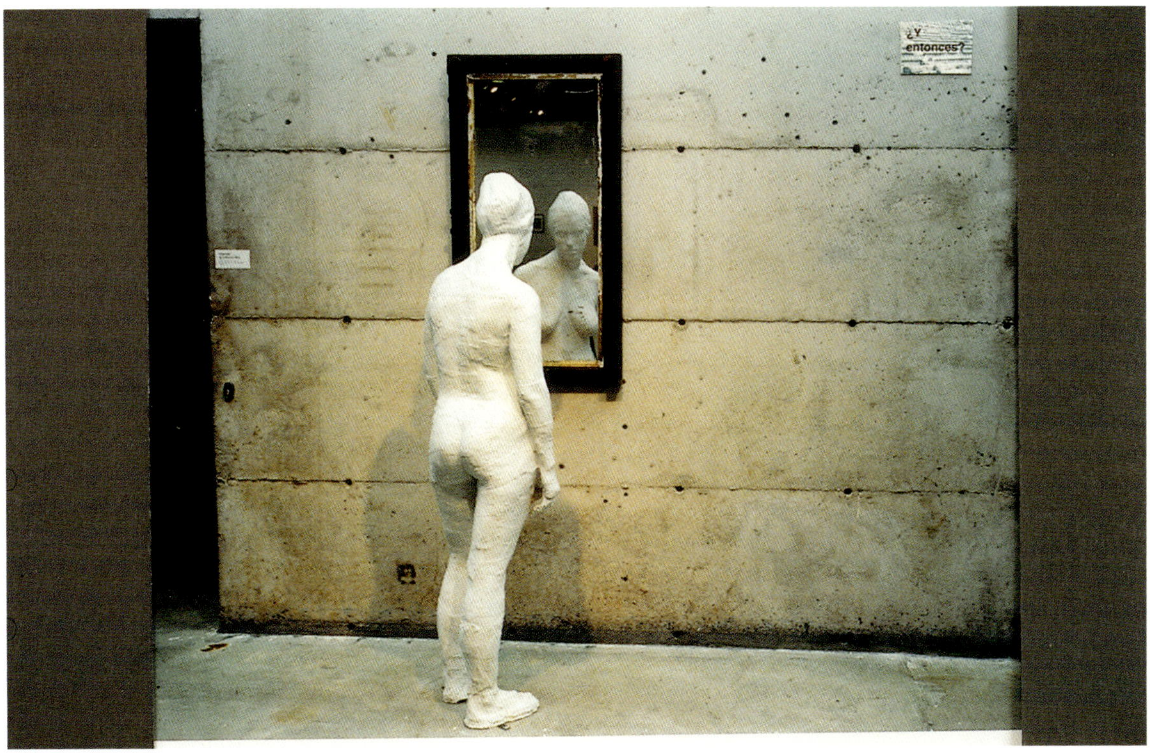

Installation at the Berkeley Art Museum, Berkeley

Les Témoins (The Witnesses) **Cahors, 1998**

Posters, giant-size transparencies, publications in newspapers
An edition of 48 photo portraits with texts mounted into them
In the course of the week of that preceded the verdict in the trial of Maurice Papon—a functionary of the Vichy regime, as well as a Minister in the post-war period, who was responsible for the deportation of many Jews in the area of Bordeaux—Jochen Gerz conversed with forty-eight women who live in the city of Cahors, all of whom were also members of Papon's generation. In the course of these conversations, he asked them about the possible relationships they see between their personal, private truths and a public, social truth. The phrases that crystallized out of these conversations, and which seem to be a concentrate that captures a fleeting moment of these women's lives, were mounted on their photo portraits. These portraits were shown as posters in public places of the city of Cahors, and ten of the portraits were also reproduced in a special number of the newspaper *La Dépêche du Midi*. This extension of the work by way of the media was repeated shortly later in the German edition of *Le Monde Diplomatique*.

A few of the texts:

The truth lies also in the things you no longer do, and in the things you would like to do, and also in how you do things. That also includes remembering. The old people have to pass along what they know.

It's a long time ago, the household has gotten larger. We had plans, but we couldn't live them out together. We saw things that still today make one shudder.

The others envy me, because I can walk without a cane. The truth isn't worth anything. What's true is that I no longer have anyone, that I cry more than I laugh.

You had to be careful about what you said. They arrested my neighbor, Madame Chapon. The militia denounced her. They tortured her. She never came back.

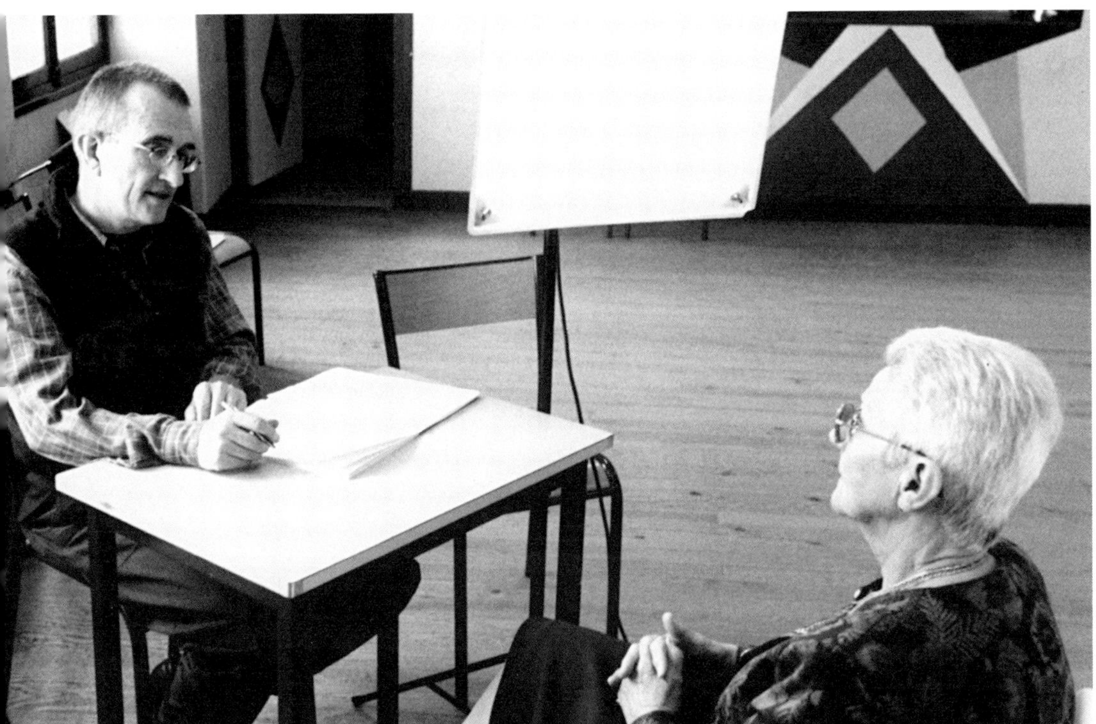

Jochen Gerz in conversation with one of the women of Cahors

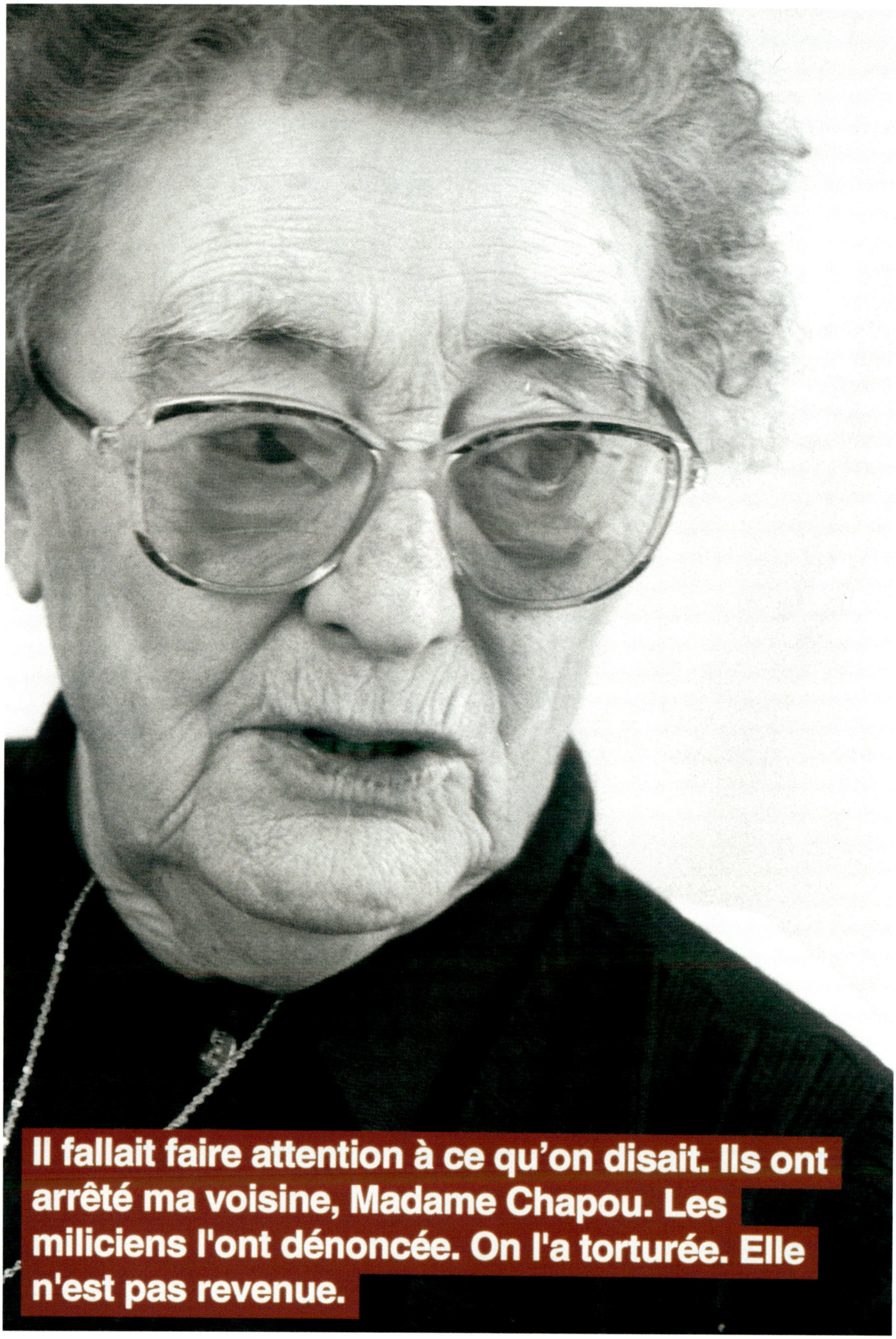
Il fallait faire attention à ce qu'on disait. Ils ont arrêté ma voisine, Madame Chapou. Les miliciens l'ont dénoncée. On l'a torturée. Elle n'est pas revenue.

Poster

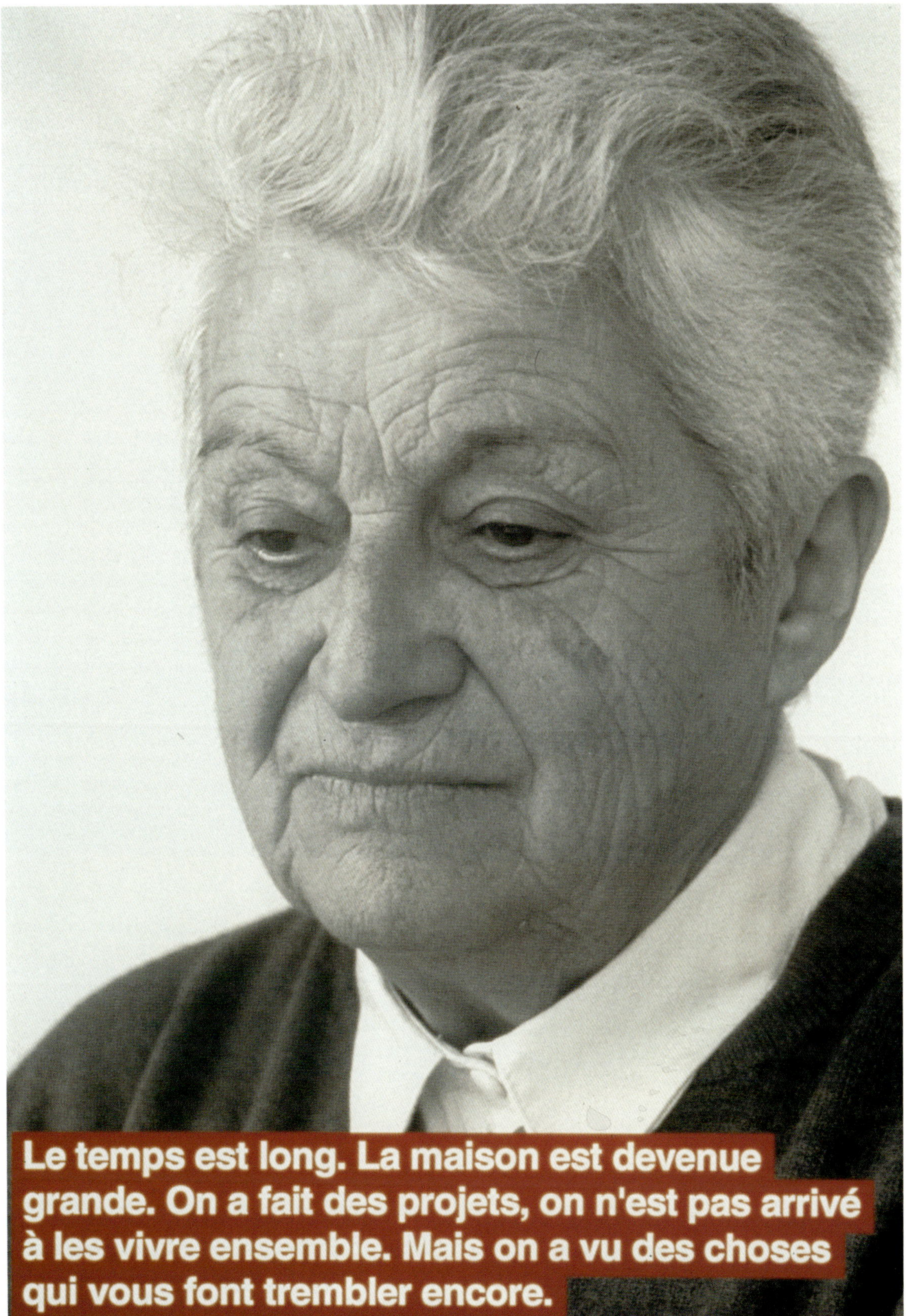
Le temps est long. La maison est devenue grande. On a fait des projets, on n'est pas arrivé à les vivre ensemble. Mais on a vu des choses qui vous font trembler encore.

Poster

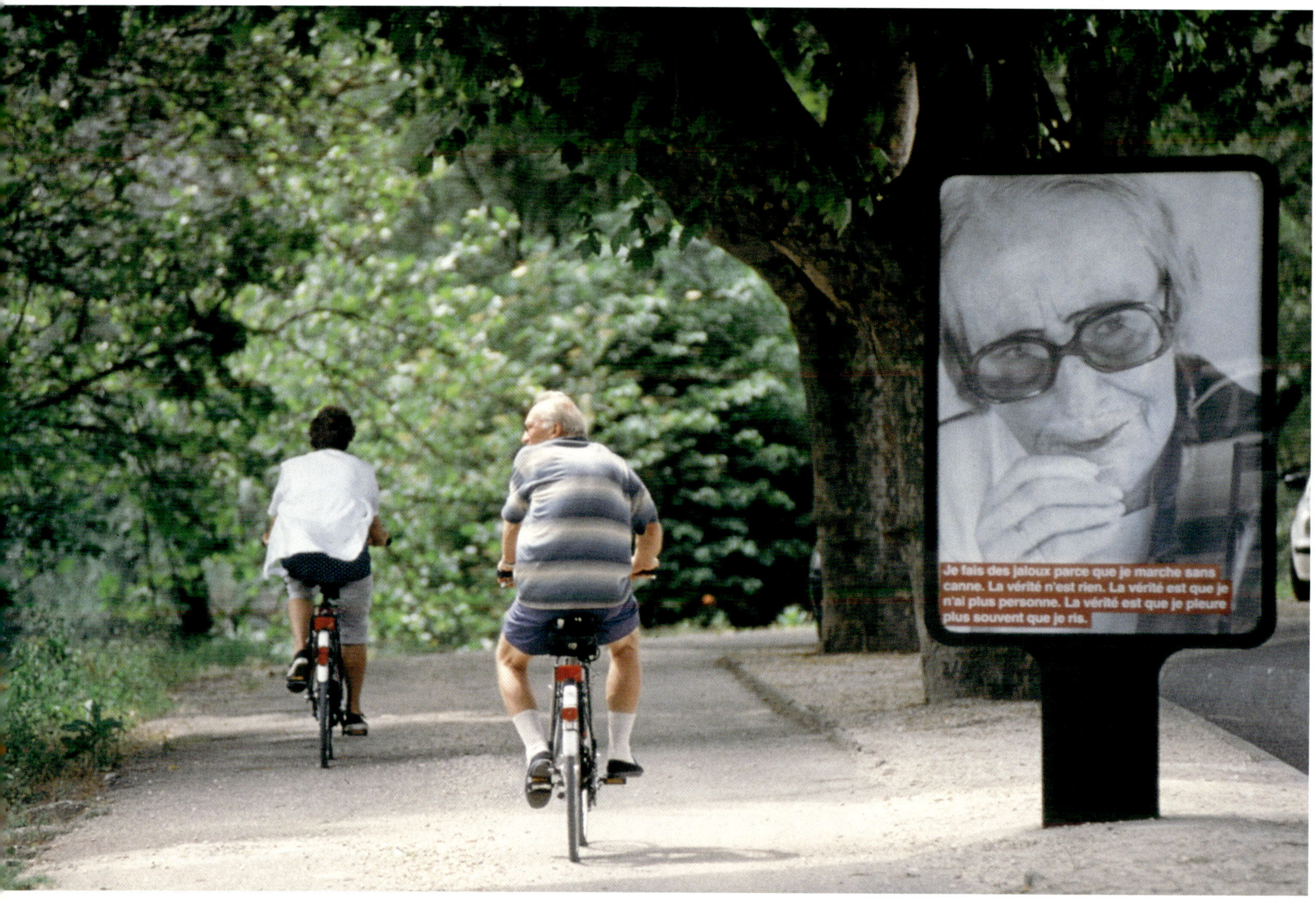

Je fais des jaloux parce que je marche sans
canne. La vérité n'est rien. La vérité est que je
n'ai plus personne. La vérité est que je pleure
plus souvent que je ris.

Cahors, 1998

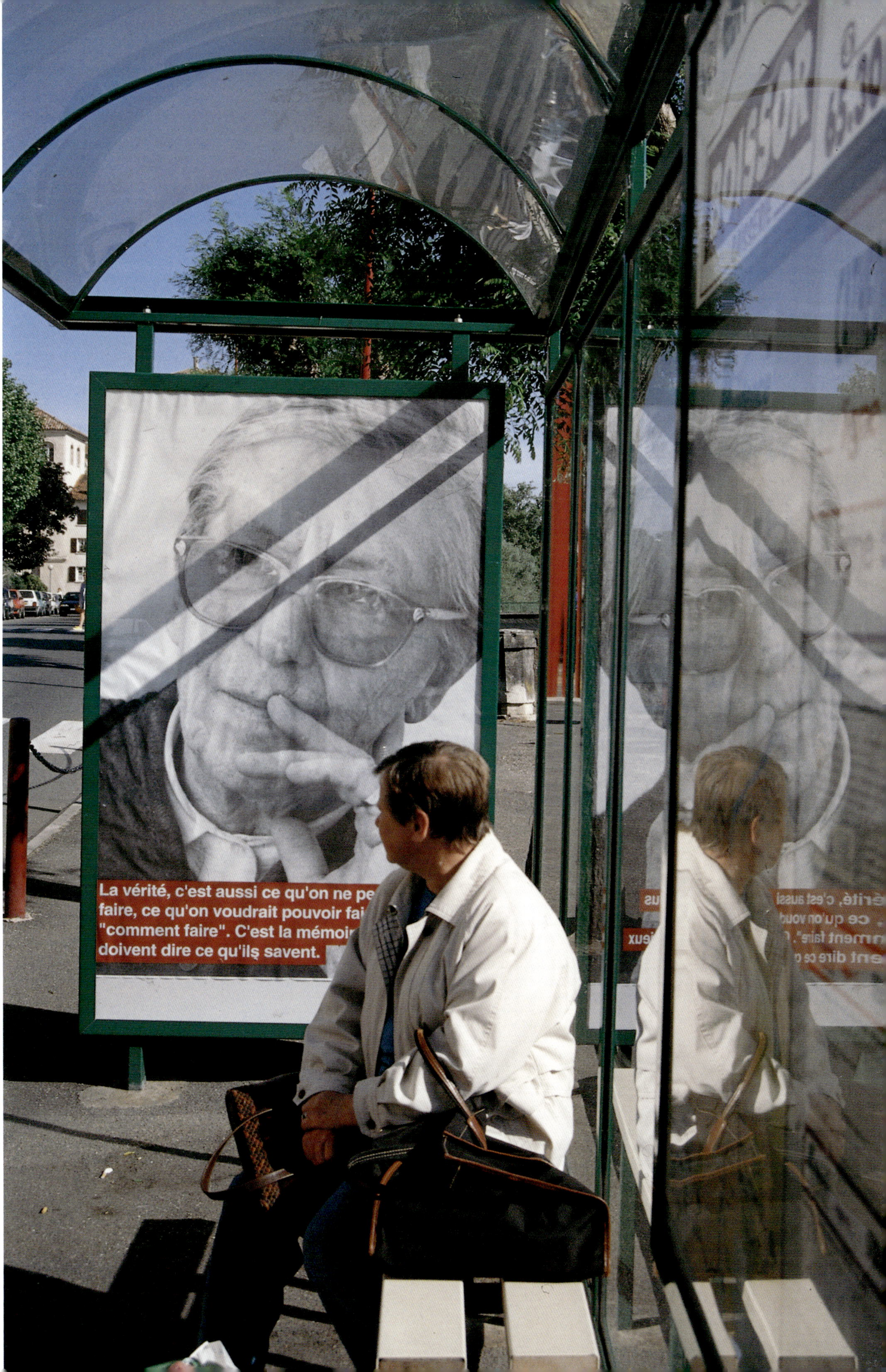
La vérité, c'est aussi ce qu'on ne
faire, ce qu'on voudrait pouvoir
"comment faire". C'est la
doivent dire ce qu'ils savent.

Documentation

Ce Soir à 23 heures 45 (This Evening at 11:45 p. m.) Paris, 1968

Sticker, offset, 10.4 x 14 cm
The sticker was pasted up in windows in public spaces, and also handed out to the public. The text reads: "Ce soir à 23 heures 45 entre la porte de Clignancourt et la rue d'Alésia 1 million de Parisiens font l'amour chez eux, vous êtes invités à participer au spectacle." (This evening at 11:45 p. m., in the area between Porte de Clignancourt and rue d'Alésia, one million Parisians will be making love in their homes. You are invited to take part in the event.)

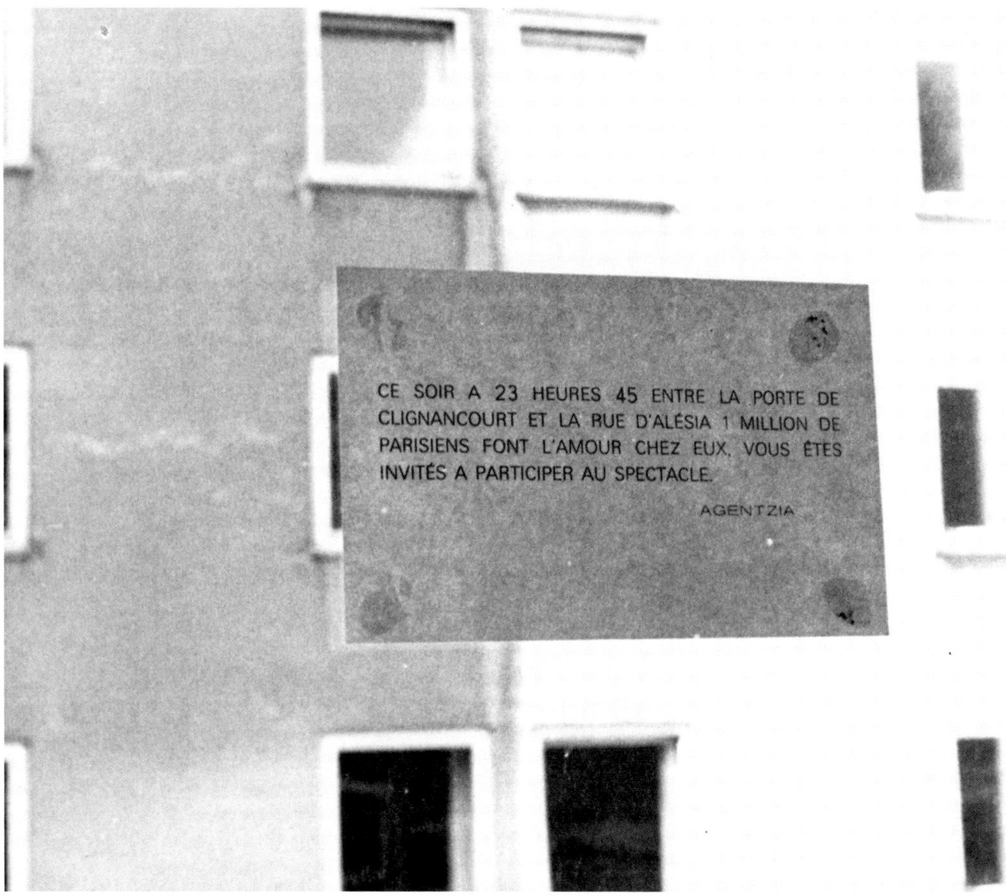

Is There Life on Earth? Paris, 1968/70

Silkscreen on clear plastic bag, 29.7 x 21 cm
Small offset on white and yellow paper, 29.7 x 21 cm
An edition of ca. 800
Friends and strangers listed in the Paris telephone book received empty plastic bags in the mail. An accompanying text invited them to put things from which they were willing to separate themselves into these bags and to send them back. The bags and the invitation, written in various languages, were also presented at various exhibitions in the period from 1968 to 1970. Of about 800 bags, more than 300 were returned, sealed, and then, on April 16, 1970, were buried in the concrete foundations, forty meters below street level, of the new Montparnasse Tower in Paris.

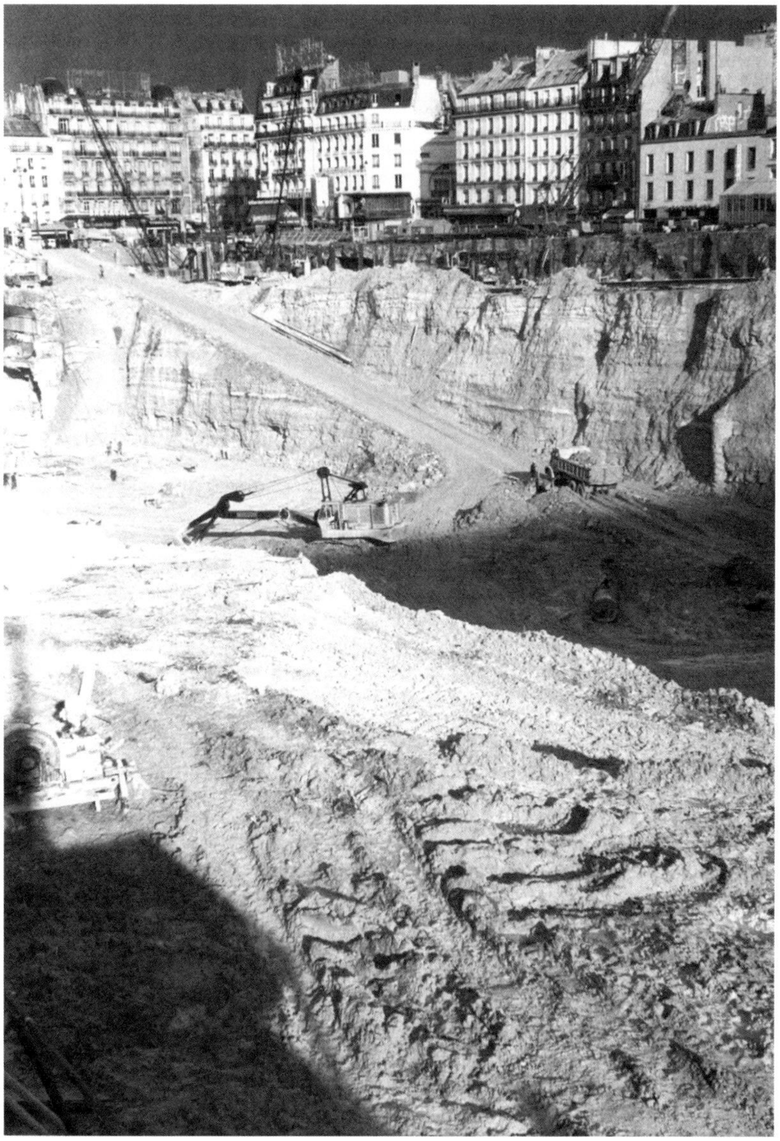

The construction site of the new Montparnasse Tower, Paris 1968

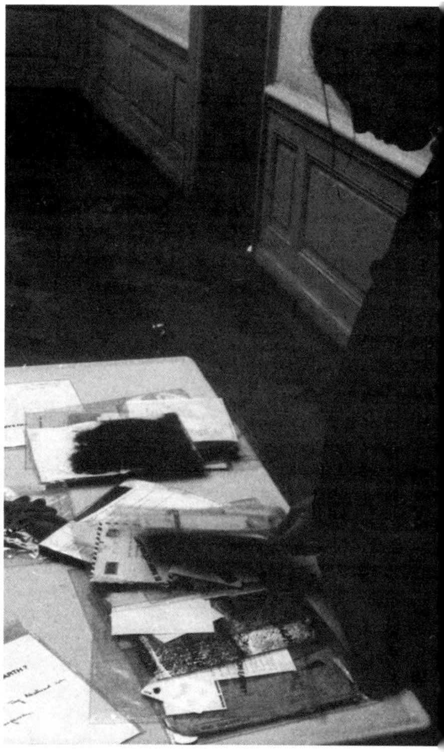

Plastic bags returned to Jochen Gerz

Das neue Telefonbuch von Paris/The New Phonebook of Paris/ Le Nouvel Annuaire de Paris/Il nuovo elenco telefonico di Parigi

Paris, 1968/71

Offset, 29.7 x 21 cm

A questionnaire in several languages was sent to strangers listed in the Paris telephone book, and also distributed to exhibition visitors. The recipients were invited to make a personal contribution to changing the structure of the Paris telephone book.

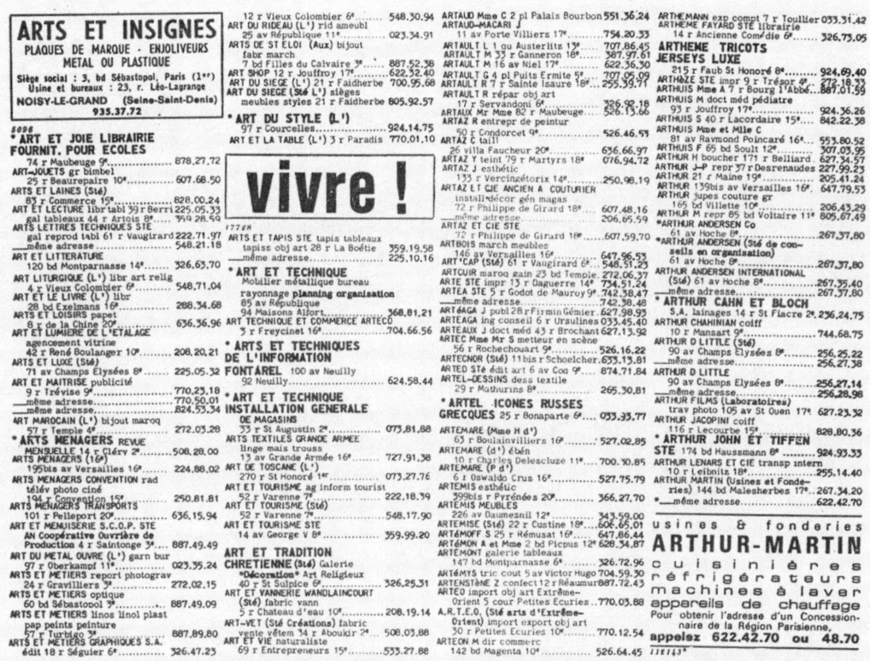

Comme tous les annuaires du monde, celui de Paris est réglementé selon un code qui tend à discréditer toute possibilité de communication non-affirmative, ludique, et satisfaisante. A peu près rien sauf "oui" et "non" n'y trouve place et les degrés les plus pauvres de fonctionnalité, niant tout principe nouveau de conscience culturel, comme le choix expérimental ou aléatoire, font de ce livre un objet hermétique et incompréhensible pour un nombre croissant de gens.

Que chacun fasse inscrire ici, pour paralyser le code de l'Annuaire de Paris, son numéro d'appel accompagné d'un mot, d'une question ou de toute phrase ayant à faire à ses préoccupations. Que tout le monde demande de même aux gens des contributions à son propre annuaire afin que chacun puisse tenter de nouvelles communications à son tour. Même des communications sans numéro d'appel peuvent permettre aux utilisateurs d'un annuaire transformé de toucher un "feedback" de sa propre pensée.

Envoyez votre communication à : Jochen Gerz, 41, rue Buffon, Paris-5e France.

As any phone-book in the world, the Phone-Book of Paris is regulated according to a code which discredits most possibilities of non-affirmative, playfull, satisfactory communication. Fairly nothing besides "yes" and "no" finds place in it and the poorest degrees of functionality denying new principles of cultural awareness, such as experimental or random choice, makes of this book a hermetic and incomprehensible object for a growing number of people.

Everybody may, in order to paralyse the code of the Phone-Book of Paris, put his phone-number down here with a word, a question, or any phrase due to his preoccupations. Everybody may as well ask people to contribute to his own phone-book so that he himself can try new communications. Even contribution without a phone-number may allow any user of the changed phone-book to touch a feedback of his own thinking.

Send your communication to : Jochen Gerz, 41, rue Buffon, Paris-5e, France.

Come tutte le guide telefoniche del mondo, anche quella di Parigi è regolata da un codice atto a discreditare qualsiasi possibilità di comunicazione non affermativa, ludica, soddisfacente. All'infuori di "sí" e "no", non c'è posto per nient'altro, e i gradi più poveri di funzionalità, negando ogni nuovo principio di coscienza culturale, come la scelta sperimentale o aleatoria, fanno della guida un oggetto ermetico ed incomprensibile per un numero crescente di persone.

Per paralizzare il codice della guida di Parigi, ciascuno scriva qui il suo numero di telefono, accompagnato da una parola, domanda o frase attinente alle sue preoccupazioni. Ciascuno domandi la stessa cosa ad altri, per ottenere contributi alla propria guida. Anche delle comunicazioni non accompagnate da un numero possono permettere all'utilizzatore di una guida trasformata di percepire un "feedback" del proprio pensiero.

Inviare la vostra comunicazione a : Jochen Gerz, 41, rue Buffon, Paris-5e,Francia.

Wie jedes Telefonbuch ist auch das Telefonbuch von Paris nach einem Kode angelegt, der alle Möglichkeiten nicht affirmativer, spielerischer und zufriedenstellender Kommunikation diskreditiert. Nahezu nichts ausser "ja" und "nein" findet Platz darin und die armseligsten Massstäbe von Funktionalität, die jedes neue Prinzip kulturellen Bewussteins (experimentelle oder zufallsbedingte Auswahl z. B.) verneinen, machen aus diesem Buch ein hermetisches und unverständliches Objekt für immer mehr Menschen.

Jeder, der helfen will, den Kode des Telefonbuchs von Paris zu paralysieren, kann hier seine Telefonnummer angeben, begleitet von einer Frage oder einem Satz, der seinen Anliegen entspricht. Jeder kann ebenfalls andere um Beiträge für sein eigenes Telefonbuch bitten, um sich auf diese Weise auch selber neue Kommunikationen zu schaffen. Auch Beiträge ohne Telefonnummer können Benutzern des veränderten Telefonbuchs zu einem "Feedback" ihres eigenen Denkens verhelfen.

Senden Sie Ihre Kommunikation an : Jochen Gerz, 41, rue Buffon, Paris-5e Frankreich.

329 Das Buch der Gesten (329 The Book of Gestures)

Heidelberg/Basel 1969; Frankfurt am Main, 1973

Performance

Printed cards, with black text on red or blue cardboard

An edition of ca. 5000 pieces, each 10.5 x 13.5 cm

During the "Intermedia" exhibition in Heidelberg, about 5000 cards with printed text were thrown from the roof of a house in the center of the city. The passers-by were also informed that the cards constituted a book: their contribution was to consist of continuing to do whatever they were doing at the time, without allowing themselves to be influenced by having found the cards.

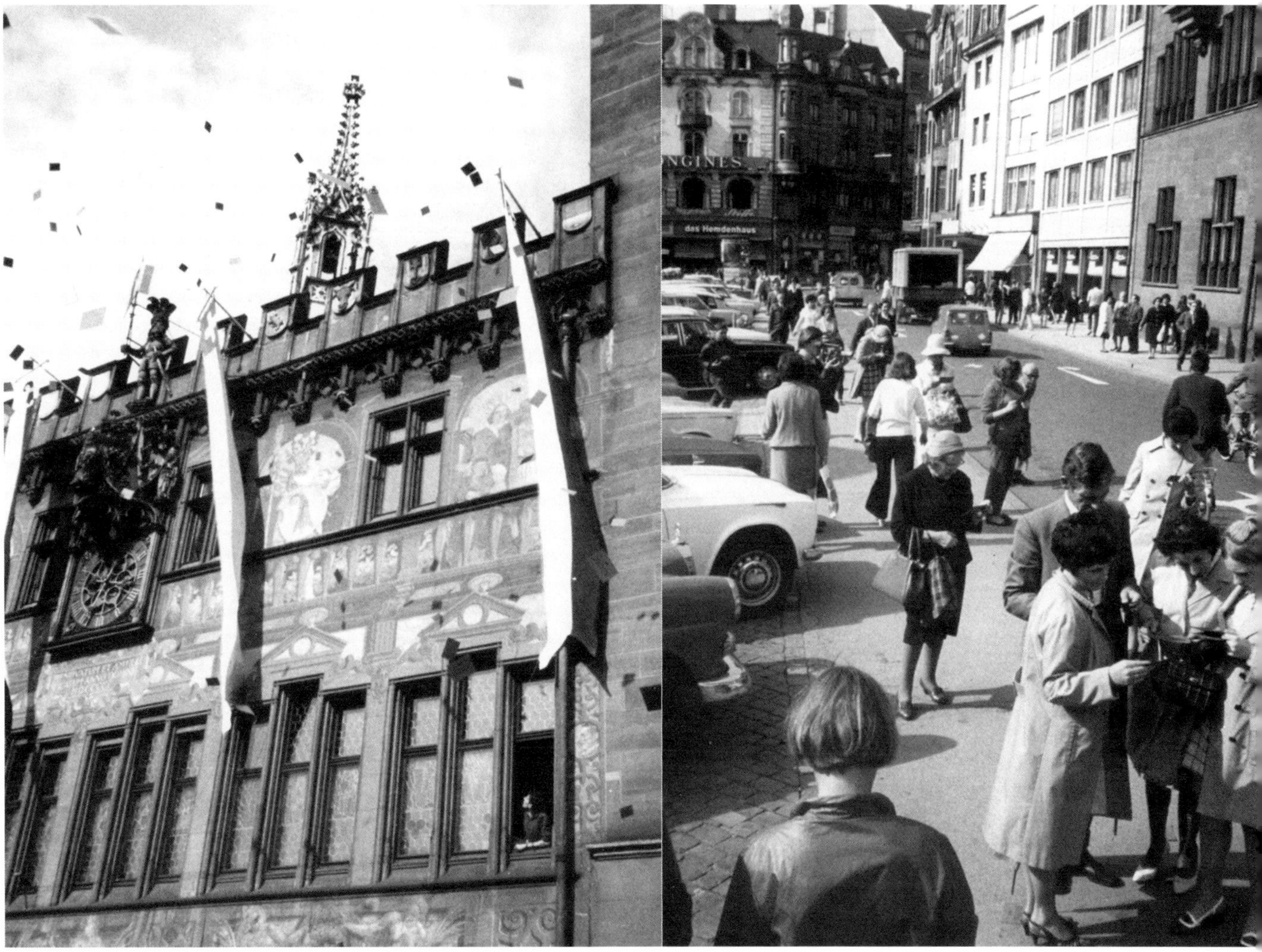

Basel, 1969

Alternatives to Memories **Basel, 1969**

Installation

A rope of a length of 300 m, 2 black-and-white photographs, 2 wooden stands, 4 gloves

During the exhibition "Für Veränderungen aller Art" (For Changes of Any and All Kinds) at Kunsthalle Basel, Jochen Gerz installed a rope that led out of the exhibition space and into the streets, and with a pair of gloves attached to each of its ends. A photograph in black and white was set up in the vicinity of each end of the rope, each photo reproducing the other extreme of the installation: the photo in the street showed the situation of the rope and the gloves within the Kunsthalle; the photo in the exhibition space showed their situation in the streets.

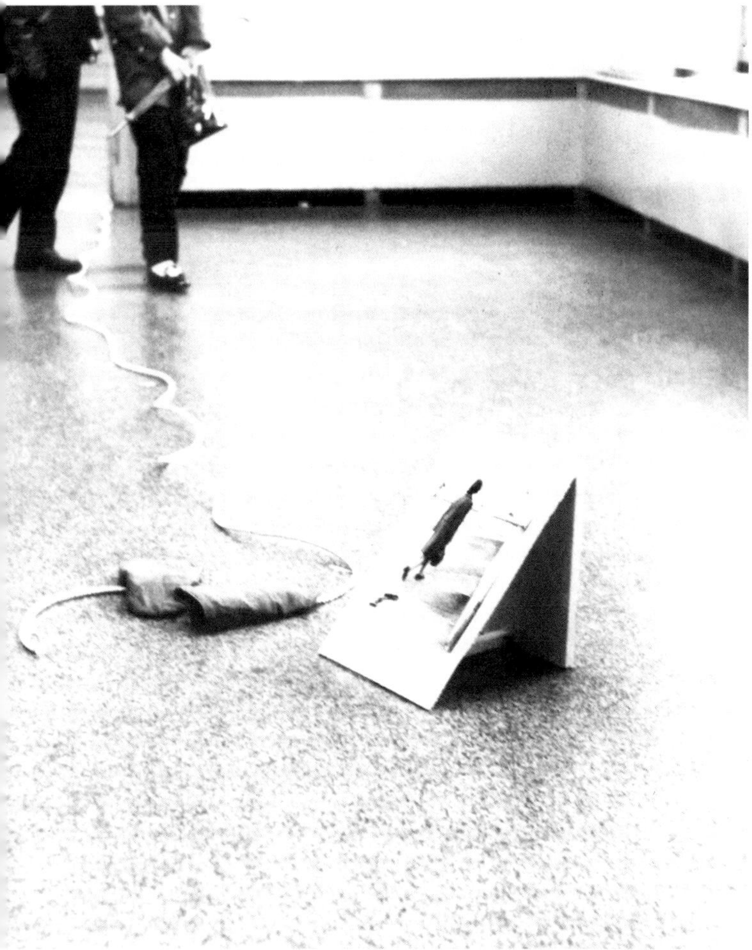

Photo of the exhibition space

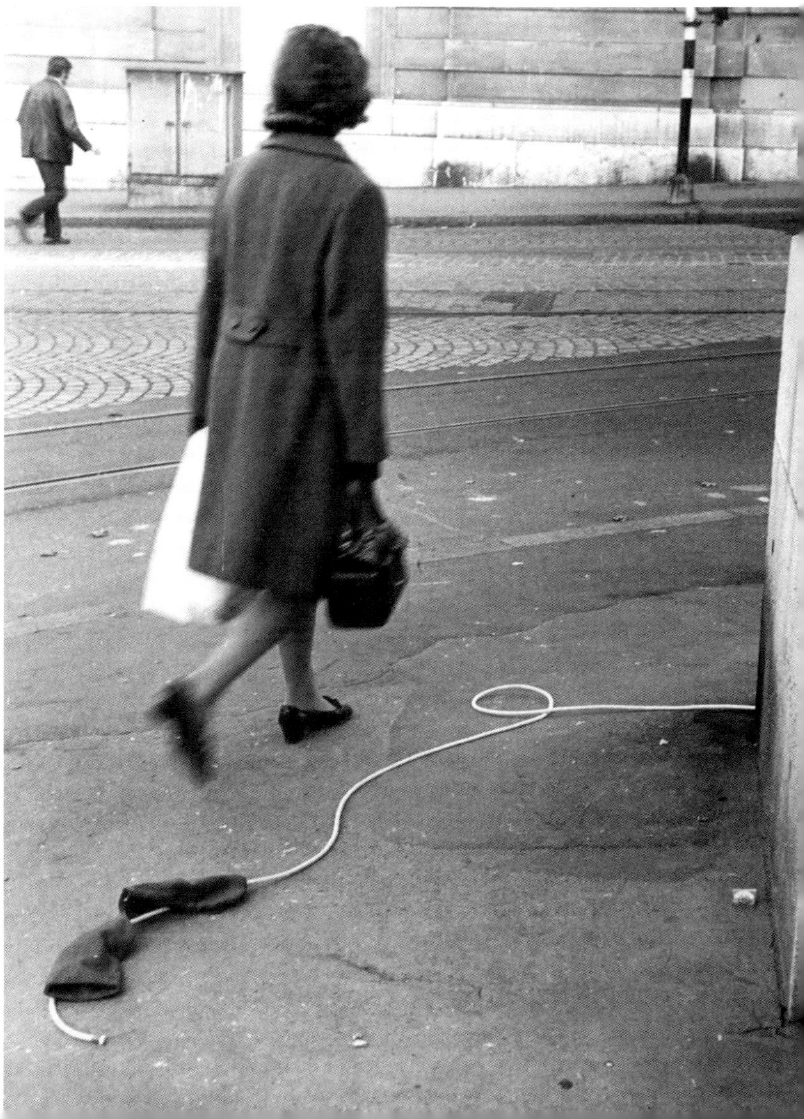

Photo of the space in the streets

Befragung über die Kunst (Art Questionnaire) Basel, 1969

Offset on paper, 29.7 x 21 cm
Questionnaires were submitted to the workers at the Hoffmann La Roche Corporation in Basel. The completed forms were shown in Basel during the exhibition "Für Veränderungen aller Art" (For Changes of Any and All Kinds).

Beruf: Arbeit .... Alter: 36 ....

Was ist Kunst für Sie ?

X a) Picasso
b) Romy Schneider
c) die Beatles
d) Schwitters
e) ....

Waren Sie schon im

a) Kunstmuseum
X b) Stadttheater
c) Konzert
X d) Jazzkeller
e) in einer Kunstgalerie
f) ....

Kennen Sie persönlich einen

a) Maler
b) Schlagersänger
c) Schauspieler
d) Schriftsteller
e) ....

Verdienen Künstler Ihrer Meinung nach

a) mehr als Sie
b) weniger als Sie
c) zu viel
d) nicht genug

und sind sie

e) reich
f) arm
g) ....

Beneiden Sie die

X a) Filmstars
b) Schlagersänger
c) Schriftsteller
d) Clowns
e) ....

Arbeiten Künstler

a) weniger als Sie
b) mehr als Sie
c) ebenso viel wie Sie
d) ....

Besitzen Künstler Ihnen gegenüber Vorteile im Leben, die sie ihrem Beruf verdanken? z.B.

a) Freiheit
b) Ruhm
c) Freizeit
d) Verantwortung
e) Glück
f) ....

An welchem Ort haben Sie bisher am meisten über das Kunstgeschehen erfahren? Im

a) Fernsehen
b) Museum
c) Radio
X d) Kino
X e) in der Zeitung/Illustrierten/Zeitschrift

Würden Sie gerne mitmachen bei

a) einem Film
b) im Schlagergeschäft
c) beim Zirkus

Haben Sie in Ihrer Jugend

a) gemalt
b) gesungen
c) Theater gespielt
d) Gedichte geschrieben
e) ....

Möchten Sie, dass Ihre Kinder

a) malen
X b) Theater spielen
c) ein Instrument spielen
d) Ballett machen
e) ....

Tram-Projekt (Tram Project) **Basel, 1969**

Installation

On the occasion of the exhibition "Für Veränderungen aller Art" (For Changes of Any and All Kinds), Basel 1969, Jochen Gerz developed the project of using white lines to detour the trams along lines 3, 4, and 14 into the Basel Kunsthalle.

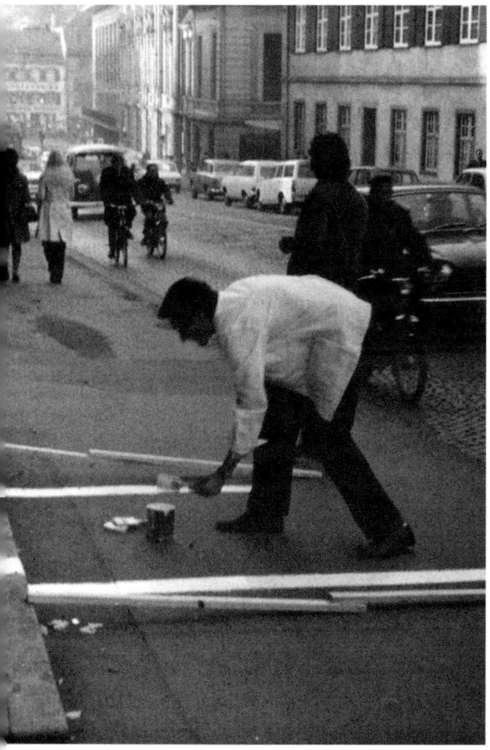

Jochen Gerz during the realization of the work

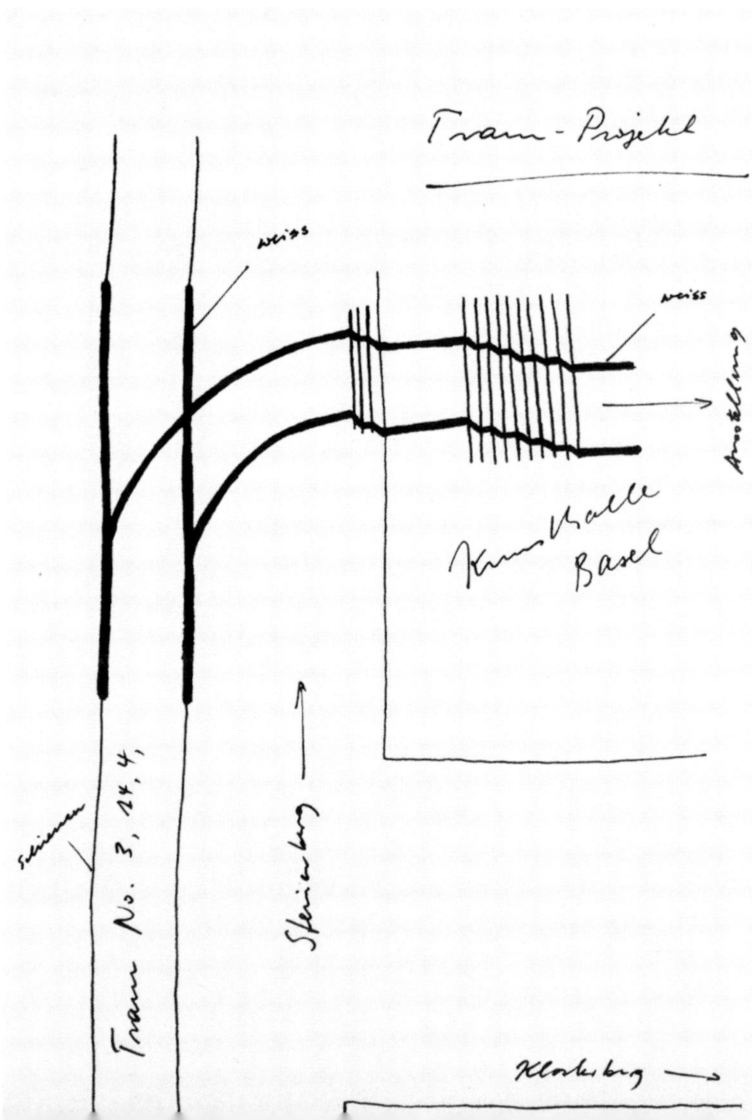

Sketch for the project

Es findet woanders statt
(The Event Is Taking Place Somewhere Else)
Basel, 1969

Card, offset, 10.5 x 14 cm
In an otherwise empty room at Kunsthalle Basel, the text *Es findet woanders statt* (The event Is taking place somewhere else) was displayed.

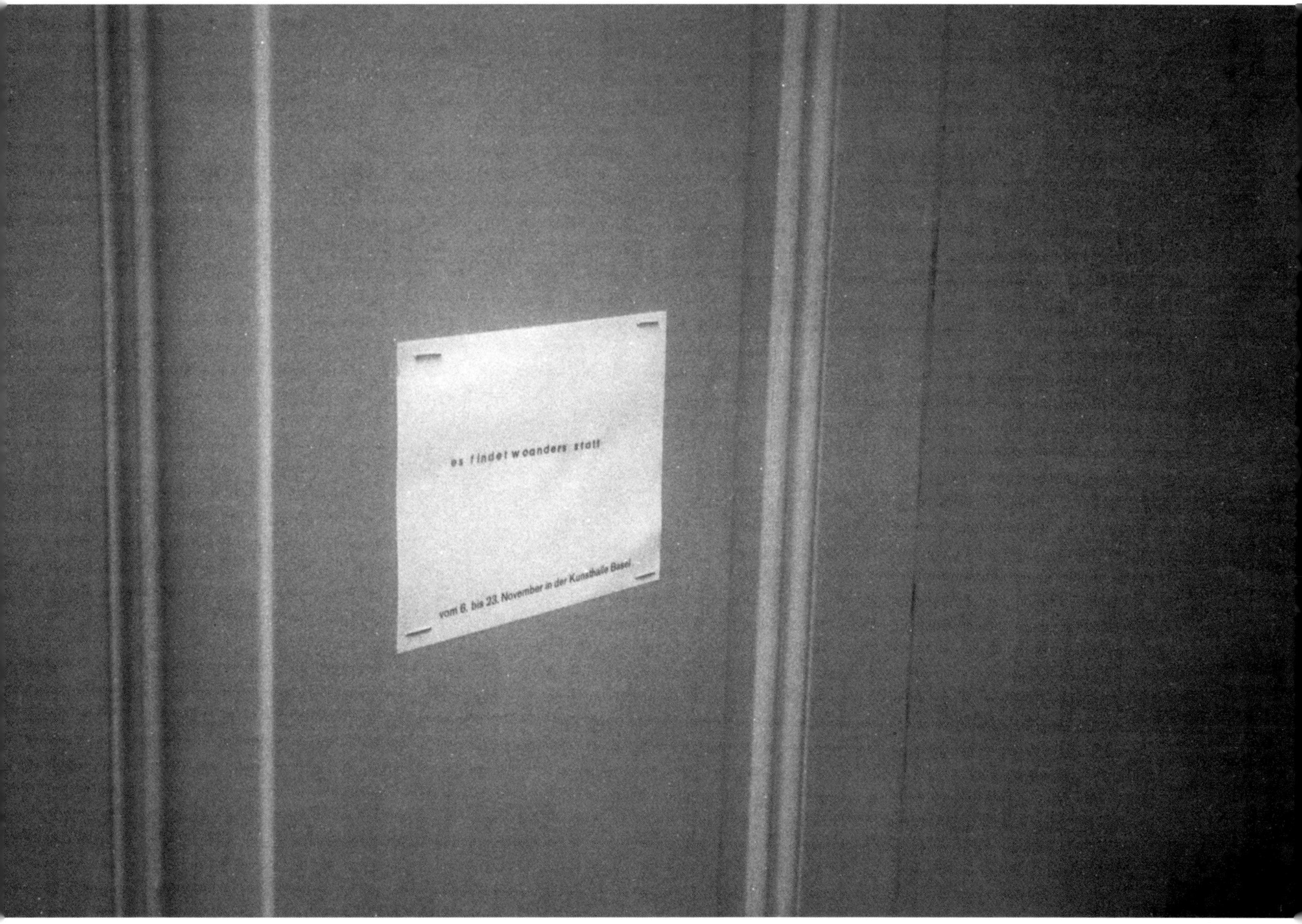

Karten (Cards) Paris, 1970

Cards, offset, each 10.5 x 14 cm
The cards were distributed and sent to various people in the art world, and to persons chosen from the telephone book. One of them, for example, bears the message: "J'ai vu quelqu'un faire un geste pour son propre plaisir. (Il n'y aura pas d'exposition). Du 4 avril 1940 au ... Jochen Gerz" (I have watched a person perform a gesture for their own personal pleasure (There will be no exhibition). From April 4, 1940 until ... Jochen Gerz).

M. Li Hô est mort.	**Mr. Li Hô is dead.**
M. Cavalcanti est mort.	**Mr. Cavalcanti is dead.**
M. da Vinci est mort.	**Mr. da Vinci is dead.**
M. Tatlin est mort.	**Mr. Tatlin is dead.**
Merci.	**Thank you.**
Du 4 avril 1940 au	**Jochen Gerz**

Pièce avec un aveugle (Piece with a Blind Man) Paris, 1970

Performance
"When we reached the sidewalk, I asked him if I could lead him back to where we had started from. He agreed, and we repeated the crossing several times, as I held his arm. We didn't talk a great deal with each another, but I nonetheless had the feeling that he found the procedure fairly normal."
(photo/text)

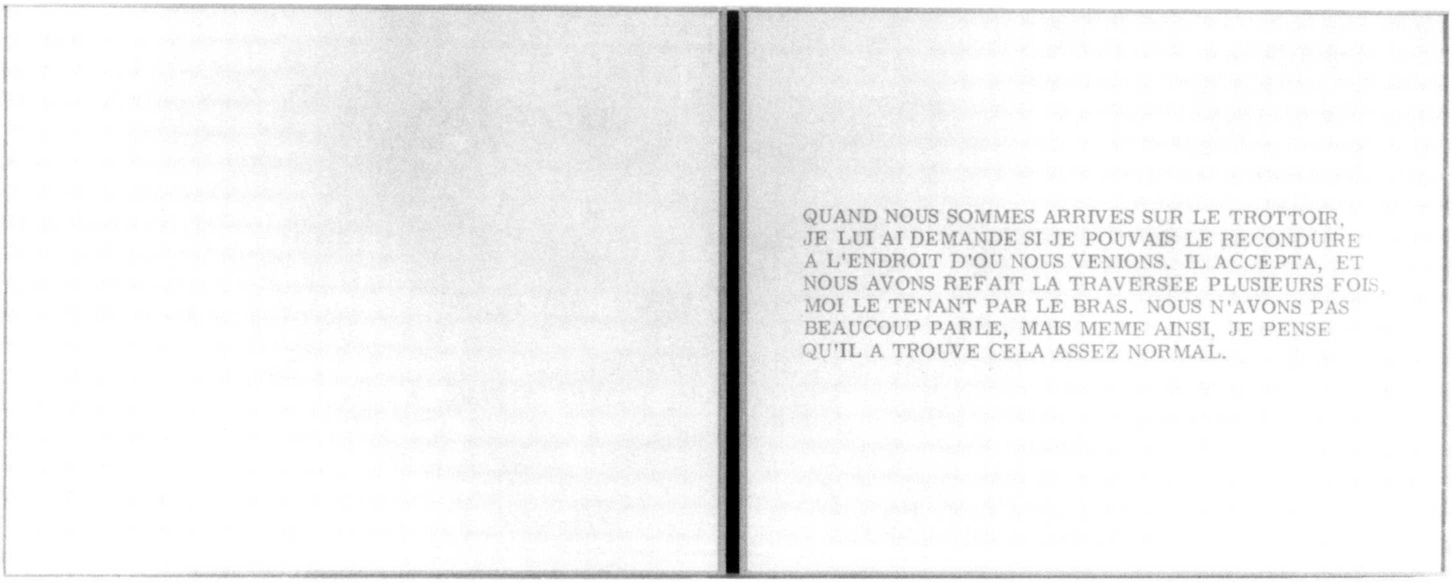

QUAND NOUS SOMMES ARRIVES SUR LE TROTTOIR, JE LUI AI DEMANDE SI JE POUVAIS LE RECONDUIRE A L'ENDROIT D'OU NOUS VENIONS. IL ACCEPTA, ET NOUS AVONS REFAIT LA TRAVERSEE PLUSIEURS FOIS, MOI LE TENANT PAR LE BRAS. NOUS N'AVONS PAS BEAUCOUP PARLE, MAIS MEME AINSI, JE PENSE QU'IL A TROUVE CELA ASSEZ NORMAL.

12 x La Santé **Paris, 1971**

Performance

Notebook, 21 x 27 cm

The score for this piece establishes that a photo is to be taken from a specific place at the start of every month in the course of a year. The work began on January 2, 1971. The photos show a part of the La Santé prison in Paris. The piece ended with the artist's arrest on March 2, 1971. In the course of the arrest, the film in his camera was exposed to the light.

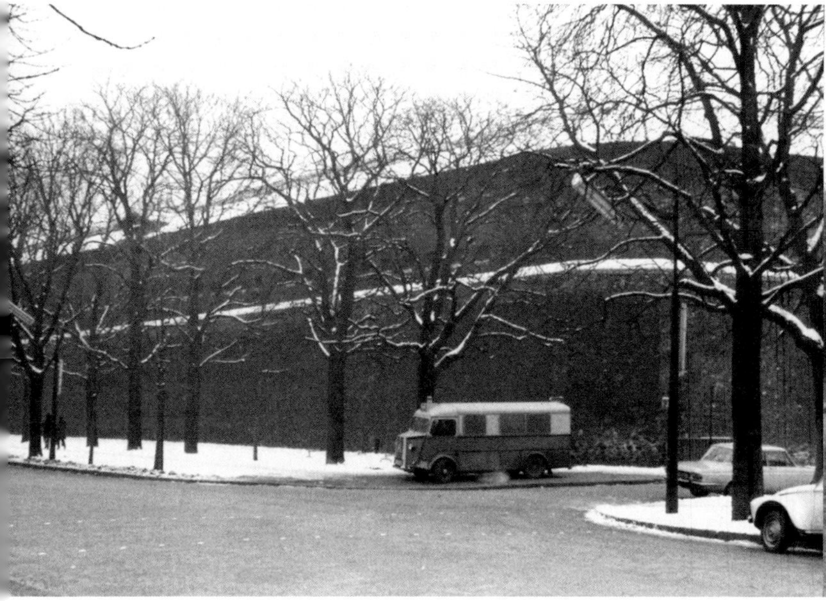

January 2, 1971, Paris

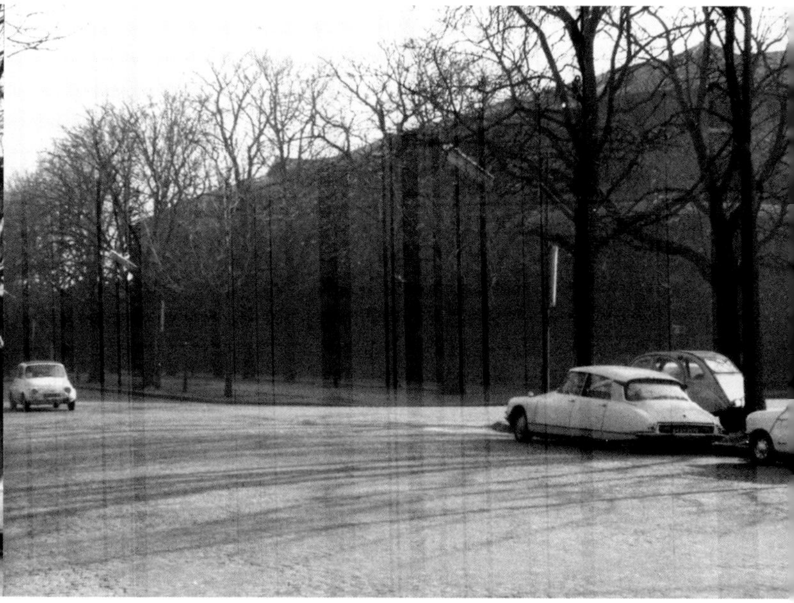

February 2, 1971, Paris

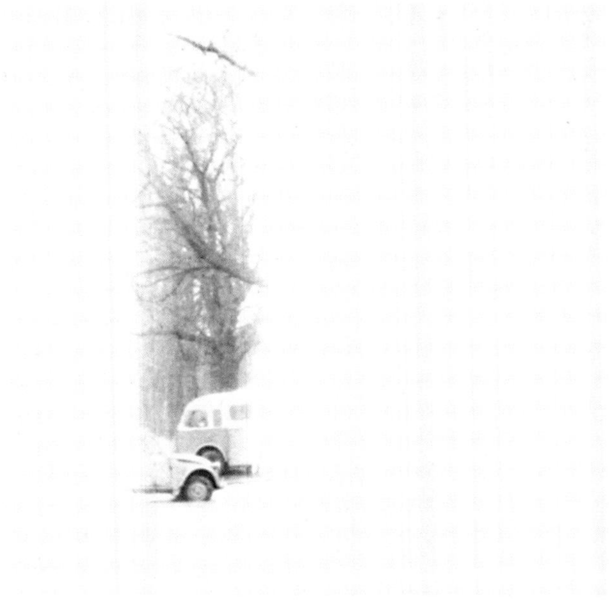

Film exposed to the light, March 2, 1971, Paris

Pièce pour un laveur de carreaux (Piece for a Window Washer) **Paris, 1971**

Performance

Duration: 90 minutes

The piece was performed by a window washer, who was photographed during his work at the Musée de l'Histoire Naturelle.

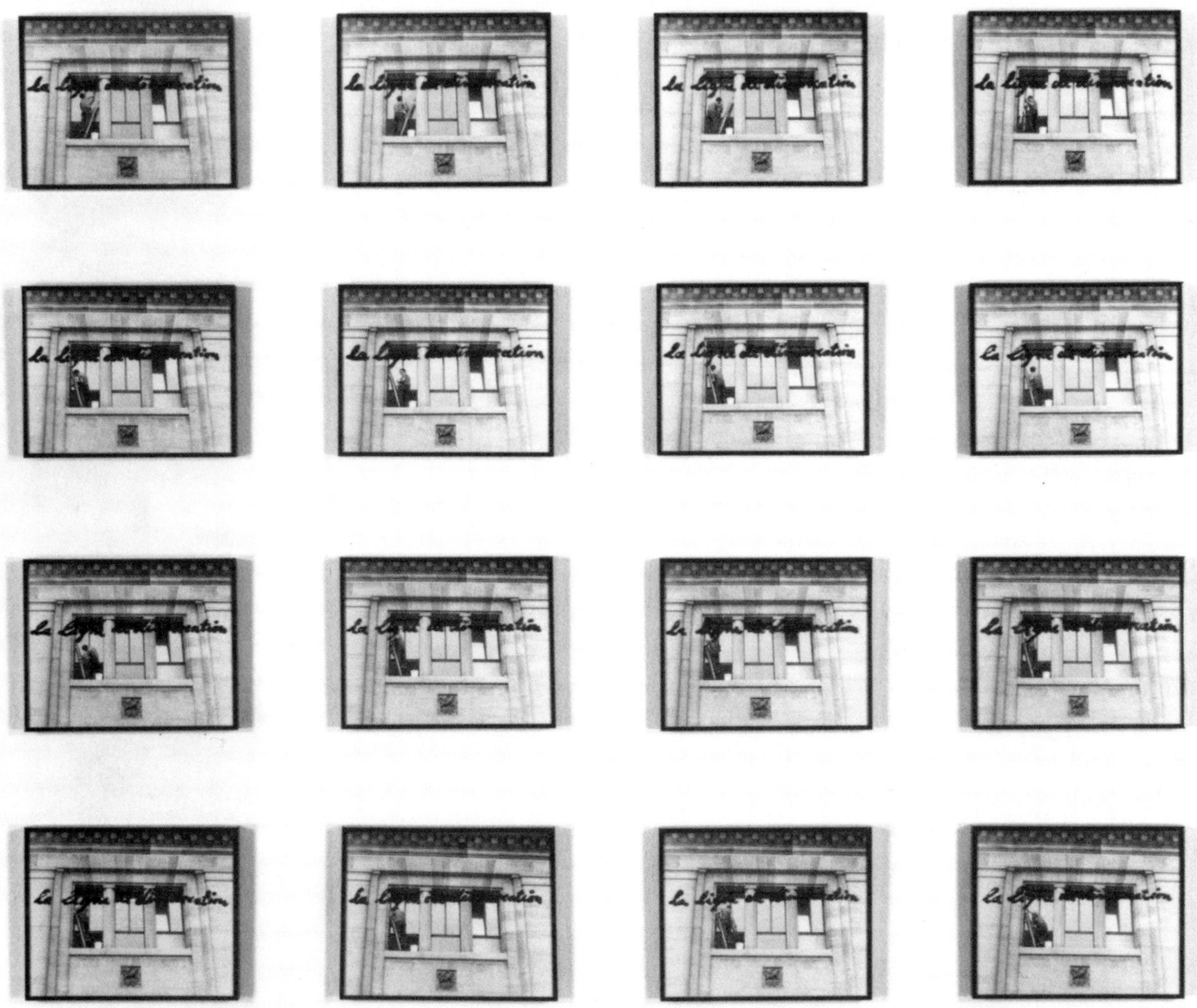

La Ligne de démarcation (The Line of Demarcation), photo/text, 1971

Pièce pour 1, 2, 3, 4, (Piece for 1, 2, 3, 4) Paris, 1971

Performance

Duration: 3 hours

The piece was performed on March 16, 1971, by three gardeners at the Jardin des Plantes, in Paris: "Between 2:00 p. m and 5:00 p. m., three gardeners were at work in the flower beds at the side of the Museum. A few days previously, a Caterpillar tractor had covered these beds with new earth, and the gardeners' task was to pack the fresh earth down, so as to prepare it for seeding. They did this by treading their way across it with tiny, trampling footsteps." (photo/text)

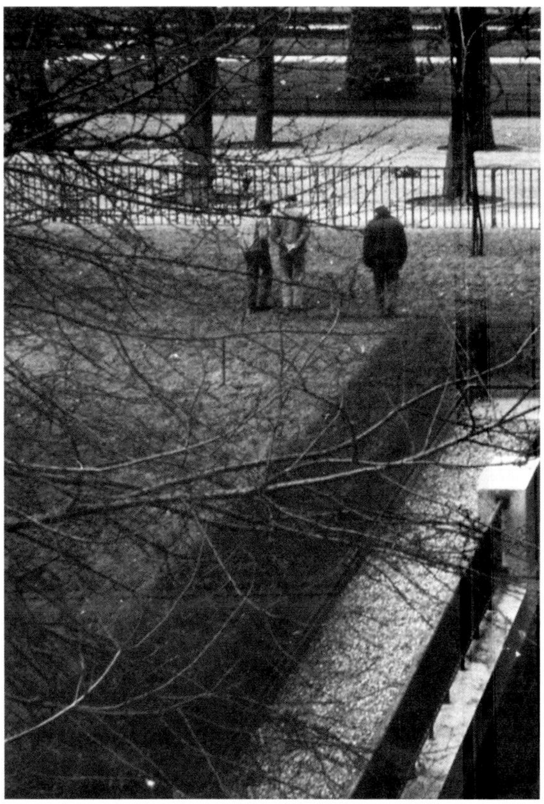

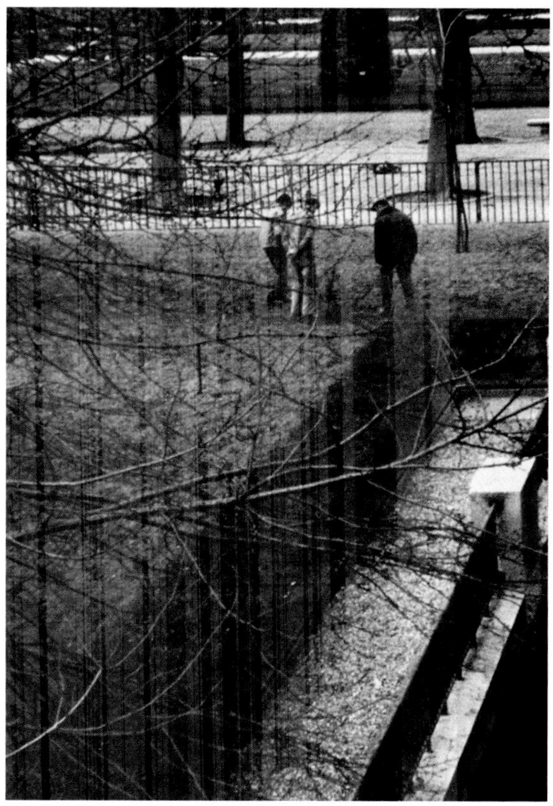

Piece for 1, 2, 3, 4, photo/text, 1971

Donner de l'eau (Giving Water) **Paris, 1971**

Die Entwicklung des Schreibens (The Development of Writing) # 2
Performance
Duration: 90 minutes
The piece was performed by a water sprinkler, photographed while in action at the Jardin des Plantes, in Paris.

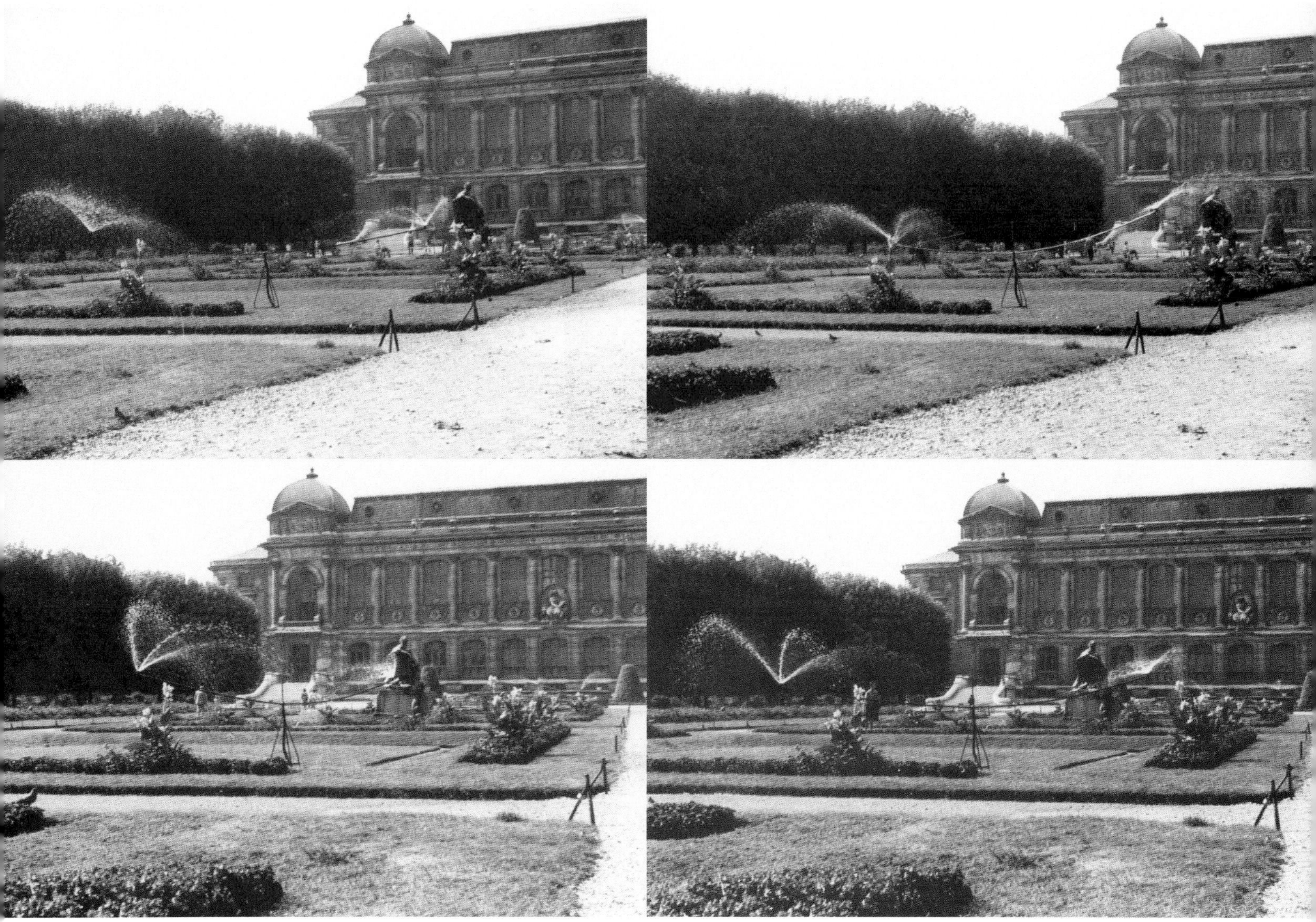

La Défoliation (Defoliation) Paris, 1971

Performance

Duration: 6 weeks

From the end of September until the middle of November, 1971, an avenue of trees which were gradually losing their leaves, in the Jardin des Plantes, in Paris, was photographed day by day.

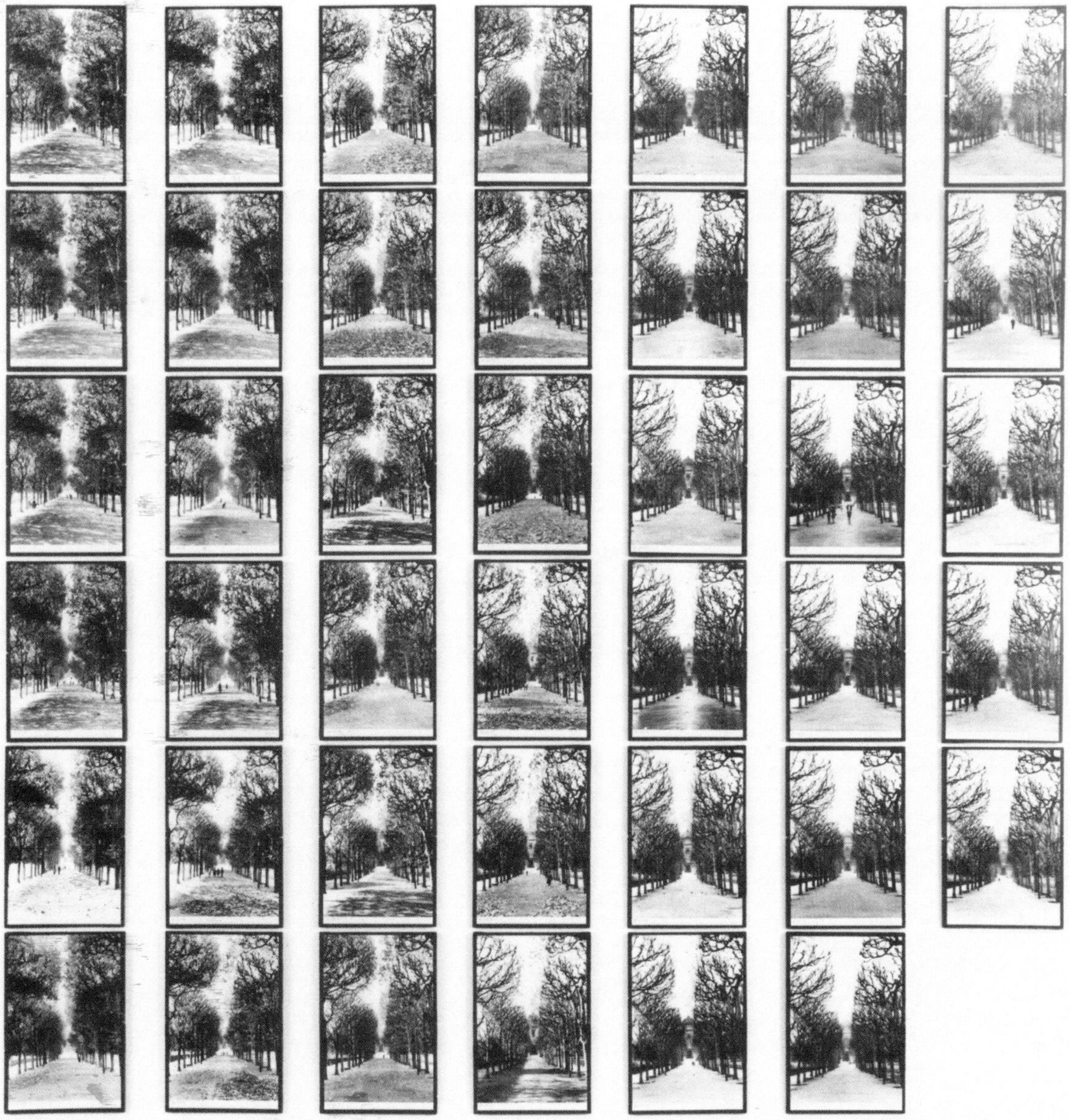

Atmosphärische Drucke (Atmospheric Prints) **Beindersheim, 1971**

Offset, 32 x 24 cm, variable in number
Sheets of paper bearing the printed phrase "Ein Tag, ein Monat, ein Jahr" (A day, a month, a year) were released in the open and then collected after a certain period of time. They were later exhibited. The work was also carried out in London, Buenos Aires, Liège, Vienna and Paris.

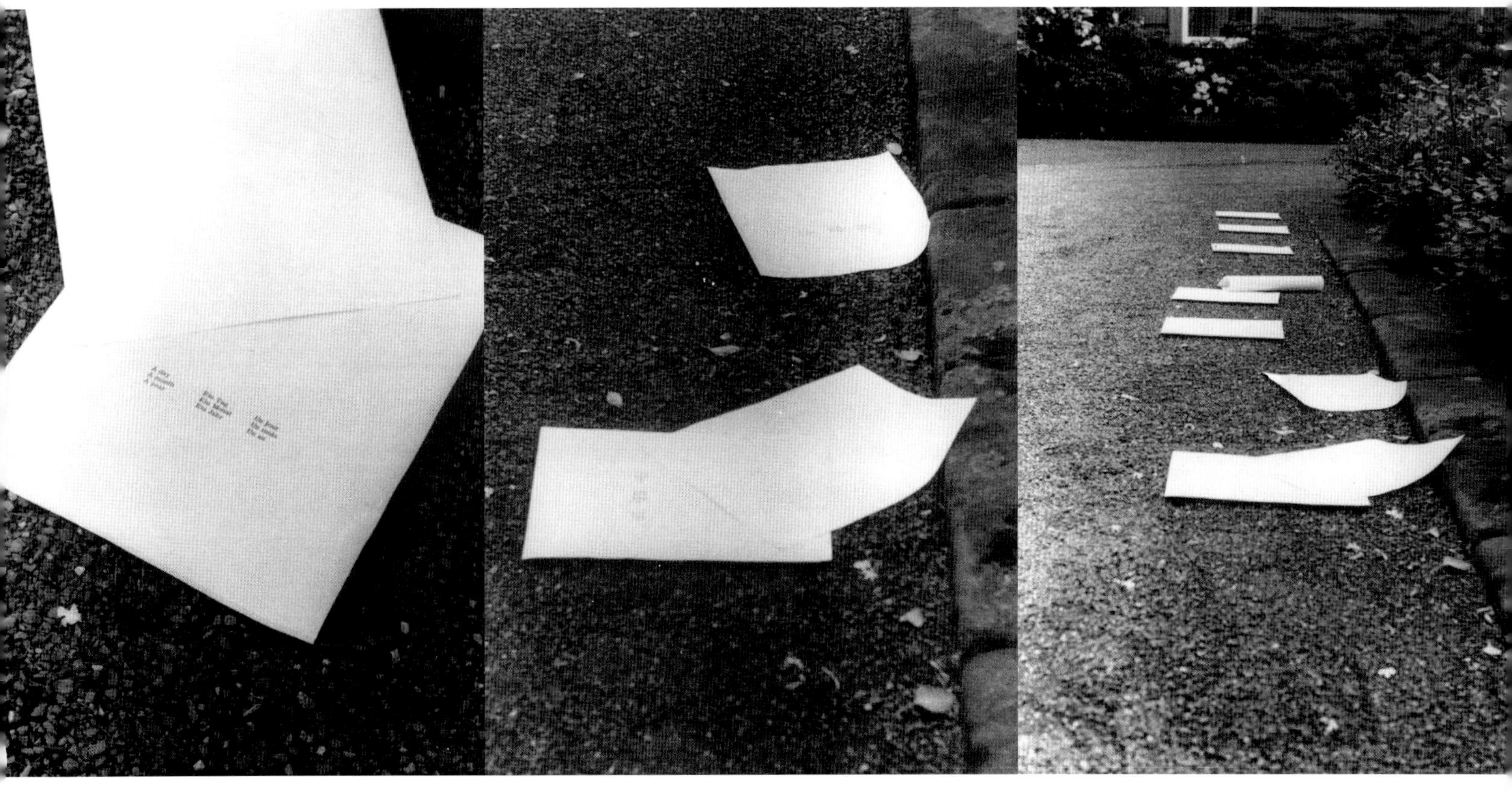

L' Arbre, sa reproduction (The Tree and Its Reproduction) **Paris, 1971**

Die Entwicklung des Schreibens (The Development of Writing) # 3

Performance

The polaroid photo of a tree was hung in the tree it portrayed, and then a new photo was made, and again suspended among the branches. The process then continued. The final photo shows the tree, decked with five pictures of itself.

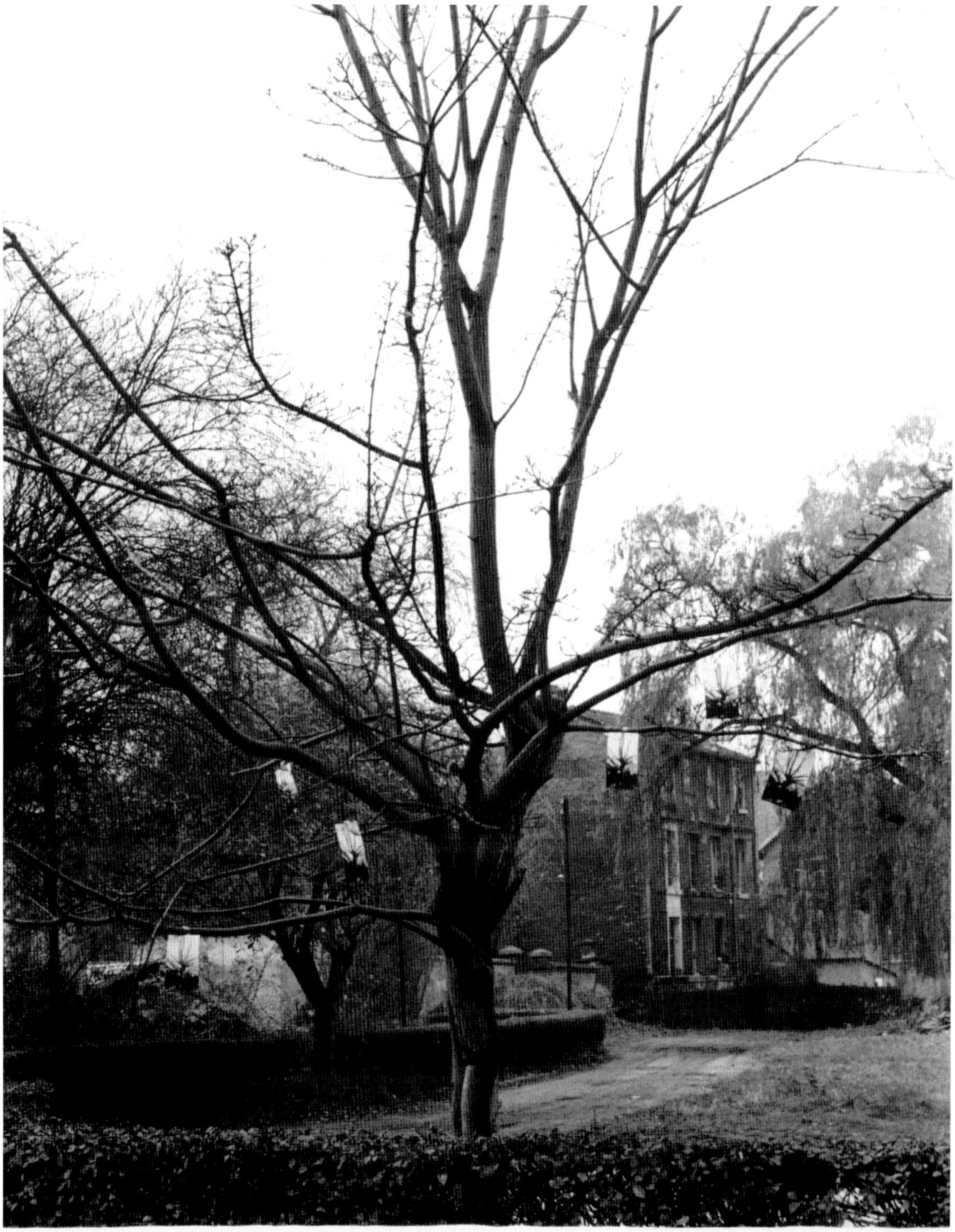

Schreiben mit der Hand (Hand-Writing) **Frankfurt am Main, 1972**

Die Entwicklung des Schreibens (The Development of Writing) # 7
Performance, videotaped by the Hessisch TV Station
Jochen Gerz, the wall of a house; duration: 3 minutes
Using his hand, without any other instrument, the artist wrote this phrase on the outside wall of a house: "Diese Worte sind mein Fleisch und mein Blut" (These words are my flesh and blood.) Towards the end of the sentence, blood began to make traces of the letters visible.

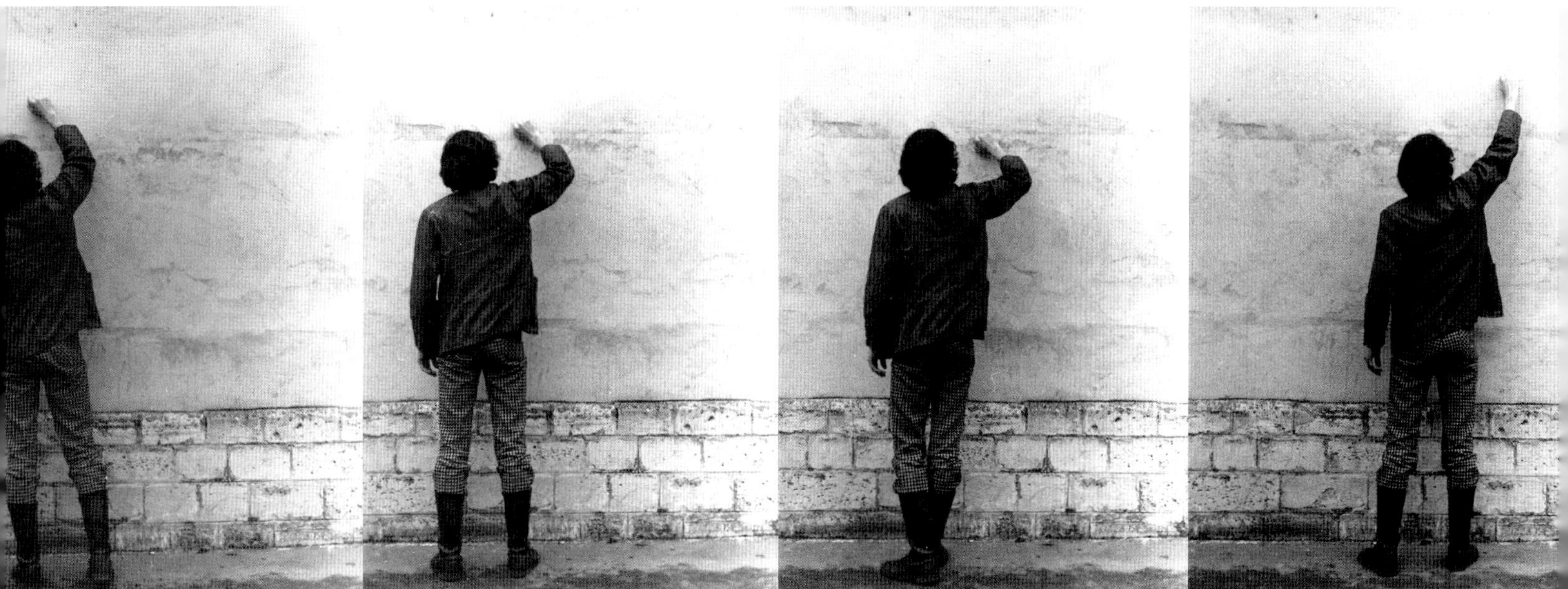

Ausstellung von Jochen Gerz neben seiner fotografischen Wiedergabe (Exhibition of Jochen Gerz beside His Photographic Reproduction)

Basel, 1972

Die Entwicklung des Schreibens (The Development of Writing) # 8
Performance
Jochen Gerz, black and white photo, 58 x 65 cm; duration: 2 hours
Videotape of the performance in Paris; duration: 25 minutes
Jochen Gerz stood for two hours at a location in the center of the city of Basel, beside to a photographic portrait of himself, taken on the same day. The performance was later repeated in Paris on Boulevard du 4 Septembre.

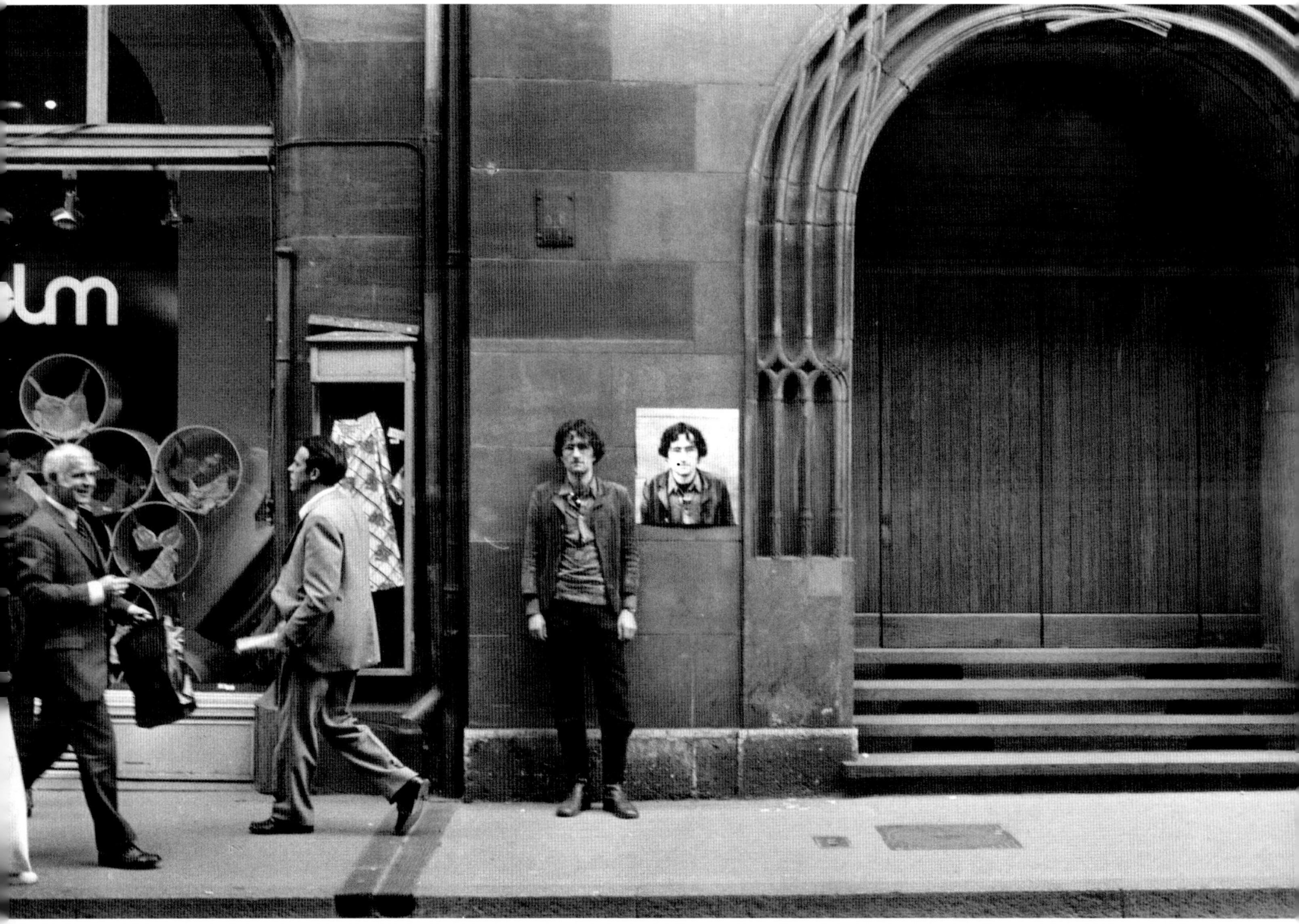

Der Goldene Schnitt (The Golden Section) **Essen, 1987**

Posters of various sizes: 260 x 360 cm, 160 x 60 cm and 300 x 60 cm
The posters show montages of two photos of the city of Essen, taken by city photographers in 1945 and 1987 from the same standpoint, accompanied by the phrase: "die Ordnung, die ihr Vergessen nennt" (The order you call forgetfulness.) They were shown for a month on billboards at various points in the city, as well as on three tram lines. The work was a part of the "im Auftrag" (On Commission) project of Essen's Folkwang Museum.

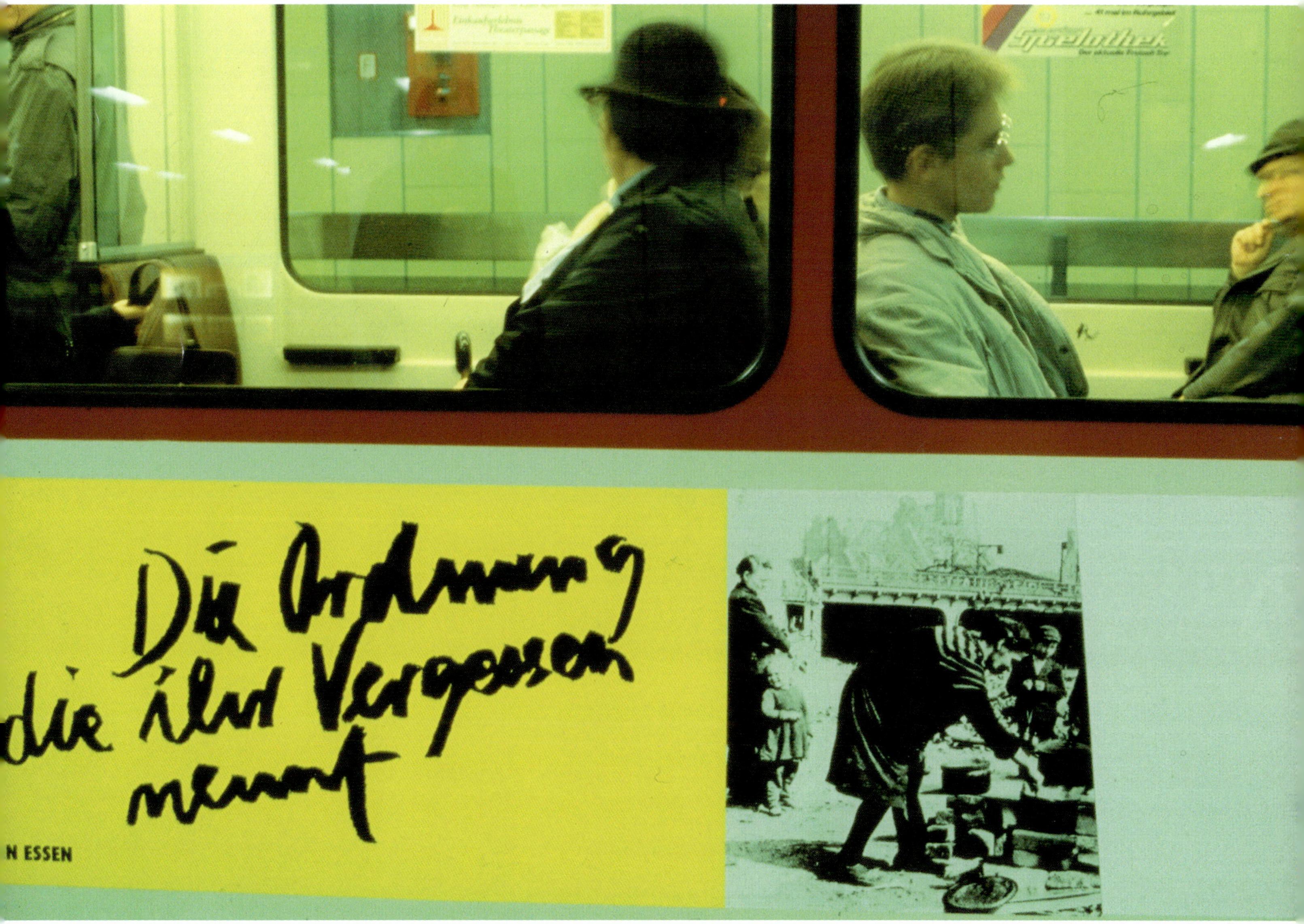

Der Grazer Anschluß–Heute ist gestern
(The Annexation of Graz–Today is Yesterday)
Graz, 1989

Scannachrome, printed on both sides; Front: 226 x 230 cm; rear: 226 x 110 cm
The poster is printed on both sides with an image from an advertisement for the Graz tourist trade. On one side, the words "Der Grazer" and "heute" can be read, one above the other. On the other, the words "Anschuß" and "gestern." The phrase can be read in two ways, dependent on the viewer's position and inclination: "Der Grazer heute – Anschluß ist gestern" (Graz' Today – the Annexation is Yesterday), or "Der Grazer Anschluß – heute ist gestern" (The Annexation of Graz – Today Is Yesterday). The work found realization as a part of the exhibition "Bezugspunkte, 50 Jahre Anschluß" (Points of Reference, 50 Years after the Annexation).

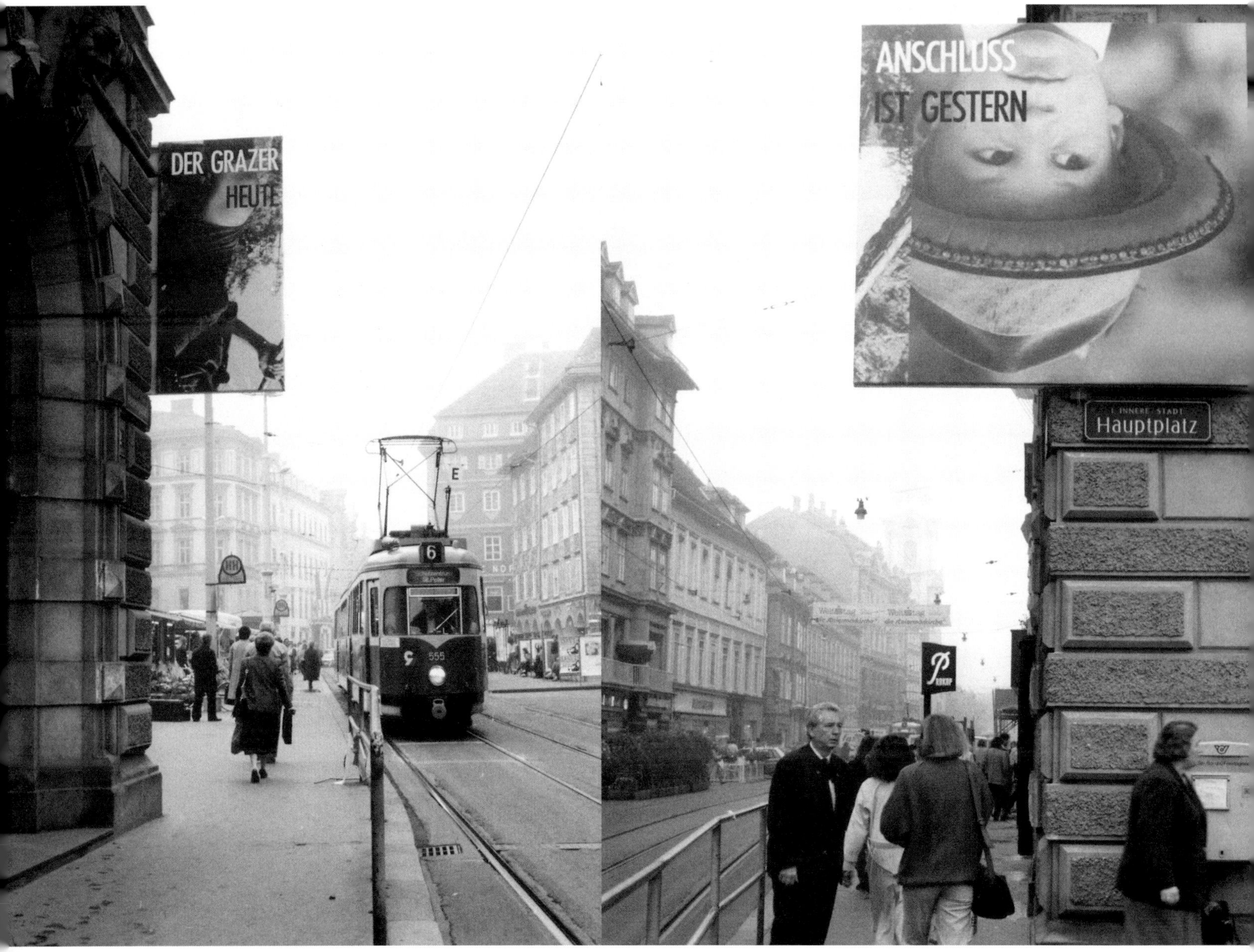

Immobilité (Immobility) Montreal, 1989

Scannachrome, 260 x 300 cm

The silhouette of a bird in the sky stands above the printed text "Pour l'art aussi l'immobilité est une tentation cruelle" (Immobility is a cruel temptation for art as well) and the logo of the Musée d'Art Contemporain de Montréal. The poster was first exhibited at the Mirabel Airport, in Montreal, and can be read as a work in a public space, and also as an advertisement for the museum.

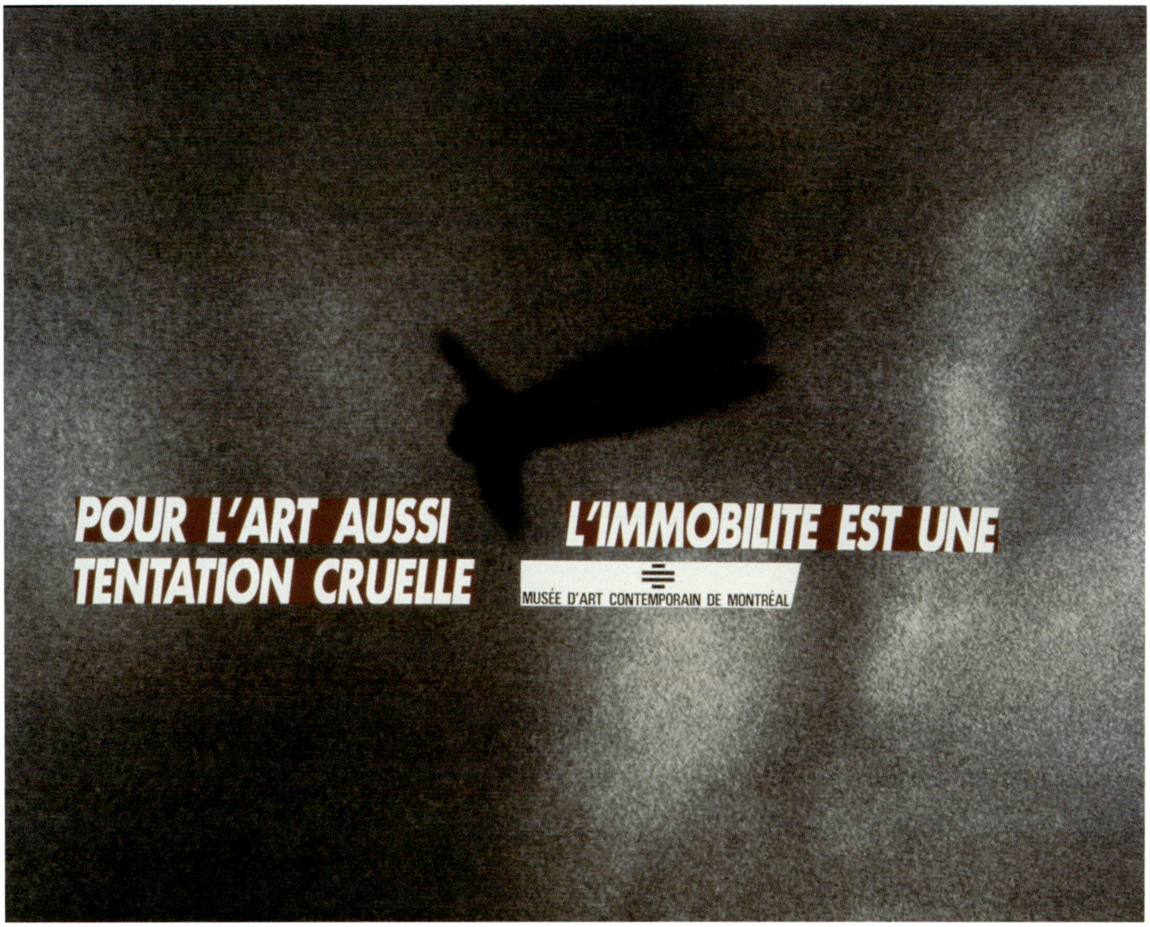

Bilder einer Ausstellung (Pictures at an Exhibition) Hamburg, 1989

Electronic billboard, Hamburg central train station
During "Eine Ausstellung" (An Exhibition) at the Hamburg Kunsthalle, the ten commandments of *Bilder einer Ausstellung* (Pictures at an Exhibition),1973–75 were fed into the computer-guided, electronic billboard at Hamburg's central train station and flashed in color for two seconds each: FORM NO IMAGE OF ME/DO NOT DESCRIBE ME/DO NOT COMPARE ME/DO NOT JUDGE ME/DO NOT APPROACH ME/DO NOT LOOK AT ME/DO NOT REMEMBER ME/DO NOT REFER TO ME/DO NOT REPRODUCE ME/GIVE ME NO NAME

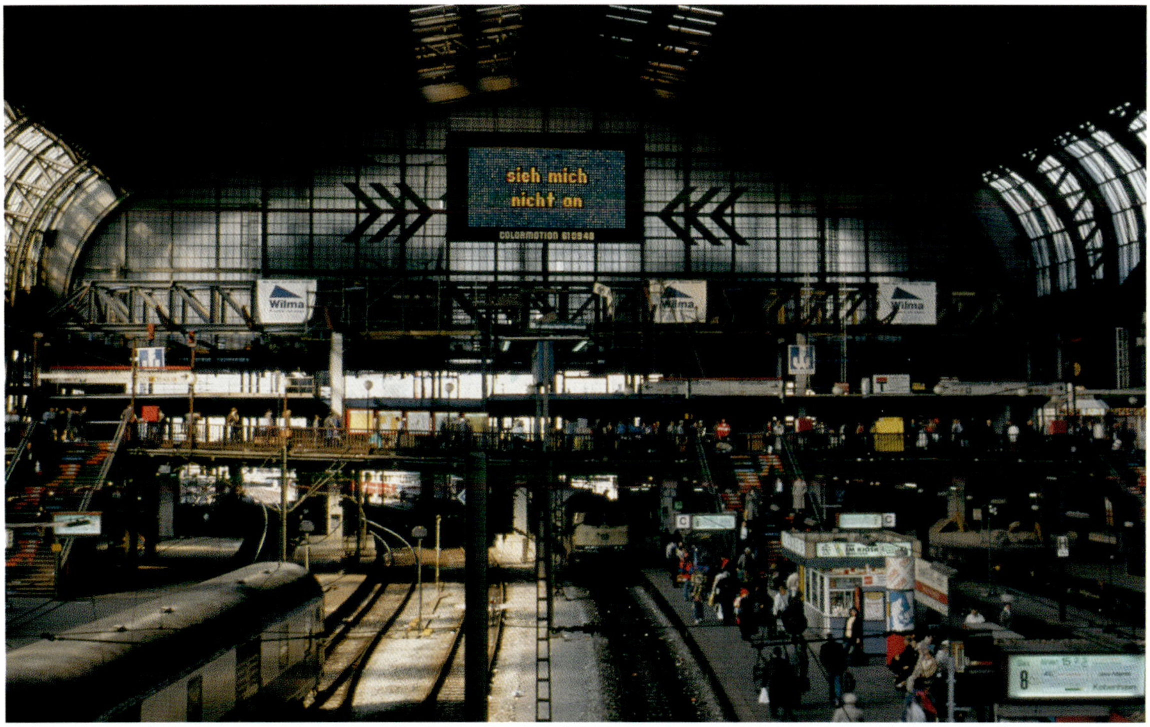

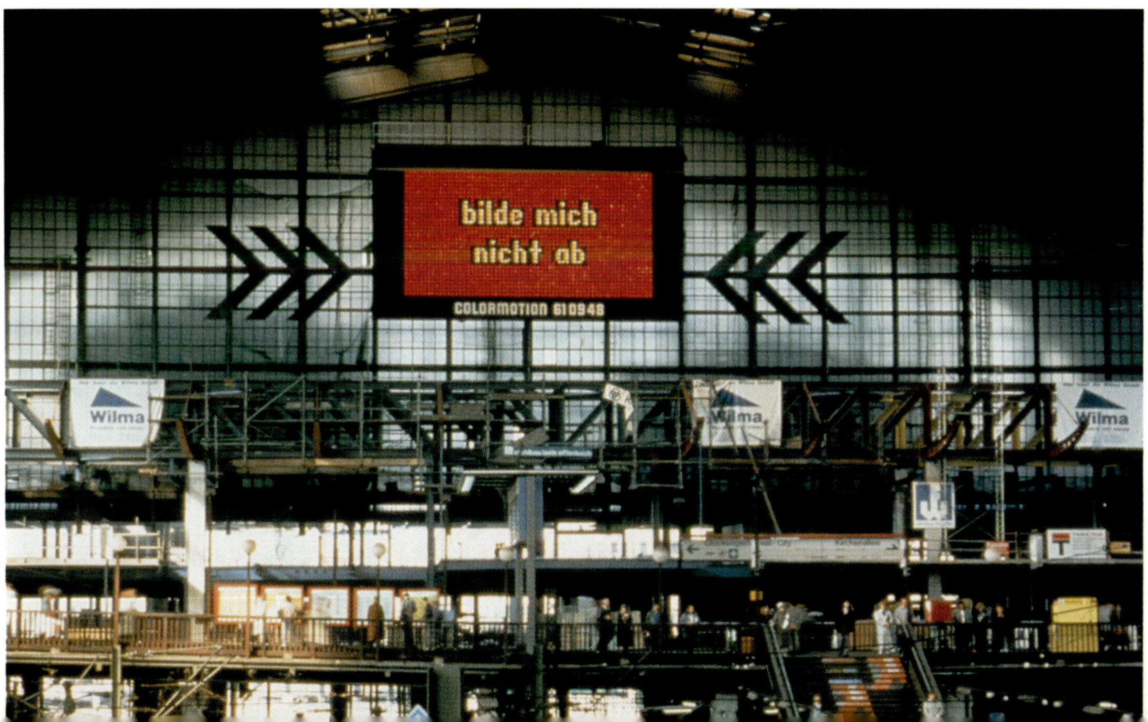

The New Derision # 2 **Montreal, 1989**

Poster, 260 x 300 cm

The poster in front of the Musée d'Art Contemporain, in Montreal, bore the following words: "A man who had been blindfol/ded was brought to a place he/did not know. Once there he said to his kidnappers: am I to/suppose there are no electricity/poles here, no newspapers, no/pictures on the wall? It would/take longer than my lifetime/for me to forget all that I have/seen. This kidnapping is nothing/in comparison, said the man/settling down for a long stay." *The New Derision #1*–another version of the same work–was simultaneously shown within the museum. The two works were made for the exhibition "Viewpoints."

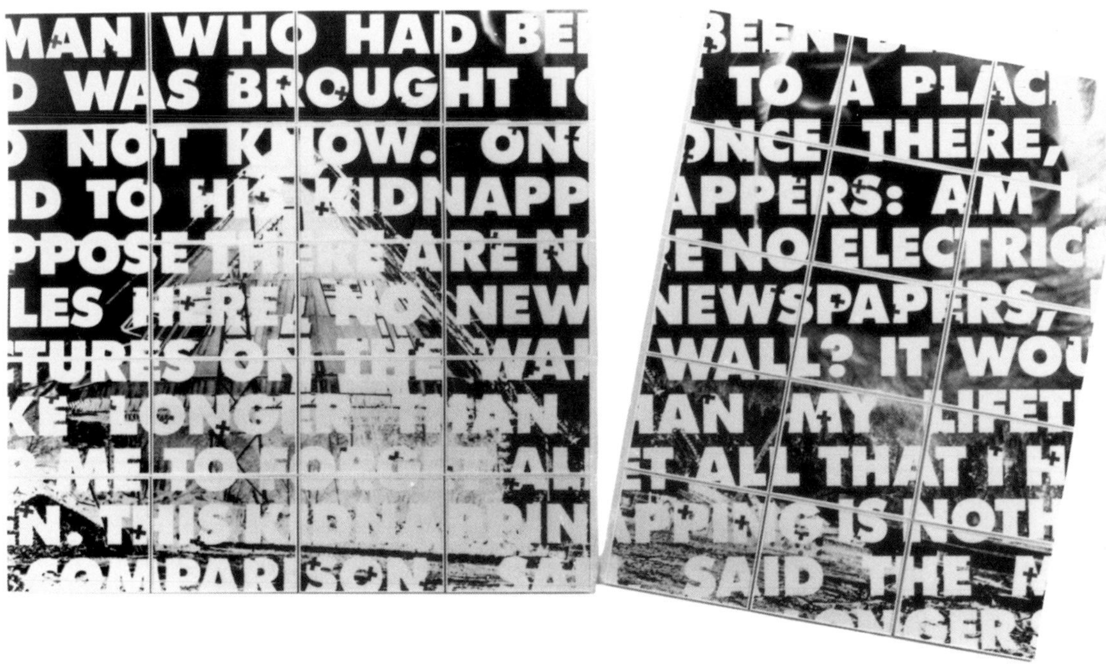

Uwolnić Stalina, Uwolnić Coca Cole **Łodz, 1990**

White vinyl letters on a black and white photograph, 240 x 360 cm
The poster, consisting of a giant-size photograph in the center of the city of Łodz, shows a negative print of a view of the industrial area of Bitterfeld, shifted 90°. The phrase printed across it in Polish reads "Freedom for Stalin, freedom for Coca Cola."

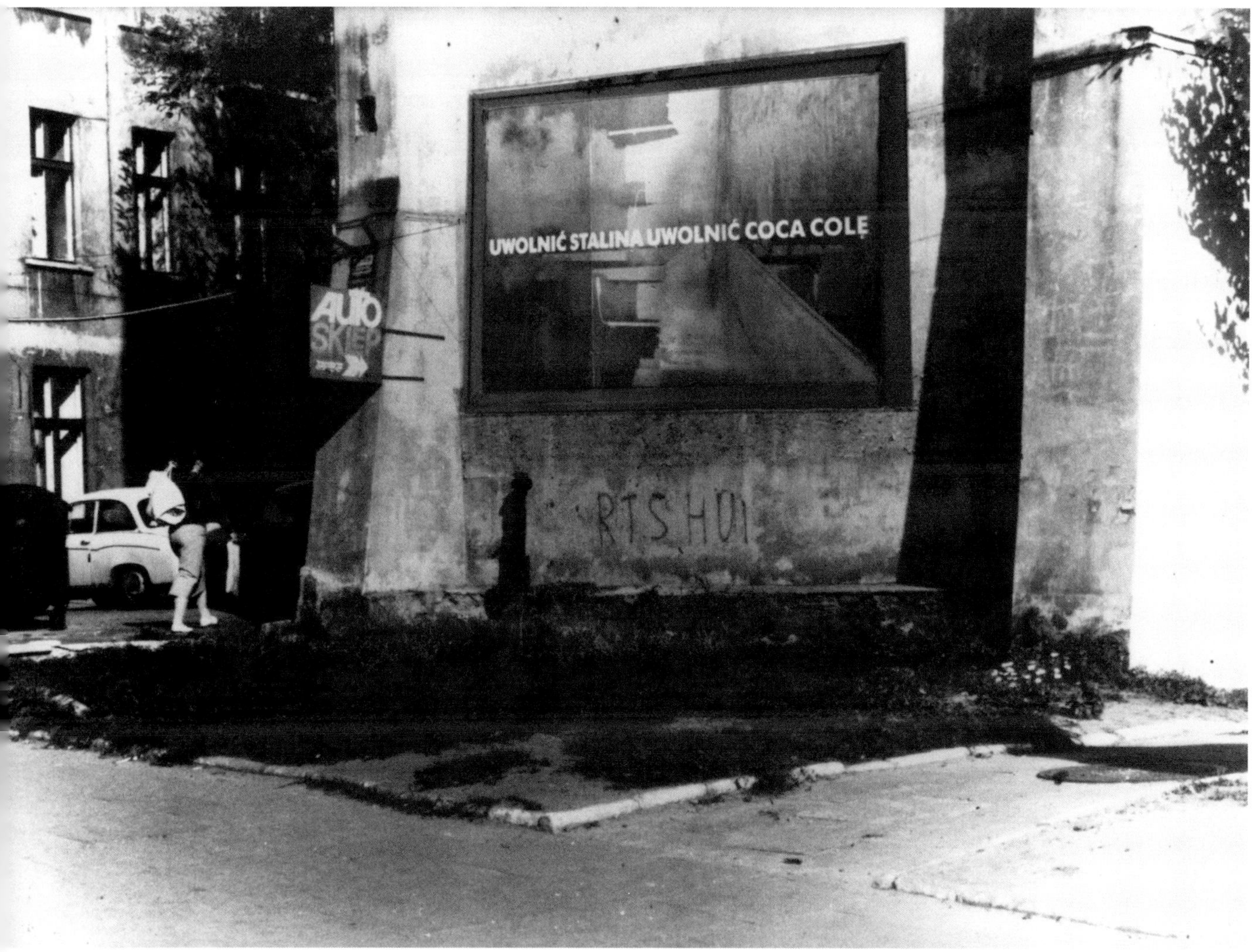

Das Pult (The Lectern) **Hanover 1991/Geneva, 1995**

Installation

Iron stand, acrylic glass: 50 x 64 x 1.5 cm, vinyl letters; total measurements: 140 x 64 x 30 cm

The first installation took place in front of the facade of the distillery in Hanover. The placard bore the following text, in German: "Among the art manifestos/there is also, and it might be mistaken for/one of them, a lectern. It stands back a little/from the wall, as though it/were a part (no matter of what) on the one hand/and on the other its description/or caption. Behind it the wall is empty/and it has long since ceased to be possible/to say how it got there. /Or whether it is art or its denunciation,/or a sign of something wrong or/a (fruitless) presentiment."

An identical lectern, accompanied by a different text which bore the title *Le monument à la paix* (The Peace Monument) was shown in 1995 in the UNESCO park in Geneva, in the near vicinity of the Soviet monument *The Conquest of Space*. The text, in French, was as follows: "Not far away from a monument lay/two jackets in the grass. They seemed lost/in these surroundings, almost touching. How/could they bear it, to be so/alone? Passers-by came and went,/their stern gaze directed to the monument, which a/genius created in honor of the pioneers/who fly and sleep in their space suits. The/jackets lay there for only a short while./They grew wet with rain and green/like the grass, until two uniformed/school girls found them."

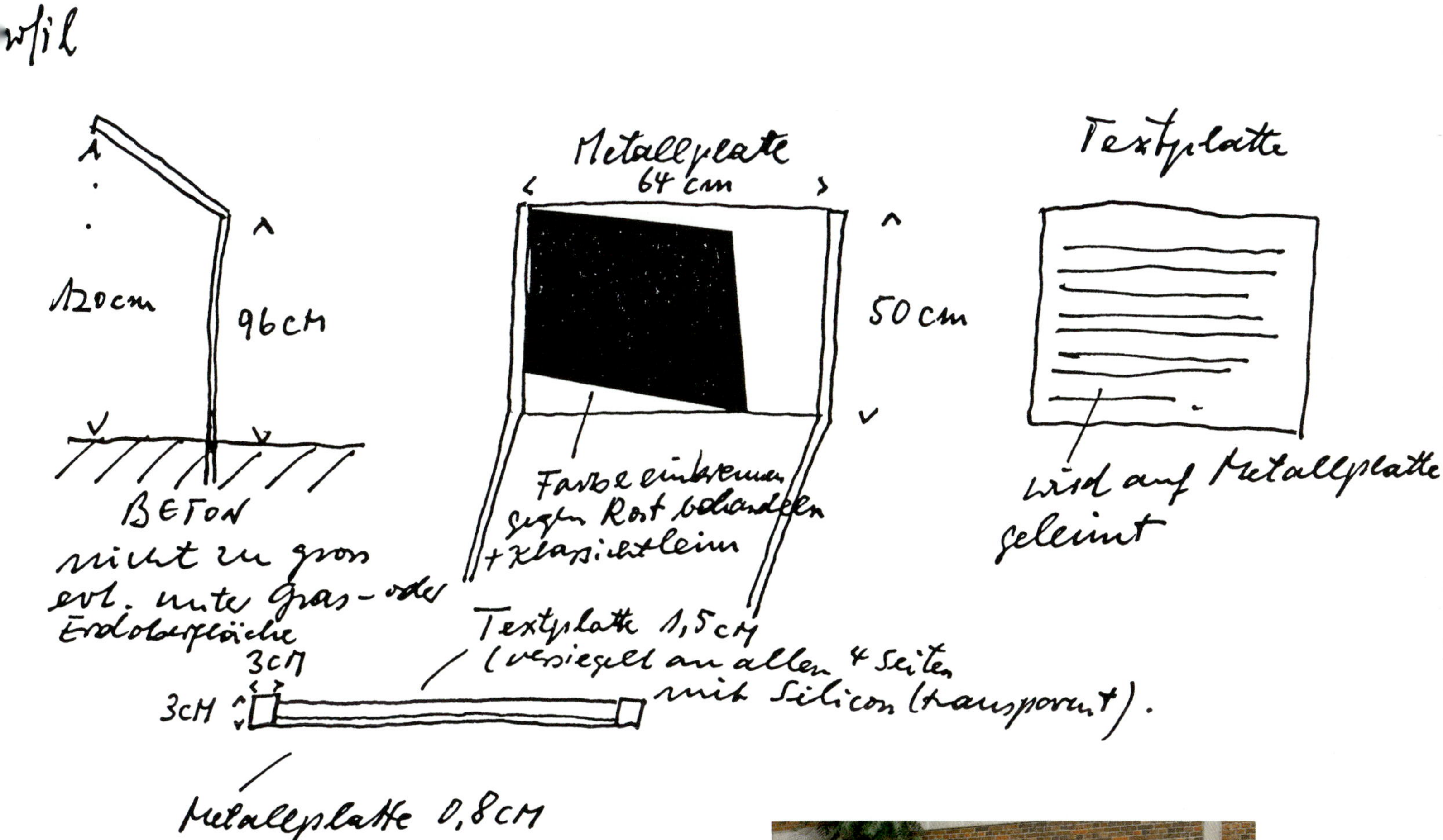

Project drawing

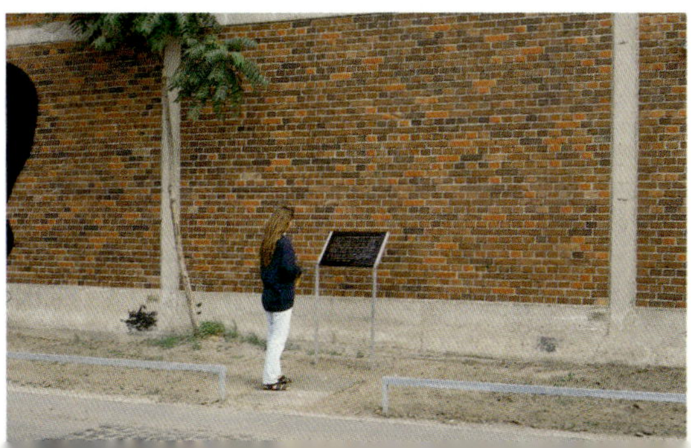

Installation photo

The Garden Project Donation **Davis, California, 1992**

Installation; 29 brass plaques, with engraved texts; 4.5 x 8.5 cm each
In collaboration with the students of the “Art Practice” seminar at the Department of Art of the University of California, at Davis
Brass plaques were set up at various points on the campus, bearing answers to the question: “What would you do if someone ordered you to change your religion?” This work was a continuation of the photo work *The Answer*, which resulted from a collaboration with the students at the University of California. The students appropriated the artist’s concept and directed to others the question which *The Answer* had directed to them.

A few of the answers:

I don’t have a problem with this./It might be good to go through/life without structure. Without/it, people lash out aggressively but/eventually they fall into another.

In the existential modification of/most you find the conundrum of/fear and annihilistic attitudes./They try to force us to be robots.

Without it we have no/standard to base our/opinion on. It is more/than just the motions./I’m not really active.

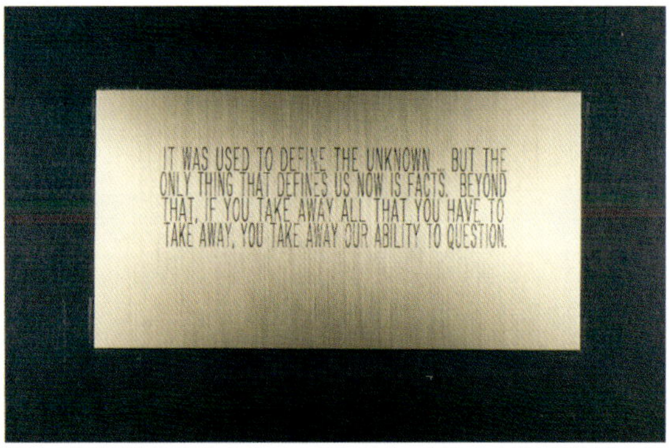

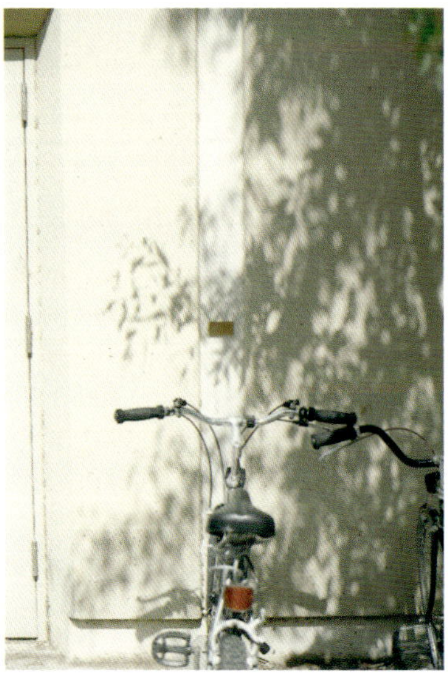

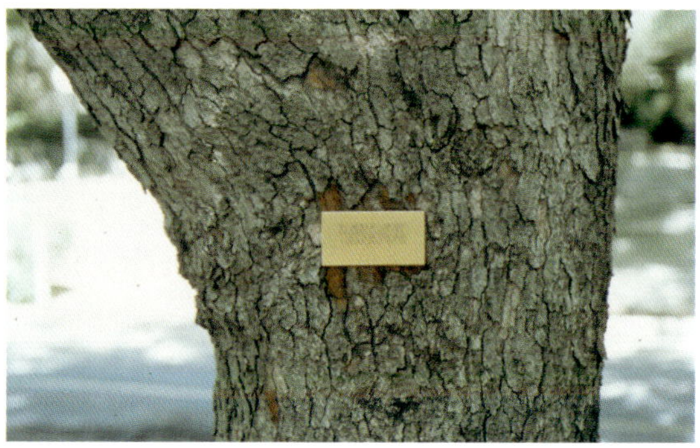

Comment vivre–How Can You Live **Paris/New York, 1992**

2 posters, offset; 110 x 150 cm each
Two posters which were set up simultaneously in the Paris Métro and the New York Subway on the occasion of the "Transvoices" exhibition show the profile of a woman. The text reads: "Right now in Paris a man turns around struck by the same thought: How can you live at the dawn of the 21st century–with religion?" In Paris, the French version of the same text referred to a person in New York.

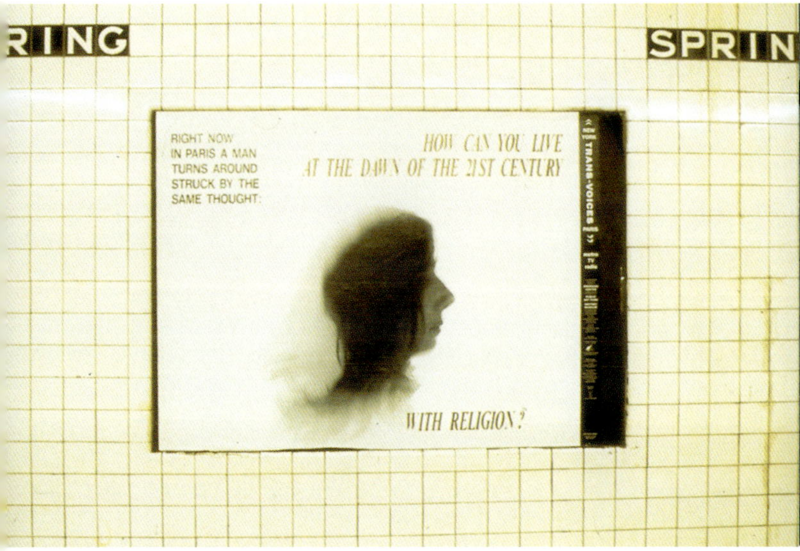

Subway, New York, 1992

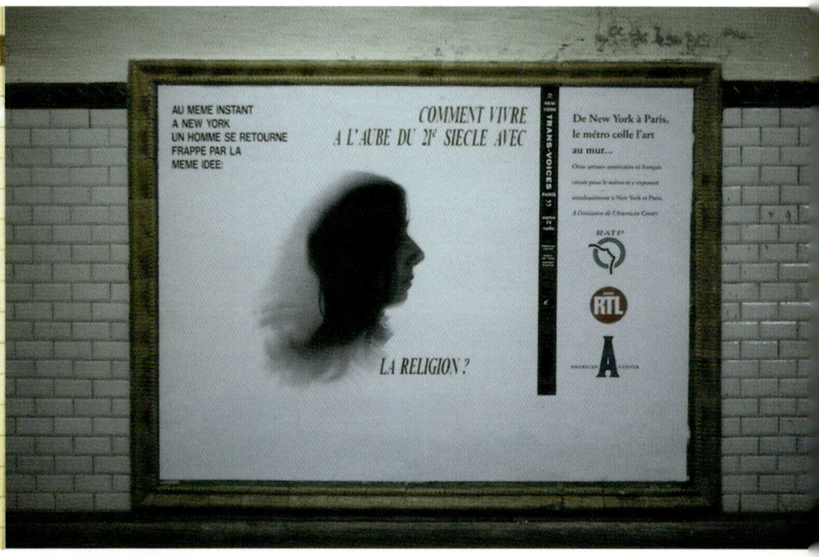

Métro, Paris, 1992

Der Eintrag (The Entry) **Düsseldorf, 1993**

Installation
Duratrans transparency projection, 181.5 x 598.5 cm, aluminum light-box, 183 x 601 x 20 cm
Poster, 240 x 360 cm
The work was presented as a light-box on the outdoor premises of Kunstsammlung Nordrhein-Westfalen, and as an exhibition poster at Kunsthalle Düsseldorf. The text reads: "Barbarian, *Gr. sb. masc.*, a person who allows himself to be blinded by *see* morality,/therefore losing the ability to recognize his fellow human beings as such, *i. e.* becoming/capable of their annihilation in the name of morality. *Hence*/Barbarity, *Gr. sb. fem.*, as a cultural phenomenon (mostly applied to deeds committed by groups, *see* Germany)."

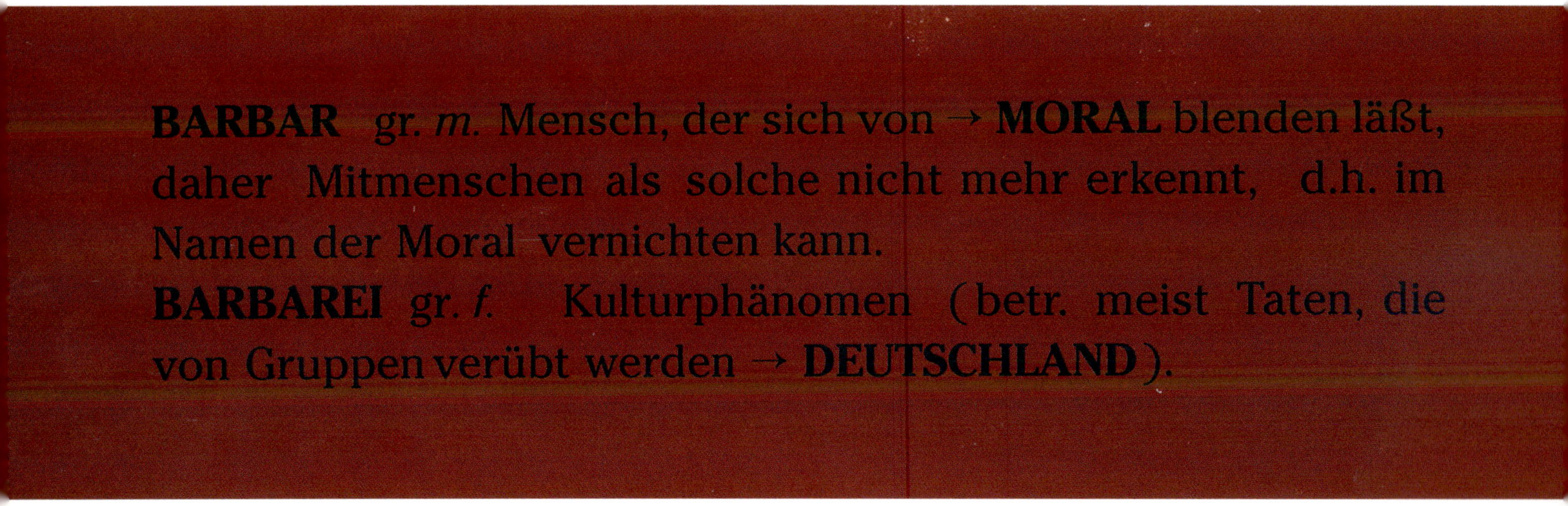

The Entry, 1993

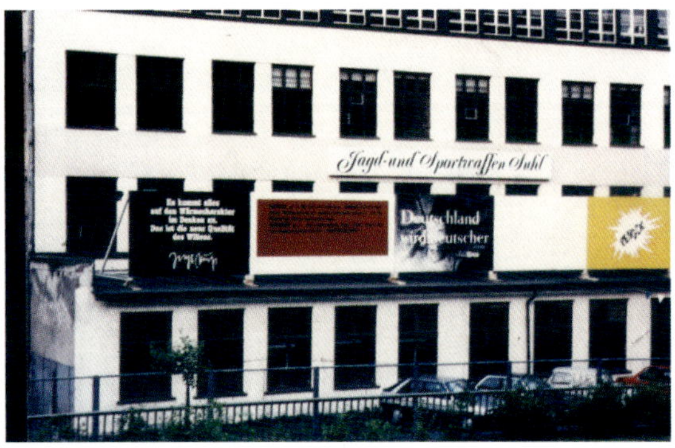

Installation photo

Hierophanie # 1 (Hierophany # 1) **Hamburg, 1993**

Performance, video

Duration: 4 hours

As a part of the *Stadtfahrt* (City Tour) manifestation, about 40 people signed up for a bus trip with Jochen Gerz. Once having boarded the bus, they were asked to specify destinations within the city of Hamburg, and this was the basis for establishing the itinerary. At each of the destinations, the person who chose it explained the reason for having chosen it. The performance was recorded on video tape.

Vergangenheit (meine) · eine angenehme Störung · Anekdoten · lokale Geschichten · souvenirs, souvenirs · sich an einen anderen Ort, an etwas ähnliches erinnern · der Freud'sche Bericht · geschichtliche, politische Andenken · die archimedische Position · Deportation · die von einem Reisenden erlebte Reise · Indiskretion · das Gerücht · die Version der Penelope · Geschichte(n) machen · die Initiation · die Einsamkeit mit den Wörtern · sich vergessen, in situ · Gesellschaftsspiel · Geschichten zum Zeitvertreib · Rückkehr · Intimes für Fremde · die Lächerlichkeit · ein Traum · Geständnis · sich schämen · eine aus Angst vor einer Falle verbrachte Zeit · die Erfindung · Zeit anhalten · schlafen, währenddem · mein Nachbar, ein Exhibitionist · etc.

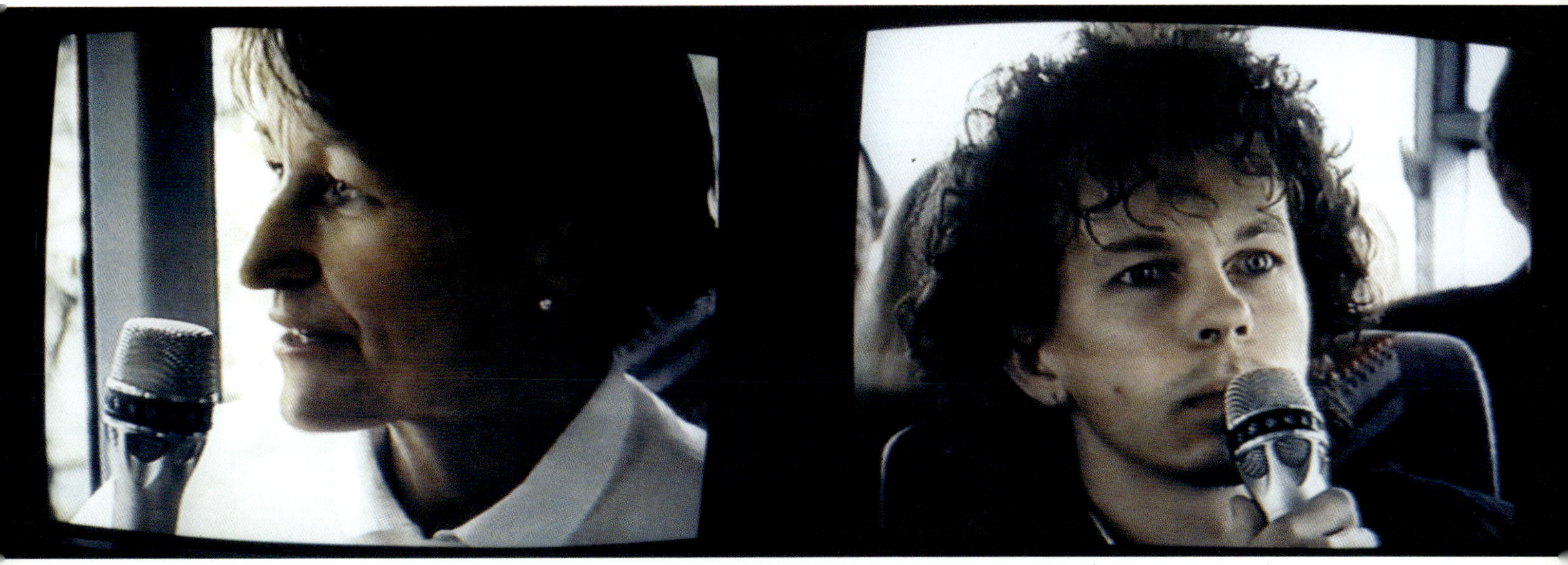

Participants at their chosen destinations

La Dispersion des semences, la récolte des cendres (The Dispersal of Seeds, the Collection of Ashes)

Geneva, 1995

Esther and Jochen Gerz; permanent installation
2 aluminum masts, each 1800 cm tall, Ø 20 cm, on a base 80 x 80 x 160 cm; 3 aluminum plates, each 40 x 40 cm
Site: the park grounds of the Palais des Nations, Geneva
Two identical, vertical aluminum masts are anchored into the lawn at the distance of 120 cm from one another. One mast ends with a simple, single platform, the other with two platforms. The work is a gift of the German Federal Republic to the United Nations, on the occasion of its fiftieth anniversary. It was inaugurated on Human Rights Day, December 10, 1995.

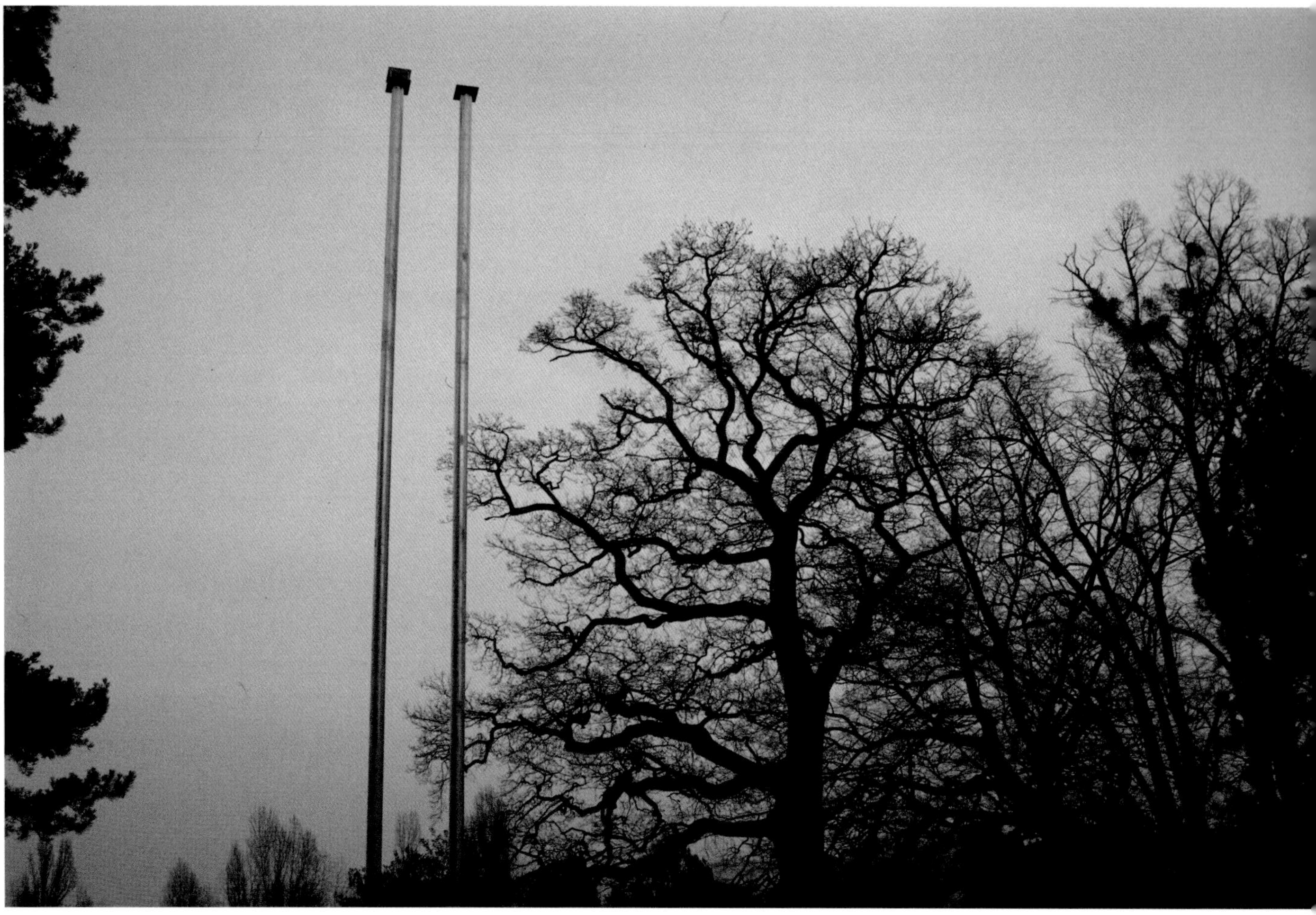

Das zwanzigste Jahrhundert (The Twentieth Century) **Oberhausen, 1996**

Esther and Jochen Gerz; Questionnaire/Installation
8 full-page newspaper announcements, published in the *Abend Blatt* of Oberhausen, Mühlheim and Marl (from February 27 to April 17); Skulpturenmuseum, Marl
Between February and April of 1996, the readers of two daily newspapers in the Ruhr were asked to respond to the following question: "Wenn das 20. Jahrhundert noch einmal stattfände, was würden Sie ändern?" (If the twentieth century were to take place again, what would you change about it?) The 228 replies were shown at Oberhausen's Gasometer.

A few of the replies:

If I had the chance to change something about this century, I would happily strike all notions of atomic energy from the heads of the physicists. I don't really think that this would result in the creation of something else, but it would be worth the try. Tschernobyl, Hiroshima and so forth speak for themselves, against atomic energy.

The elimination of nearly all problems with: the promotion of the introduction of birth control in all the nations of the world. For the elimination of all the problems of all living creatures and the sufferings of nature. There are far too many of us and we cause: trash and the destruction of the environment, oil catastrophes, excess emissions, and the devastation of the ozone layer. Pension financing by way of fewer children, since the unemployed can't pay for pension plans and aren't even "needed" as tank drivers, since even weapons technology requires fewer people; ... on the example of France, the elimination of compulsory military service. "Water wars," "excessive use of fertilizers," "child abuse."

The persecution of foreigners (Jews, Poles, Gypsies). I find it frightening to have to ask, at the age of 38, "Has the generation after our parents learned absolutely nothing?"

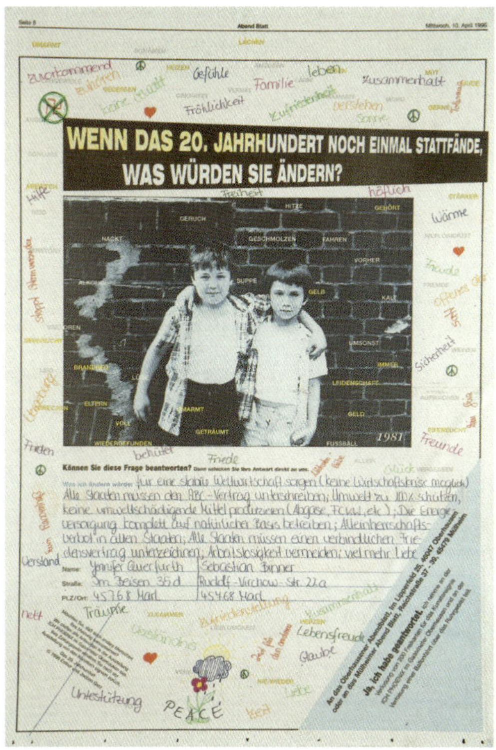

Die Heimkehr der Erinnerung (Fragen an Walter Benjamin) (The Return of Memory [Questions for Walter Benjamin])

Frankfurt am Main, 1996

Installation
Glass shelves, consisting of two side elements and 14 floors, 52 x 300 x 539 cm; glass thickness ca. 4 cm, several times smelted and sealed; stainless steel tracks on the floor, length 1700 cm, width 11 cm, thickness 0.2 cm; lectern with a reddish-brown enameled surface and white writing, 50 x 64 x 1.5 cm; stand in stainless steel, 140 x 64 x 30 cm; visible cement surface, 539 x 574 cm, partially painted green
Site: The Deutsche Bibliothek, Adickesallee, Frankfurt am Main, Federal Republic of Germany
The terrace on the roof of the new building for the Deutsche Bibliothek holds a glass book case on two library tracks, embedded into the floor, which lead to the wall of the neighboring building. On the wall, the outline of the bookshelf is marked in color. A lectern stands before it.

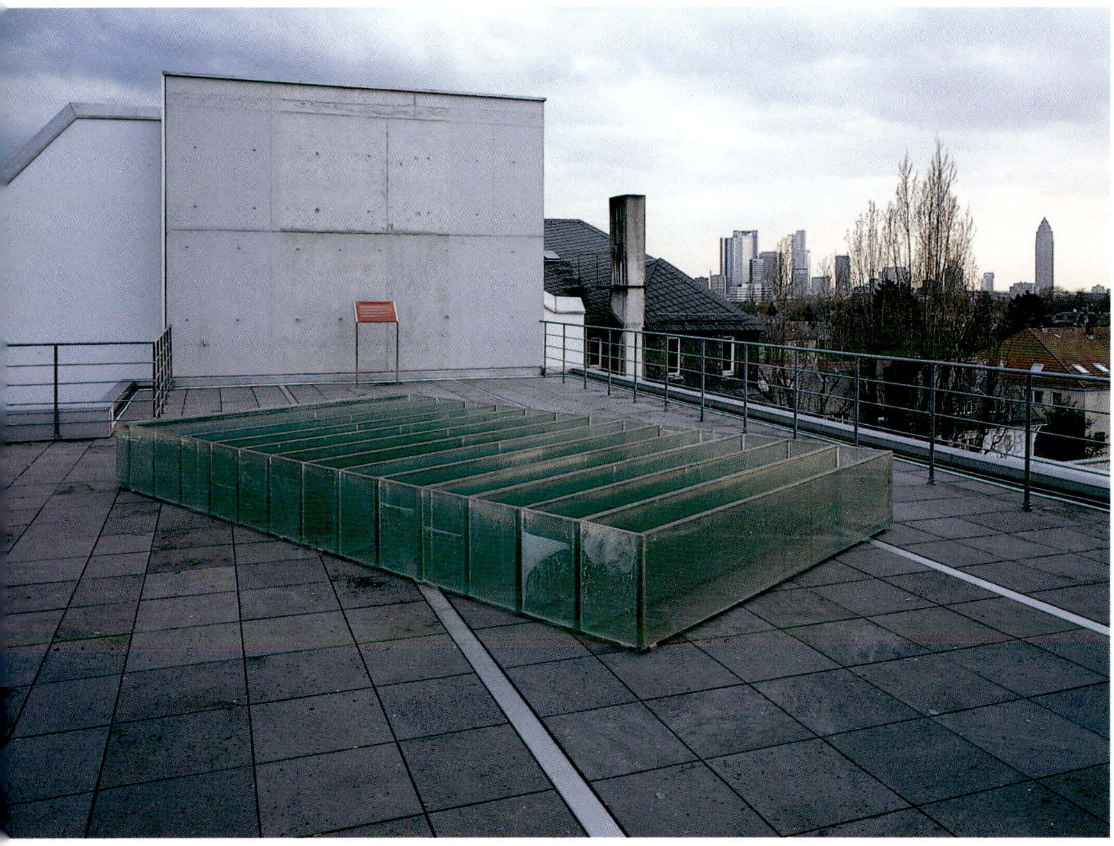

Installation on the roof of the Deutsche Bibliothek

Die Gänse vom Feliferhof (The Feliferhof Geese) **Graz, 1996**

Esther and Jochen Gerz; Installation (unrealized)

4 flag poles, at intervals of ten meters; four white flags with red texts; information stand

The competition for the construction of a memorial to the members of the resistance against National Socialism who were shot between 1941 and 1945 concluded with the recommendation for the execution of the project of Esther and Jochen Gerz. On the grounds of the Feliferhof military base, and for the course of a year, the recruits were daily to raise and lower four flags bearing the inscriptions: "Courage Courts Death," "Treason to the Nation Must Be Decorated," "Barbarity Is the Soldier's Bride," "You Can Also Call Us Soldiers." At the end of this period of time, the recruits themselves were to suggest inscriptions for future flags. The flags which were no longer used were to be preserved in the Vienna Museum of Military History and exhibited next to the standards of the Austro-Hungarian monarchy. The realization of the project was obstructed by the Steiermark Military Command. The project was accompanied by a hefty debate in the Austrian press.

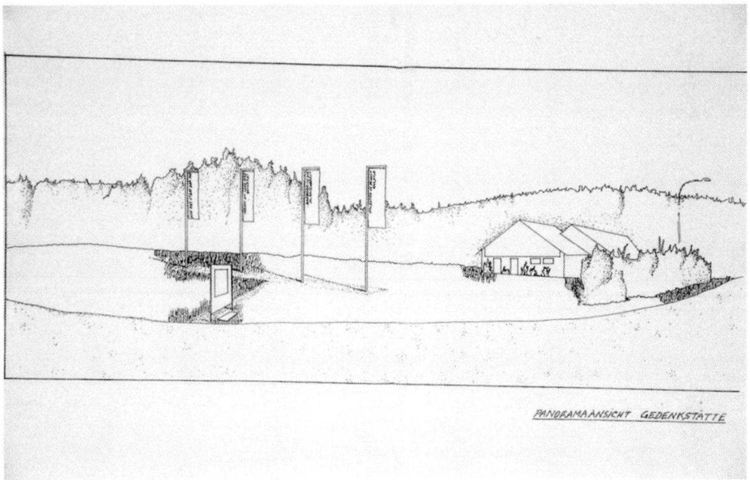

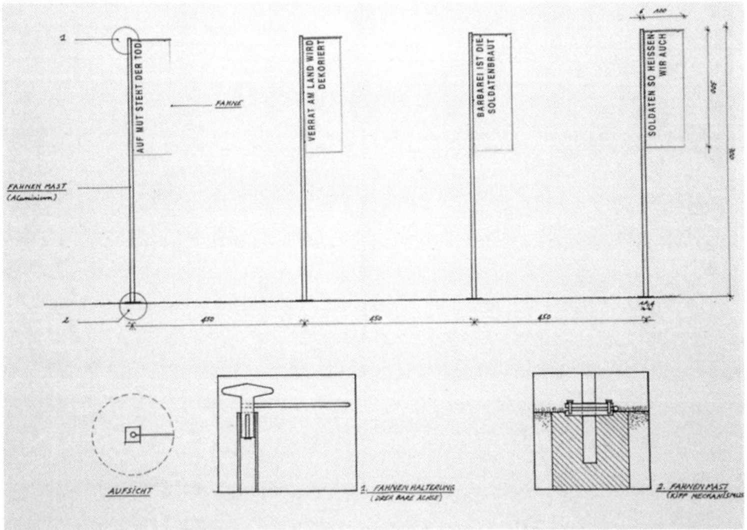

Project drawings

Raisons de sourire/Gründe zu lächeln/Reasons for Smiles **1996**

Esther and Jochen Gerz; work in progress

Text on electronic billboard, newspaper announcements; workshop; realization: framed black and white negatives on sheets of mirror glass, of various sizes

Invitations to take part in the project first began to appear in October 1966 on the electronic billboards of the city of the Paris. Shortly later, newspaper announcements appeared with the following text (extract):

"Send an undeveloped film of pictures of your smile, and you will become a part of the work. Simply think about something that makes you smile. There are apparently as many reasons for smiling as there are people, and so far as we know, these reasons are as fleeting as the smiles they cause to arise. In reality, there seem to be more reasons for not smiling. But we smile all the same. All contributions will become a part of *Reasons for Smiles* and will be seen in exhibitions as a fragment which will continue to change until one of the artists dies."

Anzeige

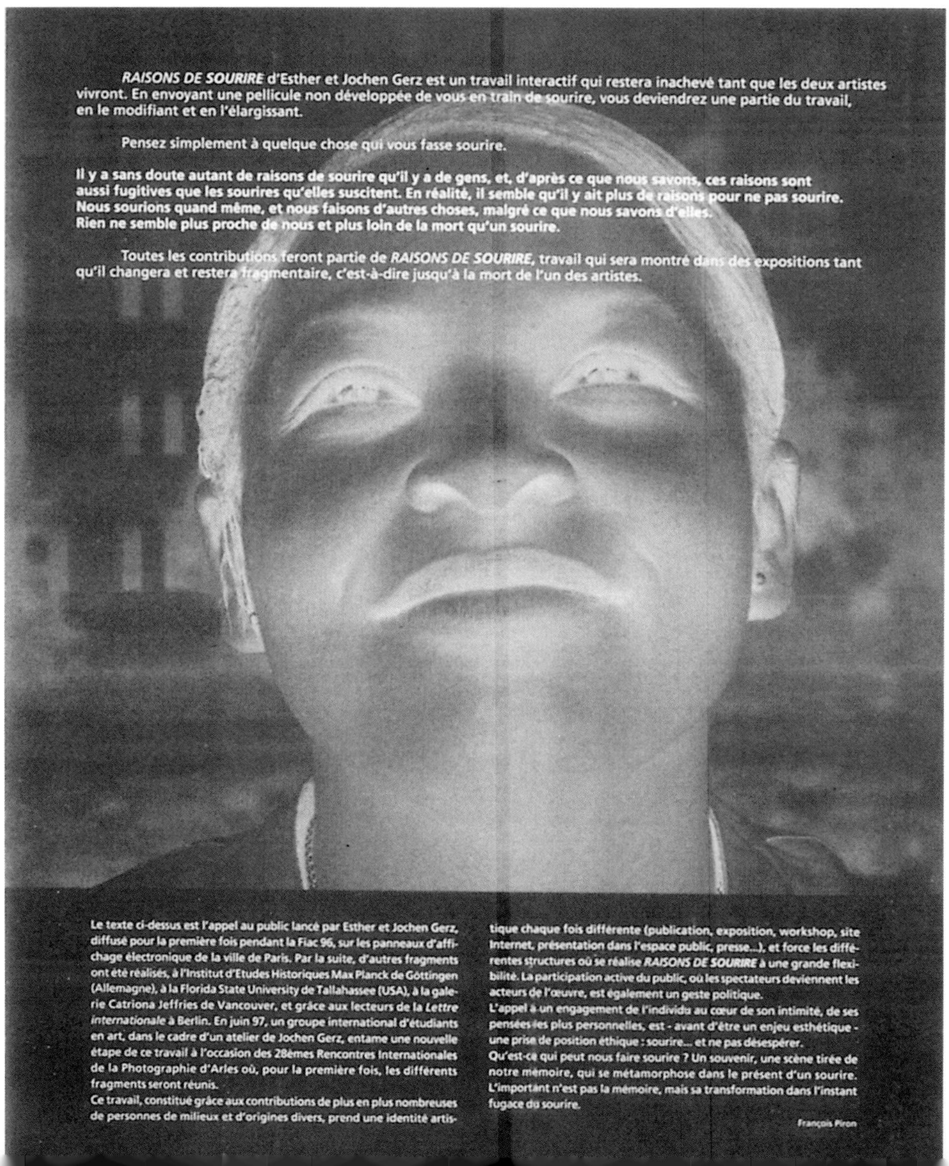

The Empty Plinth **London, 1996**

A speculative proposal for a work in a public space
Grass on a stone bed on the empty plinth in Trafalgar Square in London
Ca. 280 x 150 x 26 cm
As a speculative project for a public space, the Public Art Commissions Agency (PACA) invited Jochen Gerz to make a proposal for the fourth (empty) plinth in Trafalgar Square in London. The proposal is to raise the edge of the plinth by a few centimeters, so as to create a bed for a patch of grass, which will be removed from the home stadium of whatever the current British soccer champions. When the champions change, the patch of grass will also change. From the surrounding streets, the patch of grass remains invisible, and can't even be seen from the floor of the square. As with the other three plinths in the square, a plaque announces the source of the patch of grass on *The Empty Plinth*.

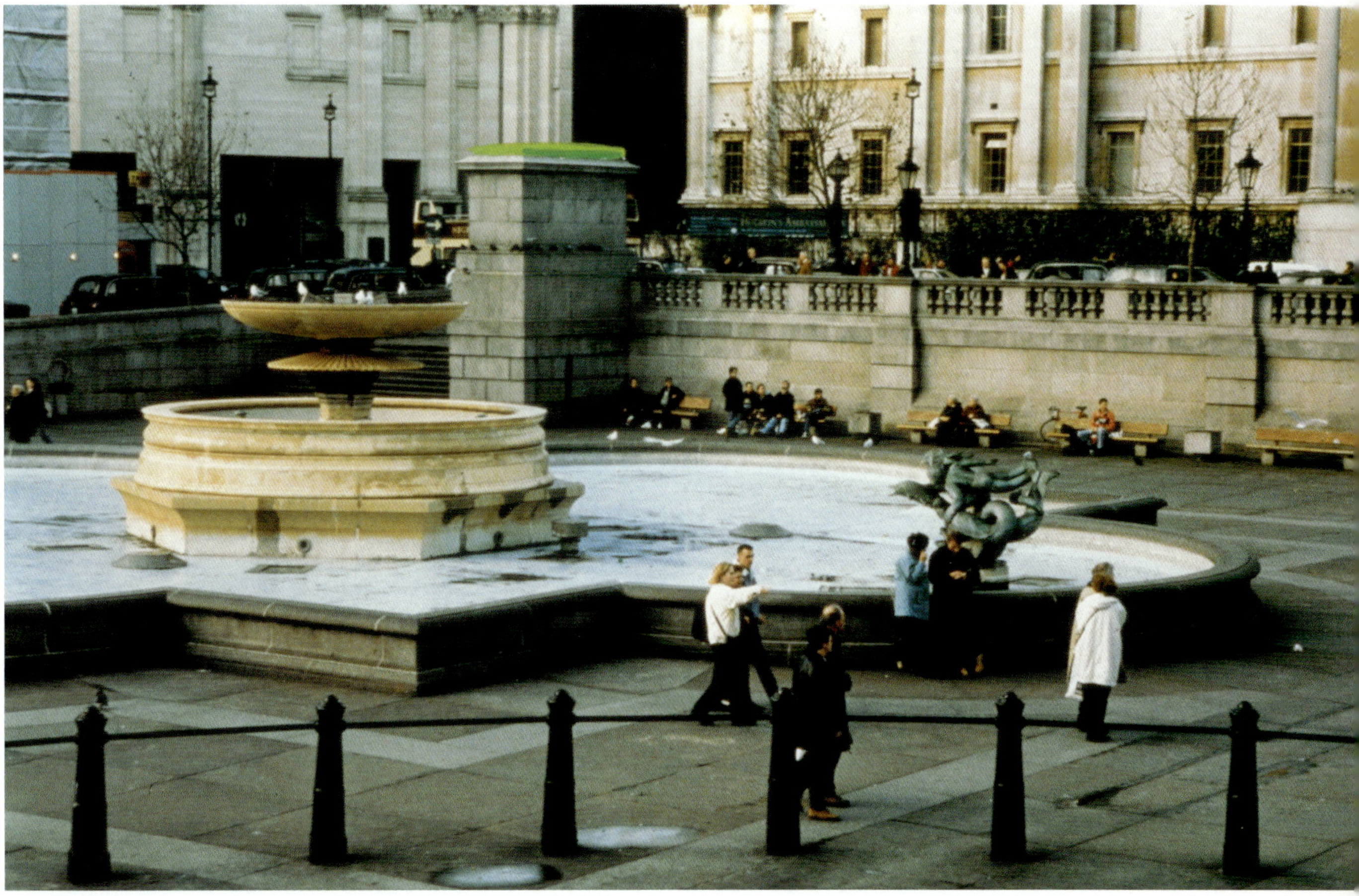

Manipulated photo

Die Berliner Ermittlungen, nach einem Oratorium von Peter Weiss (The Berlin Investigation, on an Oratorium by Peter Weiss) Berlin, 1998

Esther and Jochen Gerz
A production on the part of the Hebbel Theater, the Berliner Ensemble, and the Volksbühne am Rosa Luxemburg Platz, in collaboration with *Der Tagesspiegel*, ZDF, Deutschlandradio and SFB-Hörfunk; Director: Lukas Hemleb; spoken composition: Uwe Mengel; Production Manager: Niels Ewerbeck; With the use of the Installation *EXIT/Materialien zum Dachau-Projekt* (Exit/Materials for the Dachau Project), 1972

In January 1998, letters were sent to 10,000 subscribers and friends of the three Berlin theaters, inviting them to take part in the realization of the piece. As many as 500 participants worked in seminars on the text of *Die Ermittlung*, by Peter Weiss. 150 participants declared themselves ready to permit the appearance of their photograph as an accompaniment to a passage from *Die Ermittlung* as an announcement in the Berlin daily paper, *Der Tagesspiegel.* The announcements appeared in April 1998. For the proposed speech composition, parts of the text were taped, as recited by fifteen Berlin children and thirty immigrants who were learning to speak German. Members of the audience of the radio stations SFB, NRD, HR and Deutschlandradio recited passages onto an answering machine. The sequences were the source of radio spots, which were inserted into the stations' programs. The ZDF television program *Aspekte* broadcast four spots in which public personalities read short texts from *Die Ermittlung.* In the five performances from May 25 to June 1 at the Hebbel Theater, the Berliner Ensemble, and the Volksbühne am Rosa Luxemburg Platz, persons from the public read the piece. On the stage, which the public could visit as an exhibition, *EXIT/Materialien zum Dachau-Projekt* (Exit/Materials for the Dachau Project), 1972, was installed.

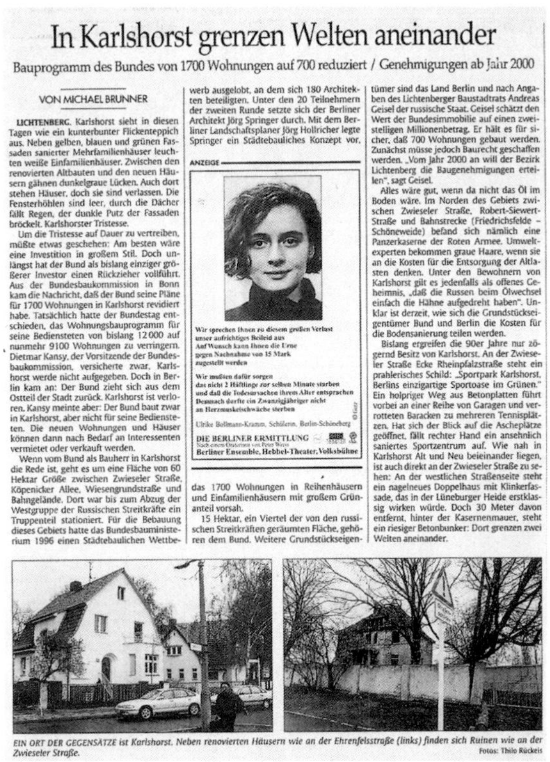

In Karlshorst grenzen Welten aneinander

Bauprogramm des Bundes von 1700 Wohnungen auf 700 reduziert / Genehmigungen ab Jahr 2000

VON MICHAEL BRUNNER

LICHTENBERG. Karlshorst sieht in diesen Tagen wie ein kunterbunter Flickenteppich aus. Neben gelben, blauen und grünen Fassaden sanierter Mehrfamilienhäuser leuchten weiße Einfamilienhäuser. Zwischen den renovierten Altbauten und den neuen Häusern gähnen dunkelgraue Lücken. Auch dort stehen Häuser, doch sie sind verlassen. Die Fensterhöhlen sind leer, durch die Dächer fällt Regen, der dunkle Putz der Fassaden bröckelt. Karlshorster Tristesse.

Um die Tristesse auf Dauer zu vertreiben, müßte etwas geschehen: Am besten wäre eine Investition in großem Stil. Doch unlängst hat der Bund als bislang einziger größerer Investor einen Rückzieher vollführt. Aus der Bundesbaukommission in Bonn kam die Nachricht, daß der Bund seine Pläne für 1700 Wohnungen in Karlshorst revidiert habe. Tatsächlich hatte der Bundestag entschieden, das Wohnungsbauprogramm für seine Bediensteten von bislang 12000 auf nunmehr 9100 Wohnungen zu verringern. Dietmar Kansy, der Vorsitzende der Bundesbaukommission, versicherte zwar, Karlshorst werde nicht aufgegeben. Doch in Berlin kam an: Der Bund zieht sich aus dem Ostteil der Stadt zurück. Karlshorst ist verloren. Kansy meinte aber: Der Bund baut zwar in Karlshorst, aber nicht für seine Bediensteten. Die neuen Wohnungen und Häuser können dann nach Bedarf an Interessenten vermietet oder verkauft werden.

Wenn vom Bund als Bauherr in Karlshorst die Rede ist, geht es um eine Fläche von 60 Hektar Größe zwischen Zwieseler Straße, Köpenicker Allee, Wiesengrundstraße und Bahngelände. Dort war bis zum Abzug der Westgruppe der Russischen Streitkräfte ein Truppenteil stationiert. Für die Bebauung dieses Gebiets hatte das Bundesbauministerium 1996 einen Städtebaulichen Wettbewerb ausgelobt, an dem sich 180 Architekten beteiligten. Unter den 20 Teilnehmern der zweiten Runde setzte sich der Berliner Architekt Jörg Springer durch. Mit dem Berliner Landschaftsplaner Jörg Hollricher legte Springer ein Städtebauliches Konzept vor, das 1700 Wohnungen in Reihenhäusern und Einfamilienhäusern mit großem Grünanteil vorsah.

15 Hektar, ein Viertel der von den russischen Streitkräften geräumten Fläche, gehören dem Bund. Weitere Grundstückseigentümer sind das Land Berlin und nach Angaben des Lichtenberger Baustadtrats Andreas Geisel der russische Staat. Geisel schätzt den Wert der Bundesimmobilie auf einen zweistelligen Millionenbetrag. Er hält es für sicher, daß 700 Wohnungen gebaut werden. Zunächst müsse jedoch Baurecht geschaffen werden. „Vom Jahr 2000 an will der Bezirk Lichtenberg die Baugenehmigungen erteilen", sagt Geisel.

Alles wäre gut, wenn da nicht das Öl im Boden wäre. Im Norden des Gebiets zwischen Zwieseler Straße, Robert-Siewert-Straße und Bahnstrecke (Friedrichsfelde – Schöneweide) befand sich nämlich eine Panzerkaserne der Roten Armee. Umweltexperten bekommen graue Haare, wenn sie an die Kosten für die Entsorgung der Altlasten denken. Unter den Bewohnern von Karlshorst gilt es jedenfalls als offenes Geheimnis, „daß die Russen beim Ölwechsel einfach die Hähne aufgedreht haben". Unklar ist derzeit, wie sich die Grundstückseigentümer Bund und Berlin die Kosten für die Bodensanierung teilen werden.

Bislang ergreifen die 90er Jahre nur zögernd Besitz von Karlshorst. An der Zwieseler Straße Ecke Rheinpfalzstraße steht ein prahlerisches Schild: „Sportpark Karlshorst, Berlins einzigartige Sportoase im Grünen." Ein holpriger Weg aus Betonplatten führt vorbei an einer Reihe von Garagen und verrotteten Baracken zu mehreren Tennisplätzen. Hat sich der Blick auf die Ascheplätze geöffnet, fällt rechter Hand ein ansehnlich saniertes Sportzentrum auf. Wie nah in Karlshorst Alt und Neu beieinander liegen, ist auch direkt an der Zwieseler Straße zu sehen: An der westlichen Straßenseite steht ein nagelneues Doppelhaus mit Klinkerfassade, das in der Lüneburger Heide erstklassig wirken würde. Doch 30 Meter davon entfernt, hinter der Kasernenmauer, steht ein riesiger Betonbunker: Dort grenzen zwei Welten aneinander.

ANZEIGE

Wir sprechen Ihnen zu diesem großen Verlust
unser aufrichtiges Beileid aus
Auf Wunsch kann Ihnen die Urne
gegen Nachnahme von 15 Mark
zugestellt werden

Wir mußten dafür sorgen
das nicht 2 Häftlinge zur selben Minute starben
und daß die Todesursachen ihrem Alter entsprachen
Demnach durfte ein Zwanzigjähriger nicht
an Herzmuskelschwäche sterben

Ulrike Bollmann-Kramm, Schülerin, Berlin-Schöneberg

DIE BERLINER ERMITTLUNG
Berliner Ensemble, Hebbel-Theater, Volksbühne

EIN ORT DER GEGENSÄTZE ist Karlshorst. Neben renovierten Häusern wie an der Ehrenfelsstraße (links) finden sich Ruinen wie an der Zwieseler Straße.
Fotos: Thilo Rückeis

Announcement in *Der Tagesspiegel*

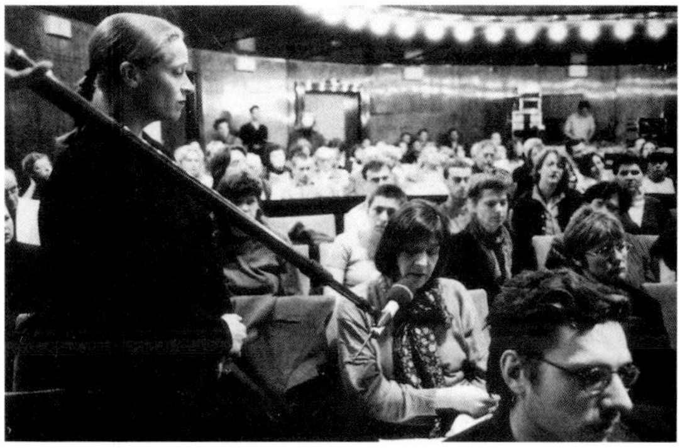

Performance at the Hebbel Theater

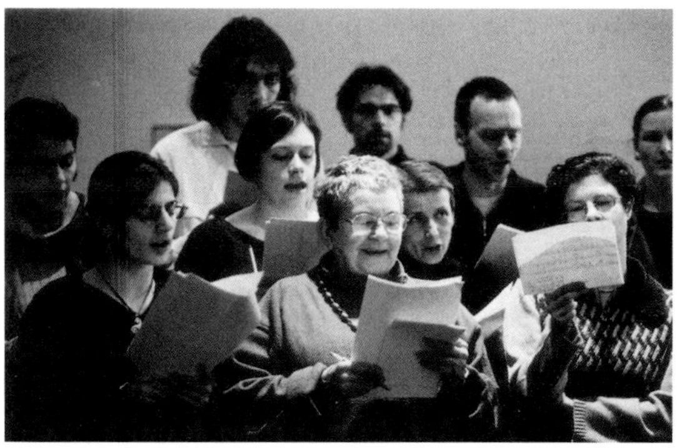

Chorus rehearsal

Miami Islet **Thurgau, 1998/99**

Installation, posters, announcements in the *Thurgauer Zeitung* and in *Cashual,* Zürich
October 18, 1998 until April 20, 1999
This work is a homage to the project by Robert Smithson which was blocked by the intervention of the environmental organization Greenpeace: Smithson's project was to cover the island crag known as Miami Islet, off the west coast of Canada, with glass, and Jochen Gerz's homage consisted of the realization of a two-part, interactive work at the Ittingen Cloisters, in Thurgau. Posters and announcements invited the visitors to bring an empty bottle into the museum, and then, in a perfectly dark room—after making their way across it—to throw it against a wall. The invitation reads: "What can we do? Destroy? Play? Create? What today is the 'I'? Ethical? Shameless? In vain? Beautiful and too late? When the empty bottle has been shattered against the wall and the shards have fallen into the pile of glass, then don't ask 'why' of art."

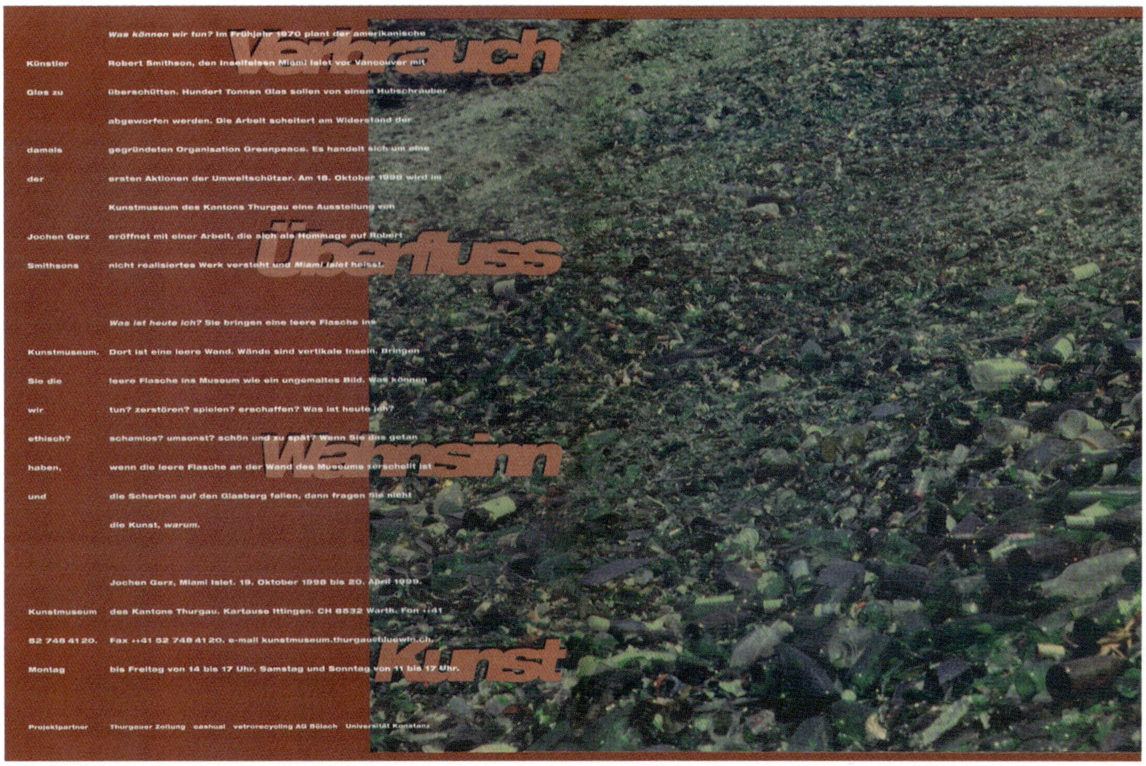

Announcement in *Cashual*, October 1998

Künstlers Traum–Goethe in Buchenwald (Artist's Dream–Goethe in Buchenwald) **Weimar, 1999**

Poster, 260 x 360 cm, neon installation; May 1 to December 31, 1999
Jochen Gerz tells the story about a rumor concerning a light that connects Belvedere Castle with the chimney at Buchenwald. The story begins when the city commissions the artist to come to grips with the rumor about the light on Weimar, and to liberate the great cultural achievements of the classics from the shadow of the genocide. It's the story of the truth. Can one play with the truth? For seven months, commercial billboards in the city of Weimar recount the city's past... Real persons speak out, debating the history and the present of the city. On December 22, during the night of the winter solstice, the green light becomes true.

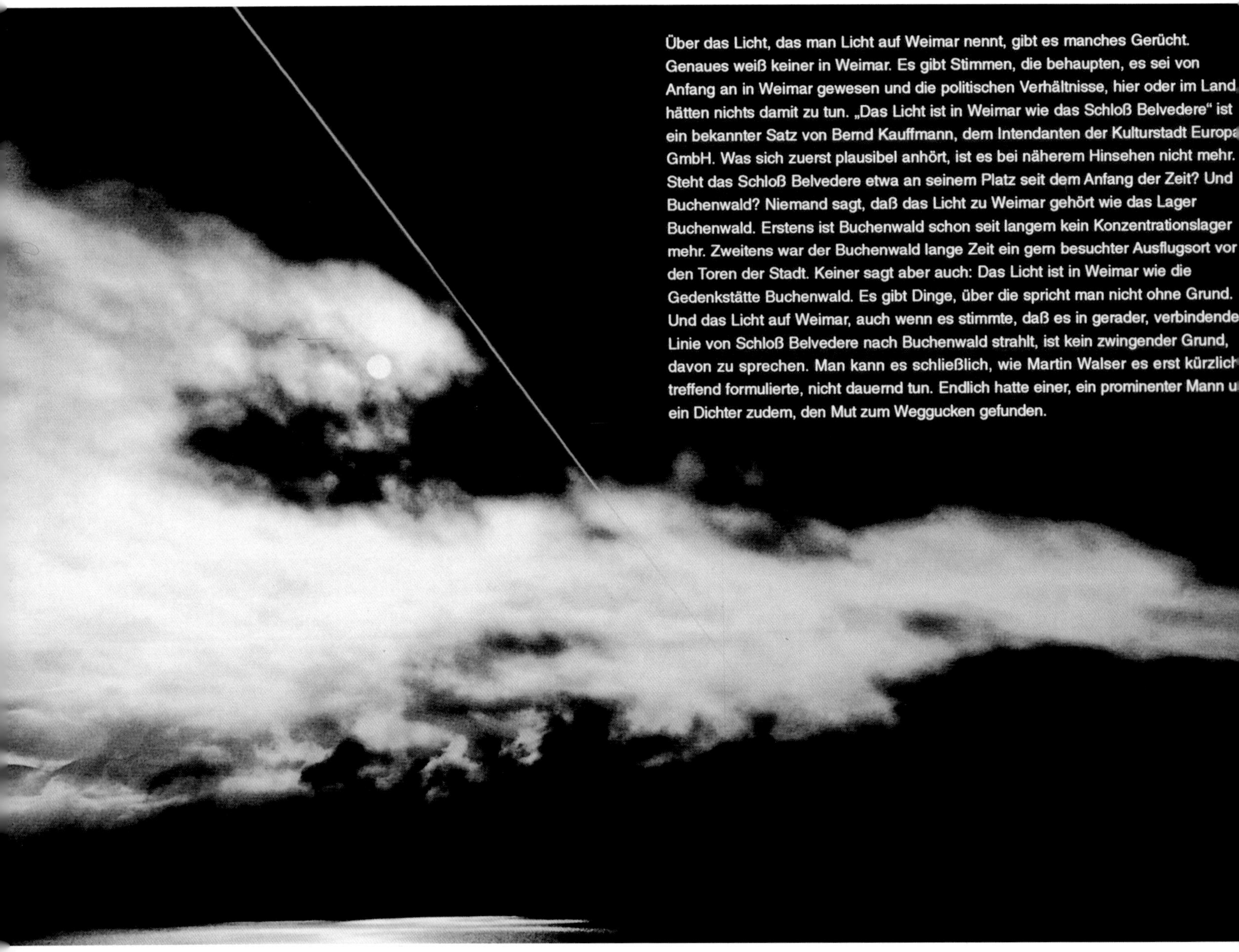

Poster sketch

Appendix

Biography

Lives and works in Paris **1940** born in Berlin **1958** studies in Chinese, English and German language and literature at the University of Cologne **1959** texts, and translations from the works, among others, of Ezra Pound and Henri Gaudier-Brzeka **1960** resides in London **1962** studies in paleontology at the University of Basel **since 1966** resides in Paris, founds the authors' cooperative press *Agentzia* in collaboration with Jean F. Bory (until 1969) **since 1968** publications, and interventions in public spaces **since 1969** photo/text works **since 1971** video works, installations, performances **1972** founds the "Society for the Practical Study of Daily Life" (until 1978) **since 1976** workshops, lectures, teaching activities **since 1984** installations in public spaces **since 1990** Roland Prize, Bremen (1990); German Art Critics' Prize, Berlin (1996); National Order of Merit, Paris(1996); Peter Weiss Prize, Berlin (1996); National Grand Prize for the Plastic Arts, Paris (1998); Artistic Contribution Award, Festival of Films on Art, Montreal (1999) **since 1995** internet works

Solo Shows

[K] is used to indicate that the show was accompanied by a catalogue.

1968 Libreria Rinascita, Modena **1969** Galerie Groh, Oldenburg [K] **1970** Aktionsraum 1, Munich [K]; Centro La Comune, Brescia; Galerie Ben Doute de Tout, Nice; Galerie Yellow, Liège; Galerie Mediacontact, Düsseldorf **1971** Centro Tool, Milan; Galerie NW/8, Beindersheim; Galerie Yellow, Liège **1972** Galerie Bama, Paris; Galerie Danert, Copenhagen; Galerie Stampa, Basel **1973** Galerie Bama, Paris; Goethe-Institut, Paris; Goethe-Institut, Amsterdam; Goethe-Institut, Lille; Goethe-Institut, Bordeaux; Centro diffusione grafica, Florence; Galerie Delta, Brussels; Gap Studio d'Arte Contemporanea, Rome [K] **1974** Kunsthalle zu Kiel, Kiel [K]; Galerie Stampa, Basel [K]; Galerie und Edition S Press, Hattingen; Galerie Entre, Paris [K]; Galerie Klein, Bonn; Galerie Bama, Paris; Kunstmuseum, Bochum **1975** Galerie bei Antpöhlers, Bremen; Musée d'Art et d'Industrie de Saint-Etienne; Musée d'Art Moderne de la Ville de Paris/ARC 2, Paris [K]; Galerie Art in Progress, Munich; Galerie nächst St. Stephan, Vienna; Badischer Kunstverein, Karlsruhe – Wilhelm Lembruck-Museum, Duisburg – Kunstverein, Braunschweig [K] **1976** Tranegaarden Gentofte Kunstbibliothek, Gent [K]; Galerie Art in Progress, Düsseldorf; Kunstraum München, Munich **1977** Studio d'Arte Cannaviello, Rome; Painting Box, Zurich; Museum van hedendaagse kunst te Gent, Gent; Cultureel informatief centrum, Gent; Galerie Stampa, Basel; Galerie Anselm Dreher, Berlin; Videostudio Mike Steiner, Berlin; Galerie Bama, Paris; Galerie Art in Progress, Munich; Städtische Galerie im Lenbachhaus, Munich **1978** Bündner Kunstmuseum, Chur [K]; Neue Galerie Landesmuseum Joanneum, Graz [K]; Galerie Klein, Bonn; Kestner-Gesellschaft, Hanover [K]; Centro de Arte Contemporãnea, Museu Nacional de Soares dos Reis, Porto – Fundaçao Calouste Gulbenkian, Lisbon; Galerie Modulo, Lisbon; Westfälischer Kunstverein, Münster [K] **1979** Studio d'Arte Cannaviello, Milan; Centre d'Art Contemporain, Geneva; Ikon Gallery, Birmingham [K]; Galerie Baudoin Lebon, Paris; Galerie Art in Progress, Düsseldorf; Kunstmuseum Luzern, Lucerne [K] **1980** Frankfurter Kunstverein, Frankfurt am Main [K]; Galerie Stampa, Basel [K]; Galerie Bama, Paris; Kasseler Kunstverein, Kassel [K] **1981** Kunsthalle Bielefeld, Bielefeld [K]; The Flat, Copenhagen **1982** Kunstverein Freiburg, Friburgo [K]; Galerie ak, Frankfurt am Main; Galerie 'A', Amsterdam; Dany Keller Galerie, Munich; Galerie Bama, Paris; Goethe-Institut, Athens [K] **1983** Galerie Stampa, Basel; Espace d'art contemporain, Maison de la culture, Châlon-sur-Saône **1984** Galerie Heinz Holtmann, Cologne; Neue Galerie, Staatliche und Städtische Kunstsammlungen, Kassel [K]; Walter Phillips Gallery, Banff Centre, Banff [K]; Yuill & Crowley, Sydney – Centre for Contemporary Art, Melbourne; Wilhelm-Hack-Museum, Ludwigshafen – Heidelberger Kunstverein, Heidelberg [K] **1985** Galerie Bama, Paris; Neuer Berliner Kunstverein, Berlin [K]; Museum für Photographie, Braunschweig; Stadtgalerie Saarbrücken, Saarbrücken [K]; Galerie Elke Dröscher, Hamburg; Or Gallery, Vancouver **1986** Kunstraum München, Munich [K]; Centre d'art contemporain (Passages), Troyes [K]; Galerie de l'Ancienne Poste, Calais; Musée des Beaux-Arts de Calais, Calais – Musée des Beaux-Arts de Chartres, Chartres [K]; Galerie Cora Hölzl, Düsseldorf; Elac, Salle Mermillon, Lyon; Coburg Gallery, Vancouver **1987** La Criée, Halle d'art contemporain, Rennes [K]; Optica, A Centre for Contemporary Art, Montreal; Yuill & Crowley, Sydney; Galerie Kicken/Pauseback, Cologne **1988** Galerie Crousel-Robelin Bama, Paris; Galerie ak, Frankfurt am Main; Galerie Löhrl, Mönchengladbach; Kunstsammlung Nordrhein-Westfalen, Düsseldorf – Museum Moderner Kunst, Palais Liechtenstein – Wien, Fondation Cartier, Jouy-en-Josas – Musée d'art moderne, Saint-Etienne – Hamburger Kunsthalle, Hamburg [K]; Galerie Anselm Dreher, Berlin; Ruine der Künste, Berlin [K] **1989** Stalke Gallery, Copenhagen; Gallery Shimada, Yamaguchi and Sagacho Exhibit Space, Tokyo [K]; Archive Space, Amsterdam; Galerie Ursula Ehrhardt, Nuremberg; Galerie Harald Behm, Hamburg; Dany Keller Galerie, Munich **1990** Galeria Maria Potocka, Kraków; Gallery Shimada, Yamaguchi and Sagacho Exhibit Space, Tokyo [K]; Archive Space, Amsterdam; Galerie Ursula Ehrhardt, Nuremberg **1991** Galerie Modulo, Porto; Hirschl & Adler Modern, New York; Kunstverein Ruhr, Forum bildender Künstler, Essen [K]; Galerie Anselm Dreher, Galerie Vier, Berlin [K]; Galerie Crousel-Robelin Bama, Paris; Galerie Cora Hölzl, Düsseldorf; Galerie Löhrl, Mönchengladbach [K] **1992** Galerie ak, Frankfurt am Main; Richard L. Nelson Gallery and Fine Arts Collection, Davis [K]; Galerie Sandmann + Haak, Hanover; Pascal de Sarthe Gallery, Los Angeles; Neues Museum Weserburg, Bremen – Forum Langenstraße, Bremen – Badischer Kunstverein,

Karlsruhe – Cornerhouse, Manchester – Saarlandmuseum, Saarbrücken; Staatliches Lindenau Museum, Lindenau; Altes Rathaus, Altenburg; Kulturhaus, Potsdam [K]; Yuill & Crowley, Sydney **1993** Galerie Samuel Lallouz, Montreal; Centre Saidye Bronfman, Montreal, Musée Bossuet, Meaux [K]; Galerie von Witzleben, Karlsruhe; City Art Gallery, Manchester; Galerie Sima, Nuremberg [K] **1994** Les Musées de la Ville de Strasbourg, Musée d'Art Moderne, Strasbourg [K]; Galerie Gandy, Prague; Galerie Löhrl, Mönchengladbach [K]; Vancouver Art Gallery, Vancouver – Newport Harbor Art Museum, Newport Beach – Neuberger Museum, Purchase [K] **1995** Tel Aviv University Gallery, Tel Aviv [K]; Galerie Guy Ledune, Brussels; Galerie Chantal Crousel, Paris; Galerie Bernd Lutze, Friedrichshafen; Gallery of Contemporary Art, Warsaw **1996** Galerie Cora Hölzl, Düsseldorf; Gallery CRG, New York; Municipalité de Périgueux, ADDC, Périgueux; Galerie Sandmann + Haak, Hanover; Galerie Ernst Busche, Berlin **1997** Germanisches Nationalmuseum, Nuremberg – Kunstmuseum am Ehrenhof, Düsseldorf – Musée d'Art Moderne, Saint-Etienne [K]; Gallery RAM, Los Angeles; Museum Wiesbaden, Wiesbaden [K]; Galerie Ribbentrop, Eltville; Rencontres Internationales de la Photographie, Chapelle du Méjan, Arles [K]; Catriona Jeffries Gallery, Vancouver **1998** Berkeley Art Museum, Berkeley; ZKM–Zentrum für Kunst und Medientechnologie, Medienmuseum, Karlsruhe [K]; Kunstmuseum Thurgau, Kartause Ittingen, Warth [K]; Maison Européenne de la Photographie, Paris; Printemps de Cahors, public space, Cahors [K] **1999** Yuill & Crowley, Sydney; Kulturhauptstadt Weimar, public space, Weimar [K] **1999–2000** Museion–Museum for Modern Art, Bozen/Bolzano – Kunsthalle zu Kiel, Kiel – Sønderjyllands Kunstmuseum, Tønder – Art Gallery of Windsor, Ontario [K]

Group Shows (since 1997)

1997 *Fotografie nach der Fotografie*, Siemens Kulturprogramm, Munich – Finlands fotografiska museum, Helsinki – Institute of Contemporary Art, University of Pennsylvania, Philadelphia – Adelaide Festival, Adelaide – Institute of Contemporary Art, Philadelphia [K]; *Made in France. Art en France depuis 1945*, Centre Georges Pompidou, Paris [K]; *foto text text foto*, Museion–Museum for Modern Art, Bozen/Bolzano – Frankfurter Kunstverein, Frankfurt am Main – Fotomuseum Winterthur, Winterthur [K]; *Intermedial, Kunstsammlung im Kunstgeschichtlichen Institut der Ruhruniversität Bochum*, Ruhruniversität, Bochum; *Pro Lidice*, Tschechisches Museum für Bildende Kunst, Prague and Goethe-Institut, Prague [K]; *Temps de pose, temps de parole*, Fonds Régional d'Art Contemporain, Villa Musso, Saintes; *20 Jahre Bielefelder Colloquium Neue Poesie*, Kunsthalle Bielefeld – Richard Kaselowsky Haus, Bielefeld [K]; *Medien-Kunstwerke*, Stampa, Basel; *Standort Deutschland*, Städtisches Museum, Schloß Morsbroich, Leverkusen; *Inexplicable Presence*, Moderna galerija, Ljubljana; *Entgegen–Religion, Gedächtnis, Körper in der Gegenwartskunst*, Kulturhaus der Stadt Graz, Graz [K]; *Antonin Artaud–Tête à tête*, Galerie de France, Paris; *Livres d'artistes, l'invention d'un genre 1960–1980*, Bibliothèque nationale de France, Galerie Mansart, Paris [K]; *Sammlung zu Gast...*, Niedersächsische Sparkassenstiftung, Münden; *Sammlung Künstler-Holzpostkarten*, Galerie Köhler, Kassel; *La Rayure, l'intervalle, le jour...*, FRAC Nord-Pas de Calais, Calais; *28es Rencontres Internationales de la Photographie*, Arles [K]; *Fluctuations créatives transdisciplinaires*, Fondation D.A.N.A.E., Paris; *Deep Storage–Arsenale der Erinnerung*, Haus der Kunst, Munich – Nationalgalerie, Berlin – Kunstmuseum, Düsseldorf – New P.S.1 Exhibitions, New York – Henry Art Gallery, Washington [K]; *Arbeiten auf Papier–Kunst der Gegenwart*, Kunsthalle Barmen, Barmen; *Projet 8*, Total Museum of Contemporary Art, Tokyo [K]; *Miniaturen heute–today–aujourd'hui–oggi*, Deichtorhallen, Hamburg; *Petersburger Hängung*, Galerie Cora Hölzl, Düsseldorf; *Über Deutschland*, Galerie Anselm Dreher, Berlin; *Deutschlandbilder*, Martin-Gropius-Bau, Berlin [K]; *Positionen künstlerischer Photographie in Deutschland seit 1945*, Berlinische Galerie, Berlin [K]; *Une saison photographique allemande*, Maison Européenne de la Photographie, Paris; *Changing Places. The Artist's Role*, Cardiff Bay Arts Trust, Cardiff; *Crossings France/Hawaii*, The Contemporary Museum, Makiki; *Kunst der Gegenwart*, ZKM–Zentrum für Kunst- und Medientechnologie, Karlruhe; *Arbeiten auf Papier–Kunst der Gegenwart deutscher Künstler*, Mykola-Zilinskas-Kunstgalerie des Nationalen M. K. Ciurlionis-Kunstmuseum, Vilnius; *Auguste Rodin–Die Bürger von Calais, Werk und Wirkung*, Skulpturenmuseum Glaskasten, Marl [K]; *Rutishauser/Kuhn: Inhalt und Form*, Kunstmuseum des Kantons Thurgau, Kartause Ittingen, Warth; *Editionen, Multiple, Objekte*, Galerie Cora Hölzl, Düsseldorf **1998** *Out of Actions: Between Performance and the Object, 1949–1979*, The Geffen Contemporary, Museum of Contemporary Art, Los Angeles – MAK–Museum für angewandte Kunst, Vienna – Museum of Contemporary Art, Tokyo [K]; *Le Fragment, la durée, le montage*, La Galerie–École d'art, Quimper; *Geistesgegenwart*, Ehem. Karmelitenkirche, Munich – Diözesanmuseum, Freising – Heilig-Geist-Kirche, Landshut [K]; *Signaturen des Sichtbaren – Ein Jahrhundert der Fotografie in Deutschland*, Galerie am Fischmarkt, Erfurt [K]; *Jardin d'artiste: de mémoire d'arbre*, Musée Zadkine, Paris [K]; *Voices*, Witte de With, Rotterdam – Fundació Joan Miró, Barcelona – Le Fresnoy, Studio national des arts contemporains, Tourcoing [K]; *Le donné, le fictif*, Centre national de la photographie, Paris; *Crossings–Kunst zum Hören und Sehen*, Kunsthalle, Vienna [K]; *Sentiers battus*, FRAC Alsace, Saverne – FRAC Lorraine, Phalsbourg; *30*, Studio d'arte Cannaviello, Milan; *Exposition de groupe*, Maison européenne de la photographie, Paris; *Pro Lidice*, Schleswig-Holsteinischer Kunstverein in der Kunsthalle zu Kiel, Kiel; *Documenta*, Museum Fridericianum, Kassel; *Ponctuations*, Musée municipal, Église Saint-Nazaire, Bourbon-Lancy; *Premises–Invested Space in Visual Arts, Architecture, and Design from France 1958–1998*, Solomon R. Guggenheim Foundation, New York [K]; *L'art e(s)t la vi(ll)e, 5 propositions d'artistes pour regarder la ville autrement*, Musée d'Art Moderne, Strasbourg; *Deux générations d'artistes allemands*, Musée d'Art Moderne, Saint-Etienne **1999** *Menschen Mächte Märkte, Kunst und Erinnerung*, Städtische Galerie, Villingen-Schwenningen; *L'Art et l'Écrit, Idem+ Arts*, FRAC Nord-Pas de Calais, Espace Sculfort, Maubeuge; *Das Versprechen der Fotografie, Die Sammlung der DG BANK*, Kestner Gesellschaft, Hanover; *Fotografie in der Sammlung der Kunsthalle zu Kiel*, Kunsthalle, Kiel; *Weimar 1999, Künstlertraum*, Weimar

Artist's Books and Monographs

1968 *Footing*, Edition Approches, Paris, Anabas-Verlag, Gießen 1969 **1969** *Replay*, Edition Agentzia, Paris **1970** *Ressurection*, Edizioni amodulo, Brescia; *Burials*, Edition Howeg, Hinwil/Zurich **1971** *Recto/Verso*, Edizioni Techne, Florence; *Annoncenteil–Arbeiten auf/mit Papier*, Luchterhand Verlag, Darmstadt/Neuwied **1973** *Die Beschreibung des Papiers*, Luchterhand Verlag, Darmstadt/Neuwied **1974** *Die Zeit der Beschreibung*, Klaus Ramm Verlag, Lichtenberg **1976** *Die Schwierigkeit des Zentaurs beim vom Pferd steigen/The Centaur's difficulty when dismounting the horse*, Kunstraum München, Munich; *Piece-31, En dansk Uddrivelse/A Danish Exorcism*, Edition After Hand, Ringkobing; *Das zweite Buch (Die Zeit der Beschreibung),* Klaus Ramm Verlag, Spenge **1977** *Les livres de Gandelu*, Edition Yellow Now, Liège; *F/T 66, F/T 68*, Edition Yellow Now, Liège **1978** *Exit/Das Dachau-Projekt*, Verlag Roter Stern, Frankfurt am Main; *Paul M. 1969/70*, Edizioni Tasma, Bologna **1979** *Paare*, Folkwang Schule GH, Essen 1979; *Come on over to the dark side*, Kunstmuseum Luzern, Lucerne **1980** *Das dritte Buch (Die Zeit der Beschreibung),* Klaus Ramm Verlag, Spenge **1981** *The Fuji-Yama-Series*, AQ-Verlag, Dudweiler; *Avec/sans public (Mit/ohne Publikum). Performances 1968–80*, Éditions Cheval d'Attaque, Paris (Kunsthalle Bielefeld) **1982** *Le Grand Amour*, AQ-Verlag, Dudweiler **1983** *Das vierte Buch (Die Zeit der Beschreibung),* Klaus Ramm Verlag, Spenge **1985** *Von der Kunst/De l'Art*, AQ-Verlag, Dudweiler; *Neue Texte*, Neue Texte, Linz; *Texte*, Karl Kerber Verlag, Bielefeld **1990** *Bleu ou la vraie vie*, Buyse Éditions, Lille **1993** *2146 Steine–Mahnmal gegen Rassismus*, Saarbrücken, Verlag Gerd Hatje, Ostfildern **1994** *De l'art. Textes depuis 1969*, énsba, Paris; *Das Harburger Mahnmal gegen Faschismus* (Esther und Jochen Gerz), Verlag Gerd Hatje, Ostfildern **1995** *Die Bremer Befragung*, Cantz Verlag, Ostfildern; *Die Gegenwart der Kunst. Interviews 1970–1995*, Lindinger + Schmid, Regensburg **1996** *La question secrète. Le monument vivant de Biron*, Actes Sud, Arles; *Das 20. Jahrhundert* (Esther und Jochen Gerz), Klartext Verlag, Essen; *The French Wall*, Richter Verlag, Düsseldorf **1997** *Daran denken. Texte in Arbeiten 1980–1996*, Richter-Verlag, Düsseldorf; *Gründe zu Lächeln–Das Göttinger Fragment* (Esther und Jochen Gerz), in: Bernhard Jussen (Hg.), Von der künstlerischen Produktion der Geschichte I. Jochen Gerz, Wallstein Verlag, Göttingen 1997, 33–80 **1998** *Kunst als Beruf. Reden vor Studenten*, Institut für Buchkunst, Leipzig; *Les Témoins*, Actes Sud, Arles **1999** *Drinnen vor der Tür. Reden an Studenten*, Hatje Cantz Publishers, Ostfildern (in preparation); *The Berkeley Oracle. Questions Unanswered*, Richter Verlag, Düsseldorf (in preparation); *Werkverzeichnis*, 3 vol., Verlag für moderne Kunst, Nuremberg (in preparation); *Künstlers Traum–Goethe in Buchenwald*, Hatje Cantz Publishers (in preparation); *Miami Islet*, Kunstmuseum Thurgau, Kartause Ittingen, Warth, Hatje Cantz Publishers (in preparation)

Interviews and Articles

1971 Klaus Groh, "Ich stelle mir vor...", in: Klaus Groh (ed.), *If I Had a Mind...*, concept-art. project-art, DuMont Schauberg, Cologne, w/o pag. **1972** Béatrice Parent, "Nous n'avons pas beaucoup parlé ensemble", in: *Kunstnachrichten*, 9, no. 3 **1974** Peter Andre Bloch (ed.), *Gegenwartsliteratur. Eine Dokumentation über die literarisch-technischen und verlegerisch-ökonomischen Voraussetzungen schriftstellerischer Arbeit*, Bonn, 211/12; Carole Naggar, "Interview mit Jochen Gerz. Dialogue commémorative du 27.5.1974", in: *Jochen Gerz*, Galerie Entre, Paris; Aurel Schmidt, "Grenzen der Mittelbarkeit", in: *Nationalzeitung am Wochenende*, 25.5.1974 **1975** Suzanne Page/Bernard Ceysson, "Interview de Jochen Gerz", in: *Jochen Gerz. Les pièces*, Musee d'Art Moderne de la Ville, ARC 2, Paris – Musée d'Art et d'Industrie, Saint-Etienne, 4–8 **1977** Kevin Clarke, "Künstlerumfrage", in: *Kunst und Medien–Materialien zur documenta 6*, Kassel; Michel Giroud, "Jochen Gerz, le voyage du Transsibérien", in: *Canal*, no. 1, April 1977; Georg F. Schwarzbauer, "Über meine Arbeit", in: *Kunstforum International*, vol. 23, May 1977 **1978** Claire Gravel, "Répondre à l'imposture culturelle par la mutilation", in: *Parachute*, no. 12, fall 1978; Annelie Pohlen, "Interview mit Jochen Gerz", in: *Heute Kunst*, no. 22, May–June 1978 **1979** Michael Erlhoff, "Gespräch mit Jochen Gerz", in: *Zweitschrift*, no. 6, 13–16; John Howell/Philippe du Vignal, "Performances de Jochen Gerz", in: *Art Press*, no. 30; Martin Kunz, "Gespräch mit Jochen Gerz", in: *Kulcher Piece Nr. 5. Come on over to the Dark Side*, Kunstmuseum, Lucerne; Herbert Molderings, "Der Besucher besucht sich selbst", in: *Theater Heute*, 1979 **1980** Claus Carstensen, "Interview mit Jochen Gerz", in: *Tidsskrift for kunst og kultur*, no. 25 **1981** Amine Haase, *Gesellschaft als Kunst. Gespräche mit Künstlern*, Wiegand Verlag, Cologne, 53–54 **1982** Marie-Louise Syring, "Jochen Gerz, l'art, destructeur de la communication", in: *Canal*, no. 50, October 1982 **1983** Kerstin Martins, "Gespräch mit Jochen Gerz", in: *Performance – Eine andere Dimension*, Künstlerhaus Bethanien, Berlin, 63–65 **1986** Patrick Le Nouëne, "Entretien avec Jochen Gerz", in: *Jochen Gerz*, Musées des Beaux-Arts, Calais 1986 **1987** Stephan Schmidt-Wulffen, "Duell mit der Verdrängung", in: *Kunstforum International*, vol. 87, January/ February 1997 **1988** Hubertus von Amelunxen/Charles Grivel, "Pourquoi ne pas faire dans le pure ordinaire", in: *Revue des sciences humaines*, vol. LXXXI, no. 210, April/June 1988 **1989** Detlef Bluehmler, "Interview mit Jochen Gerz", in: *Künstlerlexikon*, Munich; Jean-Francois Chevrier, "Trafic d'origines et images de paix", in: *Galeries magazine*, no. 31, June/July 1989; Michel Nuridsany, "Effets de miroir", in: Michel Nuridsany, *Le mirroir de l'art*, Centre Photographique de l'Ile de France, IAPIF, Pontault-Combault, 169–170; Mona Thomas, *Jochen Gerz. Paris tête d'affiche*, ed. by Office d'information culturelle, Paris, June **1990** Regis Durand, "La photographie, mon fil d'Arianne", in: *art press spécial photographie*, October 1990; Pierre Martin, "Die Melodien aus der Trans.-Sib. Noch im Kopf", in: *Morgenpost*, 20.2.1990; Florian Rötzer/Sarah Rogendorfer, "Jochen Gerz. Indifferenz der Wirklichkeit", in: *Kunstforum International*, vol. 105, January/February 1990 (reprint in: *Die künstlerische Produktion von Bildern in einer Gesellschaft des Spektakels*, Suhrkamp Verlag, Frankfurt am Main); Rainer Unruh, "Wenn Bilder lügen", in: *Szene Hamburg*, no. 3 **1991** Jerome Sans, "Il n'y a pas de mystère, c'est votre savoir qui vous tuera", in: *Sous le signe*, Salle Balène, Figeac, Édition Sud, Paris **1992** Myriam Rosen, "Gerz, sous les pavés la mémoire", in: *Libération*, 17.3.1992; Thomas Wulffen, "Indifferenz als Engagement", in: *Zyma Art Today*, no. 1, January/ February 1992 **1993** Matthias Flügge/Michael Freitag, "Dem Zugriff des Wissens widerstehen", in: *neue bildende kunst*, no. 3; Peter Funken, "Frisch aus der Fabrik", *Zitty*, no. 26; Elisabeth Jappe, "Gespräch mit Jochen Gerz", in: Elisabeth Jappe, *Performance–Ritual–Prozeß: Handbuch der Aktionskunst in Europa*, Prestel, Munich; Jacqueline Lichtenstein/Gerard Wajcman, "La place du monument invisible", in: *art press*, no. 179, April 1993; Birgitt Rambalski, "Befragung zur Bremer Befragung", in: *Die Tageszeitung*, 23.10.93; S. D. Sauerbier, "Barbar gr.m.", in: *Artis*, July/August 1993 (reprint "A Conversation with Jochen Gerz", in: *New Observations*, no. 104, January/February 1995); Kirsten Voigt, "Wir selbst sind die größte Utopie, viel komplexer als jedes Werk", in: *Badisches Tagblatt*, 30.1.93 **1994** Denis-Laurent Boyer/Richard Klein, "L'Art, c'est quelque chose de normal", in: *sans titre*, no. 26, April/June 1994; Achim Könneke, "Gespräch mit Jochen Gerz und Esther Shalev-Gerz", in: Esther Shalev-Gerz/ Jochen Gerz, *Das Harburger Mahnmal gegen Faschismus*, ed. by Achim Könneke, Cantz Verlag, Ostfildern; Judith

Mastai, "A Report from the Lab", in: *VAG*, Leporello zur Ausstellung *People Speak* in der Vancouver Art Gallery, August (reprint in: *Journal of Contemporary Art*, vol. 7, no. 2); Petra Raguz, "Faire de l'art aujourd'hui", in: *Hebdoscope*, no. 450, June 1994; Annick Texier, "Fragments d'entretiens", in: *Hebdoscope*, no. 421, April 1994 **1995** Lieven van den Abeele, "Mots vivants", in: *Topos 92*, no. 16, Paris 1995; Sabine Komm, "Ein Fremdkörper auf der Brücke", in: *Foyer*, no. 11, September/November 1995; Joachim Kreibohm, "Im Gespräch mit Jochen Gerz", in: *Artis*, no. 11, 1995; Arnulf Marzluf, "Ich will die Kunst um die Kunst bringen", in: *Weser Kurier*, 6.4.1995; Thomas Wolff, "Das dekorative Gemeinwesen", in: *Die Tageszeitung*, 11.4.1995 **1996** François Barré, "Ruser avec la mort", in: Jochen Gerz, *Le monument vivant de Biron. La question secrète*, Actes Sud, Arles; Irène Berelowitch, "Grand Angle", in: *France Culture*, 9.11.1996; Geneviève Breerette, "Je ne voulais pas montrer la mémoire frigorifiée", in: *Le Monde*, 20.7.96; Britta E. Buhlmann, "Gespräch mit Jochen Gerz zu Terry Fox' Installation *Bloodline*", in: *John Cage, Terry Fox, Gudrun Wassermann*, Pfalzgalerie, Kaiserslautern; Hejo Eicker, "Das Jahrhundert neu erfinden", in: *Oberhausener Abendblatt*, 27.2.1996; Robert Fleck, "Die Gänse vom Feliferhof–Interview mit Jochen Gerz und Esther Shalev-Gerz", in: *Album*, 24.5.1996; Michael Freitag, *Theaterwäsche–Interview mit Jochen Gerz*, Haus der Kulturen der Welt, Berlin; Guillaume Hillairet/Jan Kopp/Véronique Loock, "Jochen Gerz, Le Monument Vivant de Biron", in: *Art Présence*, no. 19, summer 1996; Jacqueline Lichtenstein/Gérard Wajcman, "Wir wissen, daß das Verdrängte uns immer verfolgt", in: *Gedächtnisbilder, Vergessen und Erinnern in der Gegenwartskunst*, Reclam, Leipzig, 1996, 153–264; Jacqueline Lichtenstein/Gérard Wajcman, "Invisible Monument", in: *Ambient Fears, Random Access 2*, Pavel Büche r and Nikos Papastergiadis, Glasgow School of Arts, 205–218; Jörg Worat, "Das Wort lügt, ist pompös und nicht das, was es meint", in: *Neue Presse*, 29.10.1996 **1997** Dorothee Baer-Bogenschütz, "Die Rose wird täglich älter", in: *Wiesbadener Kurier*, 21.5.1997; Dorothee Baer-Bogenschütz, "'Zur Zeit haben die Leute keinen Spaß an der Unruhe'. Ein Gespräch mit dem Künstler Jochen Gerz, der im Museum Wiesbaden ausstellt", in: *Frankfurter Rundschau*, 23.8.1997; Doris von Drathen/Jochen Gerz, "Gespräch in Schichten", in: Bernhard Jussen (ed.), *Von der künstlerischen Produktion der Geschichte I. Jochen Gerz*, Wallstein Verlag, Göttingen 1997, 133–143; Harald Fricke, "Lebendig soll es zugehen, Interview mit Jochen Gerz", in: *Die Tageszeitung*, 22./23.11.1997; Achim Könneke, "Vanishing Memorials, Interview mit Esther Shalev-Gerz und Jochen Gerz", in: *Jahrbuch Politische Theologie*, vol. 2, 1997, 317–324; Jacqueline Lichtenstein/Gerard Wajcman, "Invisible Monument", in: *Veiled Histories. The body, place and public art*, ed. by Anna Novakov, San Francisco Art Institute, Critical Press, New York, 63–83; Philippe Mesnard, "Les Questions de Jochen Gerz, Entretien", in: *Vacarme*, no. 4–5, September/November 1997, 72–75; Olaf Metzel, "Ein Putzlappen für schlechtes Gewissen", in: *Der Spiegel*, no. 35, 24.8.1998, 176–178; Rainer Metzger, "Über den Humor nach Ausschwitz", in: *Der Standart*, 23.1.1997; Bertram Müller, "Mit dem Holocaust umgehen–wie täglich Blumengießen", in: *Rheinische Post*, 11.3.1997; Alexander Pühringer, "Wer sagt, daß Kunst gut sei?", in: *Noëma art journal*, no. 45, September/October 1997, 66–71; Hans-Peter von Däniken, "Ein Ort für die entmündeten Stimmen, Interview mit Jochen Gerz", in: *Tages-Anzeiger*, 26.11.1997 **1998** Annette Becker, "Jochen Gerz, Le Monument vivant de Biron", in: *Noësis*, 154–157; Jochen Gerz, "Les écoles d'art", in: *Beaux-Arts Magazine*, no. 169, June 1998, 96; Jochen Gerz, "Gullivers Kunst", in: *Munitionsfabrik*, no. 1, February 1998, 12–13; Jochen Gerz, "The Berkeley Oracle", in: *Neue Bildende Kunst*, no. 3, June/July 1998, 4–90; Jochen Gerz, "Welche Bedeutung hat Picasso für Sie heute?", in: *DU*, no. 9, September 1998, 72; Detlev Lücke, "Wir müssen selbst zur Skulptur werden. Der Künstler Jochen Gerz über den Wettbewerb für das Berliner Holocaust-Mahnmal", in: *Freitag*, no. 11, 6.3.1998; "L'art c'est quelque chose de normal", in: *Un Mobile Home dans le désert*, May/August 1998, 127–130; Paul Petzel, "Die Menschen sind die Denkmale, Interview mit Jochen Gerz", in: *Orientierung*, no. 7, 62, 15 April 1998, 79–83; Hans Schmidt, "Ein Platz des Lebens, Interview mit Jochen Gerz", in: *Die Woche*, 16.1.1998, 33 **1999** Franz Littmann, "Interview mit Jochen Gerz über sein Internetprojekt *The Berkeley Oracle*", in: *Klappe auf*, March 1999

Essays (since 1997)

1997 Zoe Bendt, "Die Kunst und das Mißtrauen", in: *Neue Westfälische*, 3.1.1997; Toby Clark, "Remembering War: Memorials and Anti-Monuments", in: Toby Clark, *Art and Propaganda in the Twentieth Century*, Calmann & King Ltd., New York 1997, 118–123; Jean-Max Colard, "Esther et Jochen Gerz", in: *Les Inrockuptibles*, no. 111, 2.–8.7.1997, 17; Konstanze Crüwell, "Informationen können auch Rätsel sein", in: *Frankfurter Allgemeine Sonntagszeitung*, 25 May 1997, 28; Judd D./Renée Riese Hubert, "The Book, the Museum, and Public Art", in: *Substance*, special edition: Metamorphoses of the Book, vol. XXVI, no. 1, 1997, 69–92; Christoph Danelzik-Brüggemann, "Gefrorene Bildergeschichten", in: *Die Tageszeitung*, 14.1.1997; Gabi Dolf Bonekämper, "Lügen und andere Wahrheiten", in: *Neue Zürcher Zeitung*, 15.7.1997; Gerhard Fetka, "Kränze für Mahnmal auf dem Feliferhof", in: *Neue Zeit*, 4.12.1997; Rudolf Frieling, "Ohne Probe–Aspekte prozessualer Medienkunst", in: Rudolf Frieling/Dieter Daniels, *Medien Kunst Aktion. Die 60er und 70er Jahre in Deutschland*, Vienna/New York 1997, 156–168; "Jochen Gerz. Der malende Mund", in: Rudolf Frieling/Dieter Daniels, *Medien Kunst Aktion. Die 60er und 70er Jahre in Deutschland*, Vienna/New York 1997, 203–205; Ulrich Gerster, "Jochen Gerz – In Sachen Holocaust-Mahnmal", in: *Neue Züricher Zeitung*, 11.12.1997; Jochen Gerz, "Das Berkeley Orakel–Fragen ohne Antwort", in: *Medien Kunst Aktuell–Videokunst, CD-ROM und Internetprojekte aus Deutschland*, ZKM, Karlsruhe 1997, 88–89; Cornelia Gockel, "Ein Tagebuch der Bilder", in: *Süddeutsche Zeitung*, 9.1.1997; Amine Haase, "Barbarei ist die Soldatenbraut", in: *Kölner Stadtanzeiger*, 28.1.1997; Amine Haase, "Orte des Erinnerns und Gedenkens. Das Mahnmal–an der Schnittstelle zum Nicht-Ort?", in: *Kunst und Kirche*, no. 2, May 1997, 89–90; Amine Haase, "Jochen Gerz in Wiesbaden", in: *Kunstforum International*, vol. 138, September/November 1997, 266–268; Amine Haase, "Ein Mahnmal auf Dauer", in: *Der Kölner Stadtanzeiger*, 26.11.1997; Kai-Uwe Hemken, "Jochen Gerz", in: *Deep Storage–Arsenale der Erinnerung*, Haus der Kunst, Munich 1997, 142–145; Mark Hinson, "smile", in: *Tallahassee Democrat*, 11.4. 1997; Detlef Hoffmann, "Von den Bildern auf der Leinwand zu den Bildern im Kopf. Anmerkungen zu Jochen Gerz' Geschichtsbildern", in: Bernhard Jussen (ed.), *Von der künstlerischen Produktion der Geschichte I. Jochen Gerz*, Wallstein Verlag, Göttingen 1997, 81–132; Michael Hübl, "Zwischen Leben und Lächeln", in: *Badische Neueste Nachrichten*, 22.8.1997; Bernhard Jussen, "Vom wissenschaftlichen und von künstlerischen Arbeiten an der Vergangenheit", in: Bernhard Jussen (ed.), *Von der künstlerischen Produktion der Geschichte I. Jochen Gerz*, Wallstein Verlag, Göttingen 1997, 7–32; Thomas Kliemann, "Laß uns zusammenbleiben", in: *Frankfurter Allgemeine Zeitung*, 9.1.1997; Swantje Koerner, "Die Mängel der Medien", in: *Rheinische Post*, 5.3.1997; Ralf Kulschewskij, "Widerstand gegen das, was geschah", in: *Kunstzeit*, no. 1, 1997, 58–59; Verena Kuni, "Unsichtbare Bilder", in: *nbk Chronik*, no. 4, 1997, 97–98; Eleonore Louis, "Die Gänse vom Feliferhof. Ein Mahnmal in progress von Esther und Jochen Gerz", in: *Kunsthistoriker aktuell*, Mitteilungen des österreichischen Kunsthistorikerverbandes, XIV, no. 1, 1997, 3; Eleonora Louis/Mechtild Widrich, "Die Gelassenheit des Verräters. Zur Methodik in Jochen Gerz' Foto/Text Arbeiten", in: Jochen Gerz, *Daran denken. Texte in Arbeiten 1980–1996*, Richter-Verlag, Düsseldorf 1997, 9–29; Florence Maillet, "The French Wall de Jochen Gerz", in: *Beaux-Arts Magazine*, no. 162, November 1997, 92–93; Rainer Metzger, "Über der Humor nach Auschwitz", in: *Der Standard*, 23.1.1997, 10; Werner Meyer/Paolo Bianchi, "Die Transsibirische", in: *Kunstforum International*, February/May 1997, 154–155; Anne-Marie Morice, "Le travail des images", in: *Regards sur la Création*, no. 26, July/August 1997, 44–45; N. N., "Fahnen von Gerz und Gerz", in: *Kunstzeitung*, January 1997; Natascha Pflaumbaum, "Ein Lächeln für die Geschichte", in: *Göttinger Tageblatt*, 11.6.1997; Hermann Pfütze, "Unsichtbar, Versenkt, im Traum", in: *Merkur*, January 1997, 128, 137; Hermann Pfütze, "Politik der Gesinnungstüchtigkeit, Leserbrief", in: *Berliner Zeitung*, 1.12.1997; Evelyn Roll, "Verlag Holocaust-Mahnmal: Vier Meinungen vor der Entscheidung", in: *Süddeutsche Zeitung*, 10.12.1997; Karlheinz Schmid, "Editorial", in: *Informationsdienst Kunst*, no. 152, 19 November 1997, 3–5; Rudolf Schmitz, "Die Kunst–Jochen Gerz", in: *Deutsche Bibliothek Frankfurt am Main. Ein Dialog zwischen Architekten und Bibliothekaren*, ed. by Klaus-Dieter Lehmann and Ingo Kolasa, Verlag Gerd Hatje, Stuttgart 1997, 120–121; Wilfried Schoeller, "Zeitsprung ins Unsichtbare", in: *Du*, no. 10, October 1997, 03.54–04.18;

Beate Söntgen, "Zurückgedachte Gegenwart", in: *Frankfurter Allgemeine Zeitung*, 14.6.1997, 35; Jochen Stöckemann, "Suche nach vergessenen Bildern", in: *Hannoverische Allgemeine Zeitung*, 3.6.1997; Claude This, "Mise en abyme de deux colonnes de la mémoire: la colonne de Harbourg, le monument de Guerry", in: *Figures de l'Art, revue d'études d'esthétiques*, no. 3, 1997–98, 257–263; Douglas Todd, "Smile–you are seeing yourself", in: *The Vancouver Weekend Sun*, 23.8.1997; Christiane Vielhaber, "Anrührende Privatheit", in: *Das Handelsblatt*, 7.–8.3.1997; Thomas Wagner, "Gänse im Anflug", in: *Frankfurter Allgemeine Zeitung*, 24.3.1997; Thomas Wagner, "Als sei's ein Stück von der Leber des Prometheus", in: *Frankfurter Allgemeine Zeitung*, 7.6.1997, 33; Petra Watson, "Mirror Mirror", in: *Canadian Art*, vol. 14, no. 4, winter 1997, 64; Johannes Wetzel, "Biedermann im Museum. Ein französischer Kulturkampf um die Kunst der Moderne", in: *Die Zeit*, no. 20, 9.5.1997, 47; Charlotte Wiedemann, "Niemals fertig", in: *Die Woche*, 21.11.1997; James Young, "Der Widerspruch der Künstler", in: *Der Tagesspiegel*, 10.4.1997; James E. Young, "Deutschlands Denkmal-Problem. Gedenken, Anti-Gedenken und das Ende des Monuments", in: *Deutschlandbilder. Kunst aus einem geteilten Land*, Martin-Gropius-Bau, Berlin 1997/98, 592–597; Armin Zweite, "Jochen Gerz: Exit –Materialien zum Dachau-Projekt (1972/74)", in: *Deutschlandbilder. Kunst aus einem geteilten Land*, Martin-Gropius-Bau, Berlin 1997/98, 442–444 **1998** Roland Baumann, "Jochen Gerz–Un artiste de la mémoire", in: *Regards, Tribune juive de Belgique*, 17.11.1998, 38; Helga Bittner, "Das Papier bleibt vor Dachau nicht weiß, Jochen und Esther Gerz proben in Berlin Peter Weiss' *Die Ermittlung*", in: *Rheinische Post*, 19.5.1998; Marc Bormand, "To Live", in: *Premises*, Guggenheim Museum, New York, 224–227; Florian von Butler/Stefanie Endlich, "Build? Wait? Abandon? Notes on the debate on the proposed Holocaust Memorial in Berlin", in: *Domus*, no. 808, October 1998, 97–102; Laura Evenson, "What is the answer?", in: *San Francisco Chronicle*, 11.4.1998; Friedrich Friedl/Nicolaus Ott/Bernhard Stein, *Wann Wer Wie*, Könemann-Verlag, Cologne, 246–247; Bernard Géniès, "Cahors. Le printemps est beau", in: *Le Nouvel Observateur*, no. 1753, 11–17.6.1998, 132–134; Cornelia Gockel, "Jochen Gerz, Kunst der Erinnerung. Darstellbarkeit von Erinnerung", in: *Zeige deine Wunde, Faschismusrezeption in der deutschen Gegenwartskunst*, Verlag Silke Schreiber, Munich 1998, 48–57; Clara Greed/Marion Roberts (eds.), *Introducing Urban Design. Interventions and Responses,* Longman, Harlow, 126–127; Amine Haase, "Die Diskussion um das Holocaust-Mahnmal in Berlin", in: *Kunstforum International*, vol. 140, April/June 1998, 492; Andreas Hapkemeyer, "Jochen Gerz–Erase the Past", in: *Das Versprechen der Photographie, Die Sammlung der DG BANK*, Prestel, Munich; Pierre Hazan, "Rendre le passé brûlant", in: *Le Temps*, 7.11.1998; Kai-Uwe Hemken, "Kritik der Erinnerungspraxis", in: *Gerhard Richter, 18. Oktober 1977*, Insel Verlag, Frankfurt am Main and Leipzig, 126–129; Ute Kiehn, "Kann aktives Zuschauen Wegschauen verhindern?", in: *Berliner Zeitung*, 26.2.1998; H. D. Kittsteiner, "Die Geschichte nach dem Ende der Kunst", in: *Merkur*, April 1998, 294–307; Nicola Kuhn, "Und dann wird es heiß", in: *Der Tagesspiegel*, 18.1.1998; Marion Leske, "Die Provokation liegt im Pinselstrich", in: *Die Welt*, 22.10.1998; Julia Naumann, "Viel Beifall für Jochen Gerz' Provokation", in: *Die Tageszeitung*, 19.1.1998; Brigitte Ollier, "Jochen Gerz et ses Témoins", in: *Libération*, 2.6.1998, 37; Paul Petzel, "Zur Ästhetik des Erinnerns. Das Konzept des Andernacher Spiegel-Containers", in: *Der Andernacher Spiegelcontainer. Mahnmal für die Opfer der nationalsozialistischen Euthanasie in der ehemaligen Rheinprovinz*, 66–85; Hermann Pfütze, "Die Zeit muß mitbauen", in: *Berliner Zeitung*, 16.1.1998; Mônica Riani, "No MAM, a expressão teatral interpretada pelas artes plásticas", in: *Gazeta do Rio*, 12.3.1998; Ingeborg Ruthe, "Das Ghetto Kunst verlassen", in: *Berliner Zeitung*, no. 57, 9.3.1998; Karlheinz Schmid, "Dimension Zeit. Die Plädoyers", in: *Kunstzeitung*, no. 17, January 1998, 4; Joachim Schwitzler, "Ein Kunstprojekt mit Scherben. Jochen Gerz' Installation im Thurgauer Kunstmuseum–Aufruf zu einem Flaschenwurf", in: *Thurgauer Zeitung*, 17.10.1998; Mark Siemons, "Dürfte ich das noch einmal hören? Der Wiederholungszwang zertrümmert die Sprache: 'Die Berliner Ermittlung' von Jochen Gerz", in: *Frankfurter Allgemeine Zeitung*, 28.5.1998, 43; Nathalie Simon, "Sur les ailes du désir. La 8e édtion présente trente artistes internationaux", in: *Le Figaro*, 2.6.1998, 27; Esther Slevogt, "Raus aus den Fauteuils!", in: *Die Tageszeitung*, 17.3.1998; Ika Szope, "Das Beste, was man tun kann ... Jochen Gerz und sein Projekt *The Berkeley Oracle*", in: *Munitionsfabrik*, no. 1, February 1998, 13; Kerstin Ullrich, "Ein Riesen Roman mit unendlich vielen Autoren", in: *Berliner Morgenpost*, 18.1.1998; Paul Usherwood, "Public art abhors a vacuum", in: *Art Monthly*, no. 222, 1998–99, 13; Ludmila Vachtova, "Kunst ist gefährlich, Jochen Gerz in Ittingen", in: *Die Weltwoche*, 22.10.1998; Michel Verrier, "Pour garder en mémoire les victimes de l'Holocauste", in: *Le Nouveau Quotidien*, Geneva, 2.2.1998; Thomas Wagner, "In die Schublade gehen", in: *Frankfurter Allgemeine Zeitung*, 13.7.1998; Gabriela Walde, "Stellen Sie sich vor, Sie wären im Lager", in: *Die Welt*, 25.2.1998; "Warum?", in: *Frankfurter Allgemeine Zeitung*, 19.1.1998; James E. Young, "Germany's Memorial Question:

Memory, Counter-Memory, and the End of the Monument", in: Martin Morris (ed.), *German Dis/Continuities*, Duke University Press, Durham, 1998, 859–865; James E. Young, "Holocaust Memorials", in: *Archis*, no. 5, 1998, 51, and "To build a monument. Berlin's Holocaust memorial problem", in: *ibid.*, 56 **1999** Ludwig Ammann, "Schnitzeljagd im Museum", in: *Badische Zeitung*, 16.3.99; Paolo Bianchi, "Künstler ohne Kunstwerk", in: *Basler Magazin*, no. 12, 27.3.1999, 6–7; Sigrid Feeser, "Das Berkeley Orakel", in: *Kultur*, no. 87; Michael Hübl, "Die Scherben in Ittingen und das Orakel im Internet", in: *Badische Neueste Nachrichten*, February 1999; Michael Hübl, "Kann man den Antworten entrinnen?", in: *Badische Neueste Nachrichten*, 5.3.1999; "Licht auf Weimar. Die ephemeren Medien", Weimar 99, Kulturstadt Europas, Leporello der Stadt Weimar, 1, 7–9; Thomas Michelon, "Image et Shoah. Ce que je vois, ce que je ne saurais voir", in: *Pratiques*, spring 1999, no. 6, 43; Hanno Müller, "Grünes Licht über Weimar", in: *Thüringer Allgemeine*, 1.5.1999, 1, 4; N. N., "Internet-Projekt von Jochen Gerz in Karlsruhe. Wie das Antike Orakel", in: *Badische Neueste Nachrichten*, March 1999; Arno Orzessek, "Rosinen ohne Kuchen", in: *Süddeutsche Zeitung*, 13.3.1999; Régine Robin, "Figer la mémoire allemande dans le béton", in: *Le Monde*, 12.2.1999; Marko Schacher, "Gibt es ein Leben vor dem Tod", *Stuttgarter Nachrichten*, 7.4.1999, Heinz Peter Schwerfel, "Naumann schmückt sich mit fremden Federn", in: *Art. Das Kunstmagazin*, January 1999, 101; Gerlinde Sommer, "Erhellung durch Hörensagen", in: *TLZ Weimar*, 29.4.1999